P9-CFK-193

The research that led to this book was conceived and carried out jointly by Compass Partnership and the Centre for Civil Society at the London School of Economics. The lead sponsor was the Zurich Community Trust. The supporting sponsors were the Calouste Gulbenkian Foundation, the Paul Hamlyn Foundation, and the Kings Fund.

Compass Partnership

Compass Partnership is a management consulting firm specializing in the management and development of independent, non-profit-seeking organizations. Founded in 1982, Compass has worked with over 800 nonprofit clients and has built up a body of knowledge on management in this field and a tried and tested range of approaches to consultancy. Compass specializes in working with large organizations with complex problems, combining rigorous intellectual analysis with an understanding of how organizations work and how to achieve change.

E-mail: demerson@compassnet.co.uk
Tel.: +44 (0) 1628 478 561
Web site: www.compasspartnership.co.uk

The Centre for Civil Society

The Centre for Civil Society at the London School of Economics seeks to improve understanding of the set of organizations that are distinct from the market, the state, and household institutions and that are variously referred to as nongovernmental, voluntary, nonprofit, and third-sector organizations. These institutions are part of a wider civil society and form a social economy of private organizations serving public purposes.

The mission of the Centre for Civil Society is to become the European academic center of excellence for the study of civil society, social economy, and philanthropy.

Web site: www.lse.ac.uk

Managing
at the Leading Edge

Mike Hudson

Managing at the Leading Edge

New Challenges in Managing
Nonprofit Organizations

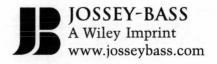
JOSSEY-BASS
A Wiley Imprint
www.josseybass.com

Published by Jossey-Bass
A Wiley Imprint
989 Market Street, San Francisco, CA 94103-1741   www.josseybass.com

Jossey-Bass books and products are available through most bookstores. To contact Jossey-Bass directly call our Customer Care Department within the U.S. at 800-956-7739, outside the U.S. at 317-572-3986, or fax 317-572-4002.

Jossey-Bass also publishes its books in a variety of electronic formats. Some content that appears in print may not be available in electronic books.

Credits begin on page 303.

Library of Congress Cataloging-in-Publication Data

Hudson, Mike.
   Managing at the leading edge: new challenges in managing nonprofit organizations / Mike Hudson.—1st ed.
      p. cm.
   Includes bibliographical references and index.
   ISBN-13 978-0-7879-7806-8 (alk. paper)
   ISBN-10 0-7879-7806-X (alk. paper)
   1. Nonprofit organizations—Management. I. Title.
   HD62.6.H83   2005
   658'.048—dc22

                                                            2005003697

Printed in the United States of America   FIRST EDITION
HB Printing   10 9 8 7 6 5 4 3 2 1

Contents

Tables, Figures, and Exhibits

Tables

Figures

Exhibits

Preface

Nonprofit organizations in many parts of the developed world were transformed during the last quarter of the twentieth century. In the 1960s and '70s, they were seen as disparate and unconnected organizations at the margins of health care, education, international development, medical research, and other fields. Most were small, employed few staff, and were run on a shoestring. Concepts of management were either not understood or were positively shunned because they were seen as being relevant only to business.

Today many countries see these organizations as the constituent parts of the *third sector*—organizations that do not exist to make profits and are not part of the public sector. They are viewed by governments and academics as critical elements of civil society, and they see themselves in this way also.

It is increasingly recognized that community, social, cultural, and even economic development all depend on a diverse and healthy nonprofit sector. Community development is almost entirely a function of nonprofit organizations such as clubs, churches, community centers, and action groups. Social development relies on local and national networks of organizations for health, disability, and social welfare, and advocacy groups have arisen for almost every facet of human and animal life. Cultural development is heavily dependent on nonprofit arts organizations, and economic development is supported by nonprofit trade and professional associations and by business promotion organizations.

These organizations play a critically important role in the democratic process. They represent people's views to local and national governments on a wide range of issues. They reflect the diverse and fragmented nature of modern society, and they provide some of the "glue" that holds that society together. They are also renowned as instigators of new ideas and social innovations. Many of the great services that people in developed countries now take for granted were incubated in nonprofit organizations before governments saw their value and made them universally available.

Recognition of the crucial roles that the sector plays has led to greatly increased government and private funding, which has in turn driven dramatic sector growth. Today nonprofit organizations deliver a huge range of essential services, and they mobilize the great campaigns of our time. Increased income from donations, foundations, bequests, and other sources has created organizations that now have significant resources at their disposal.

The Nonprofit Sector in the United States Today

Today the nonprofit sector in the United States consists of 1.6 million formally constituted organizations, a number that is growing at over 5 percent per year, twice the rate of formation of business organizations. It employs over eleven million people, and it benefits in addition from the voluntary efforts of almost six million full-time-equivalent people. This represents just over 7 percent of the total U.S. paid and voluntary workforce (INDEPENDENT SECTOR and Urban Institute, 2002).

Nonprofit organizations provide a huge range of services in health care, education, social services, culture, employment and training, housing, community development, and emergency aid. They are responsible for

- Half the nation's hospitals
- One-third of its health clinics
- Over a quarter of its nursing homes
- Nearly half (46 percent) of its higher education institutions
- Four-fifths (80 percent) of its individual and family service agencies
- 70 percent of its vocational rehabilitation services
- 30 percent of day-care services
- Over 90 percent of its orchestras and operas
- Delivering over 70 percent of its foreign disaster assistance [Salamon, 2002]

Nonprofit organizations drive campaigns for social improvement and have been responsible for creating many of the great movements for change. Campaigns against slavery and for women's suffrage, civil rights, environmental protection, and gay rights have all been orchestrated through nonprofit organizations.

These organizations "give institutional expression to two seemingly contradictory principles that are both important parts of American national character; the principle of individualism—the notion that people should have freedom to act on matters that concern them—and the principle of solidarity—the notion that people have responsibilities not only to themselves, but also to their fellow human beings and to the communities of which they are part" (Salamon, 2002, p. 11).

Giving is an essential part of the American character, and it is reflected in the $212 billion given annually by individuals, foundations, and corporations (AAFRC Trust for Philanthropy, 2002). People also give their time, with 110 million people (56 percent of the population over eighteen years of age) volunteering an average of 3.5 hours per week (INDEPENDENT SECTOR and Urban Institute, 2002). This commitment to nonprofit action derives in part from distrust of government involvement in the delivery of many services. People believe that if they want action, they must organize to make it happen. It is not that American people are against government in principle; it is that they believe government should undertake only those activities that it is uniquely positioned to carry out. This perspective is reflected in the fact that the business sector accounts for 80 percent of national income, the government sector just over 13 percent, and the nonprofit sector almost 7 percent. The income attributable to the nonprofit sector is more than half as big as that from government when assigned values for volunteers and unpaid family workers are included (INDEPENDENT SECTOR and Urban Institute, 2002).

The Professionalization of Management

Twenty to thirty years ago nonprofit organizations were often run by amateurs—people who believed in a cause and wanted to do something about it but who did not always have the necessary management expertise. Today many of these organizations are managed by talented professionals, and these professionals are supported by a growing body of knowledge about the special characteristics of nonprofit organizations and the skills required to manage them, which often differ from the skills required by public and private concerns. The techniques of working with multiple stakeholders, of juggling diverse income streams into an ever wider range of activities, and of responding to increased public scrutiny are now well understood by experienced nonprofit managers and board members.

Nonprofit organizations have been through enormous change already, but more change is undoubtedly on the horizon. The sector will grow even further over the coming years. Governments are likely to continue to contract out more of the services currently delivered by the public sector. Private income is predicted to grow as significant numbers of very wealthy people come to the end of their lives and want to benefit others through creating private foundations and bequests. Managers and board members now face a new set of questions about increasing the impact of their organizations and directing their own efforts. There are demands that in addition to their activities and finances, nonprofit organizations should report on the results they achieve. There is pressure to discover which services really make a difference, to focus activities, and to *scale up* so activities and services achieve greater impact. There is pressure to form strategic alliances, with other nonprofit organizations and with the public and private sectors, to achieve ever more demanding objectives. There is an expectation that nonprofit organizations will become more sustainable, rather than lurching from one challenge to the next. There is increased regulation, sometimes from bodies that have different and conflicting requirements. These are just a few of the many challenges that managers are now facing.

Critical Questions for the Future

This is the nonprofit context in which I set out to answer some critical questions about the future management and governance of nonprofit organizations in developed countries:

- What are the leading-edge approaches to managing nonprofit organizations?

- What should managers and board members be doing differently to enhance the performance of their organizations?

- How can the impact of the nonprofit sector be significantly increased?

The Research for This Book

I am from the United Kingdom, and I came to the United States as an outsider, able to see the activities of its nonprofits through a fresh pair of eyes. This has had the great advantage of helping me avoid preconceptions and prejudices. I came with two pads of blank paper and a list of very open and unstructured questions to ask of people involved with nonprofit organizations. So this is the story of an outsider who came to America to get an overview of the third sector and to tease out some of the most interesting developments in leading and managing nonprofit organizations.

A number of my interviewees reminded me of the journey made by the French political scientist Alexis de Tocqueville in 1831. He spent nine months touring the United States and on returning to France wrote *Democracy in America*—a treatise that is used in academic courses today and frequently referred to in the literature on nonprofits. Like de Tocqueville, I traveled to New York, Boston, and Washington, and we both had the benefit of seeing the country from the outside, of being warmly welcomed by many people, and of having time to reflect on what we learned. The parallel ends there, however, because my visit was shorter and more comfortable (he had to travel on horseback). He spent time in the Midwest and the South and did not venture further west than Michigan whereas I had the pleasure of traveling to the West Coast. His book was an enduring review of democracy whereas mine is limited to my fascination with the management and governance of nonprofit organizations.

The research that informs this book involved sixty-five face-to-face interviews with chief executives and senior managers of American nonprofit organizations and of foundations and umbrella bodies, leading academics, and consultants who specialize in the nonprofit sector. They were chosen through a process known in the academic world as *snowballing*—identifying leading figures in the field and asking them for examples of well-managed organizations and of people who were saying and writing interesting things about management. In addition the project team approached organizations and individuals mentioned in the relevant literature and reviewed lists such as the Arco list of the "100 best nonprofits to work for," the *NonProfit Times* list of the largest nonprofits, and the Foundation Center list of the largest foundations. Over 100 books and reports were gathered and reviewed to supplement the data from the interviews.

I set out with a list of headings concerned with management, governance, leadership, mergers, teams, and organizational learning. I did discuss these subjects with the interviewees, but overwhelmingly the subjects that they talked about were capacity building, performance management, strategic alliances, and the other topics that have become the chapters of this book.

The approach I adopted has potential methodological flaws. It could be argued that selecting interviewees who are at the top of organizations or who advise those at the top and combining their views with the opinions and prejudices I bring from my experience as a consultant advising nonprofit organizations in the U.K. led to the conclusions I wanted to find. To minimize this risk I interviewed academics and consultants as well as leaders of nonprofit organizations.

The ways in which people in the middle and on the front line of organizations experience the approaches to management and governance set out in this book may also be questioned. Perhaps they see these approaches as management "fads" that in practice contribute little to organizational effectiveness. No doubt some do, but the combined evidence from the interviews, the literature review, and monitoring of the nonprofit sector press (which can be highly critical) leads me to conclude that I have captured the essence of either what people think makes a difference or what has been demonstrated to work in practice. I believe this research has identified the ideas that can contribute most to the effectiveness of nonprofit organizations. The ideas discussed in this book are the cutting-edge issues on which managers and board members can have greatest impact.

Yet another methodological question concerns the timing of the research. When the economy is thriving and the sector's income is growing, managers have investment for the future at the top of their agendas. When the economy is weakening, managers have to make cutbacks and layoffs. This research was undertaken when the U.S. economy was coming to the end of a period of growth, and dollars were flowing into the sector. The economy has subsequently experienced a difficult period, and as this book goes to press, economic

growth has resumed once again. The ebb and flow of the economy
has an immediate effect on the nonprofit sector. However, one of the
enduring characteristics of the sector is its robustness in the face of
external challenge. One recent book characterizes the history of the
sector as "a story of resilience" (Salamon, 2002). So even though the
economy affects short-term priorities, the challenges that managers
and board members face in investing in development of the capacity of their organizations remain relatively unchanged in the longer
term, and my research focused mostly on those challenges.

Six Central Propositions

It took the nonprofit sector in the developed world many years to
accept notions of management and to begin to understand what is
distinctive about managing nonprofit organizations. This book
makes six central propositions, devoting a chapter to each one.
Nonprofit organizations need

1. *To strengthen their own capacity* (Chapter One). They need to
invest much more heavily in their people, systems, and infrastructure so they have the organization capacity to deliver greater
impact. Building capacity is not about creating unnecessary administration and bureaucracy—it is about systematically building organizations that have the clout to make a sustainable difference to
pressing social, economic, and environmental problems.

2. *To manage performance* (Chapter Two). They need to develop
a clear understanding of what performance means and how it should
be measured and then focus people and systems sharply on the
desired results. Reporting on what an organization does is no longer
sufficient—it is the results that matter.

3. *To create strategic alliances* (Chapter Three). They need to
work with each other and with public and private sector organizations in long-term strategic alliances. Working in isolation is not
an option. There is too much to be learned from other nonprofits
and from private and public sector organizations.

4. *To exploit changing patterns of funding* (Chapter Four). They need to understand the difference between capital and revenue funding, tap into a much wider range of sources of finance, and structure their funding to use different types of finance to suit different circumstances.

5. *To be led with integrity* (Chapter Five). Leaders need to mobilize people around the mission, focus people on results, create small teams, and invest in leadership and management development so everyone is motivated to achieve the organization's objectives.

6. *To continuously strengthen their governance* (Chapter Six). Board members and managers need to establish crystal clarity about the board's role, structure the board around governance tasks, and monitor the performance of the board and its members in an open and transparent way.

Together these propositions add up to a new agenda that encourages paying much greater attention to outcomes and focusing the whole organization on achieving them.

Application of the Propositions

One of the most vital characteristics of the nonprofit sector is its extraordinary diversity. There are organizations focused on almost every conceivable human activity. Some exist primarily to provide services and some were created to change the way people behave; some challenge the balance of power and our very conception of society and some exist to enhance the environment in which we live.

It might be assumed that this book provides an agenda that applies only to service-delivering organizations and not to advocacy organizations. That is not the case. I spoke both with leaders of organizations that exist to achieve social change and with leaders of organizations that deliver services and have a strong social change agenda. Many of the propositions are applicable to both, though their salience may vary, and they are frequently much more difficult to implement in the more politicized advocacy organizations, which often have the widest agendas and the fewest resources.

However, the propositions in this book do apply mainly to medium-sized and large organizations—those that employ ten or more staff and those with an income of $1 million per annum or more. I recognize the importance of smaller organizations and that they form the majority in the sector in many countries. But appropriate approaches to managing and governing small organizations are very different from those required by larger organizations, and my experience and interest is in the latter.

The extraordinary variety of nonprofit organizations extends beyond the causes that they champion. They all have different histories, stakeholders, and sources of finance; in addition they have different cultures. They are also full of contradictions and ambiguities. No two nonprofit organizations are quite the same. Consequently, approaches to management and governance that are appropriate for some may be entirely inappropriate for others. There are principles, but they do not always hold, and there is good practice, but it may not be right for some organizations. So although you, like me, may get excited by some of the ideas that follow, this book comes with a health warning—take those parts that really fit the needs of your organization today, and leave the rest for others to use in different circumstances and at different times.

The Audience

This book has been written for

Managers and board members of nonprofit organizations

Funders who provide the resources

Fundraisers who seek the funding

Intermediary bodies that support the sector

Academics who study the sector

Consultants who assist the sector

The chapters are set out in the order in which managers and board members might think about strengthening their organizations. It will sometimes be logical to start by building organization capacity and establishing systems for measuring performance. Once an organization is strong, it can consider creating strategic alliances and diversifying funding. It will then need stronger leadership at every level, and finally, it will need to strengthen its arrangements for governance. However, every organization has to carry out its own assessment of its performance and determine which investments in organization development will bring the greatest rewards. In practice the place to start will vary from organization to organization. Each chapter, therefore, can stand on its own, and the book may be read in any order the reader wishes.

To assist readers who are new to this field, I have included a brief history of the nonprofit sector and details of the books and reports that I found most compelling as resources at the end of the book. For readers interested in the international context, I have included some comparisons between the U.K. and the U.S. nonprofit sectors as a further resource.

I consider this book to be a work in progress. There is always more work to be done to understand what truly makes a difference in management and governance. I therefore warmly welcome challenges to what I have found, further examples of successful implementation of the ideas presented, and identification of concepts that I have overlooked. Please send your views to Compass Partnership, Greenbanks, New Road, Bourne End, Bucks, SL8 5BZ, England, or to mhudson@compassnet.co.uk. I look forward to hearing from you and promise to reply.

Bourne End, Buckinghamshire, England   Mike Hudson
March 2005

Acknowledgments

This book could not have been written without the support of many people and organizations.

I am grateful for support from James Austin, chair of the Social Enterprise Initiative, and his colleagues at Harvard Business School. James willingly provided names of leading organizations and people to visit and began the "snowball" that finally led me to the people who were interviewed for the research that underlies this book.

I am particularly grateful to the sixty-five people who were kind enough to give me time in their busy schedules for interviews, some of which lasted for more than two hours. They are named in Resource B, and their contributions are the foundation of this book.

I am also grateful to the many authors whose work I have drawn on to deepen my understanding of the context of and key developments in the management and governance of nonprofits. They are all referred to in the text, but I would particularly like to acknowledge Christine Letts, David La Piana, Peter Dobkin Hall, Lester Salamon, Paul Light, James Austin, Jane Arsenault, Jed Emerson, William Ryan, Burt Nanus, Stephen Dobbs, and Frances Hesselbein. I have drawn heavily on your work, and I hope I have reflected its significance appropriately.

The draft of this book was reviewed by many people. I am particularly grateful to Michael Edwards, director of governance and civil society at the Ford Foundation; William Ryan, independent consultant and Research Fellow at the Hauser Center for Nonprofit Organizations; Char Mollison, vice president of constituency services at the Council on Foundations; Abby Snay, executive director of Jewish Vocational Services of San Francisco; and Marilyn Wyatt, director of consulting and training at BoardSource. Thank you all for your valuable comments.

I would also like to thank Mark Rosenman, Distinguished Public Service Professor of the Union Institute, who provided valuable criticism at a seminar on the research findings.

I would also like to thank all my current and past colleagues at Compass Partnership who have contributed to and challenged my thinking. My current and past clients deserve particular thanks as they have given me the opportunity to work in this field and to learn so much from practical experience.

The research was made possible by the four funders, led by the Zurich Community Trust and supported by the Calouste Gulbenkian Foundation, the Paul Hamlyn Foundation, and the Kings Fund. I am most grateful for their financial support.

This project could not have happened without the support and advice of Helmut Anheier, director of the Center for Civil Society at the School of Public Policy and Social Research at the University of California–Los Angeles and Centennial Professor at the London School of Economics (LSE). Helmut's contacts, his willingness to help raise the funds and promote the project, and his academic oversight of the work were all invaluable.

The research was overseen by a steering group of leading figures from the U.K. voluntary sector. The group was ably chaired by Richard Gutch, who ten years earlier had traveled to the United States to look at practices of government organizations that contract with the nonprofit sector to deliver public services and the implications for nonprofit organizations.

A few people deserve special thanks for their contributions. Chris Staples, community affairs director at Zurich Financial Services, was a funder, a member of the steering group, and a consistent supporter throughout the project. Melinda Letts was also on the steering group and went through the draft manuscript with a fine-tooth comb, greatly enhancing the logic and the language of the book.

One person who deserves particular acknowledgment is Natalia Leshchenko, who while studying for her doctorate at the LSE identified many of the interviewees and researched the history of the sector.

Samantha Norrington, then my personal assistant at Compass Partnership, undertook the task of setting up the first forty interviews. Debbie Emerson set up the second trip to the United States, involving a further twenty-five interviews, and as with my last book took responsibility for converting a mixture of typescript and handwritten notes into clean manuscript. I am very grateful for their support.

Finally, I am grateful to my wife, Diana, and our four children, Jennifer, Tim, Jessy Anne, and Katherine, for putting up with my hiding in my garden office when I should have been being a husband and a father.

Notwithstanding all this support, any mistakes and misjudgments in the book are solely my responsibility.

—M. H.

The Author

Mike Hudson is the director of Compass Partnership. He was the administrative director of Friends of the Earth UK during its formative years. Following this, he worked in the United Kingdom and the United States for a business strategy consulting firm.

He has worked as a consultant to not-for-profit organizations for twenty years, leading teams that bring about major change in complex organizations. His clients include the chairs and chief executives of a wide range of national and international nonprofit organizations. He has also been a Visiting Fellow at the London School of Economics.

His previous book, *Managing Without Profit* (Directory of Social Change, 2000), sets out the theory and practice of creating highly successful nonprofit organizations. It has sold over 16,000 copies and is available from www.dsc.org.uk.

1

Building Organization Capacity

Good organization has been a characteristic of nonprofit organizations since they first emerged as distinct entities in the nineteenth century. Many, such as the YMCA and the Salvation Army, formed great national networks, which are now the cornerstones of much nonprofit activity. More recently, nonprofit organizations have striven to raise the quality of their management through organization development, strategic planning, management training, and board development. This effort has now led managers to the idea of *capacity building*.

Building organization capacity is about systematically investing in developing an organization's internal systems (for example, its people, processes, and infrastructure) and its external relationships (for example, with funders, partners, and volunteers) so that it can better realize its mission and achieve greater impact. Capacity building has to be viewed in the context of an organization's objectives and values. It is not about strengthening an organization for its own sake. It is about creating an organization that has the ability to make a serious impact on its desired mission. Nor is it about being business-like just because that is viewed by some as a characteristic to be valued. It is about having a significant impact within the context of the values and beliefs cherished by people who champion nonprofit enterprise.

Cynics might say that capacity building is just a repackaging of established ideas. It is true that the ideas are not all new. But the energy and momentum behind capacity building are indicative of the enthusiasm with which it has been embraced. The most compelling reason for its ready acceptance is a recognition that the nonprofit sector is failing to have the impact it could have on the pressing social issues the nation faces. Across the United States there is no shortage of organizations with effective programs for assisting people in need, but their potential impact is often restricted by shortfalls in both funding and capacity. They want to deliver quality services, to reach more people, to mobilize better campaigns, or just to keep pace with rising expectations for competitive salaries, effective technological support, and accountable boards. But they just don't have the capacity to do it, and this is particularly marked among the social services organizations, many of which have insufficient resources.

Capacity building is a matter for both service-delivering and advocacy organizations. To have significant impact both need effective boards, strong management teams, and good relationships with their funders. Service organizations need the capacity to manage quality, to measure performance, and to manage risk. Advocacy organizations need the capacity to publicize their cause, to hold disparate groups together, and to manage talented and creative people who often believe more in the cause than in their organization. These different organizational types may need different types of organization capacity, but neither can be effective without it.

What is most notable to a visiting outsider is the energy, enthusiasm, commitment, and funding that is being directed at capacity building. Capacity building used to be seen as a cost. Now it is seen as an essential investment that lies at the heart of effective management. It is no longer just a continuation of past efforts to strengthen organizations. Organizations at the leading edge are undertaking thorough, systematic, and rigorously evaluated capacity building initiatives. Their aim is to increase the overall impact of the nonprofit sector by creating organizations that are much more effectively and efficiently managed. They seek a step change in performance, not just gradual and halfhearted attempts at making improvements.

Clearly, achieving such change depends on having the finances to make capacity building investments, and when funding is tight, spending on capacity building is reduced. However, progress to date has convinced many people that capacity building is not an optional extra. It is an essential ingredient of effective management. So this first chapter describes why capacity building has risen to the top of the management agenda, why some funders are reluctant to pay for it, and how critical ingredients need to be brought together to implement successful capacity building initiatives.

This chapter demonstrates that leading-edge organizations

- Recognize lack of capacity as a critical constraint

- Invest in capacity building

- Identify the critical elements of organization capacity

- Adopt a systematic approach to capacity building

- Choose among four strategies for increasing impact

- Measure the impact of capacity building

Recognize Lack of Capacity as a Critical Constraint

Since the early 1980s, there has been a growing realization that nonprofit organizations need significant investment in organization capacity if they are to have greater impact. Forward-looking grant-giving foundations were among the first to raise the issue. They started asking questions about what nonprofit organizations were achieving and what could be done to increase their impact. Many people trace the start of capacity building efforts to the launch of the David and Lucile Packard Foundation capacity building program in 1983.

The theoretical context for capacity building gained much credibility from Robert Putnam's groundbreaking study of civic society organizations in Italy. Putnam (1993) demonstrated that the potential for a community to grow and thrive depended on the richness of its associations and civic organizations. His book popularized the idea of *social capital*. So today capacity building is viewed as an essential element of increasing social capital and hence of creating strong democratic societies that have the infrastructure to develop socially and economically. "The quality of the connections between people and institutions provides the basis for civil society and healthy communities," according to Urban Institute researcher Carol de Vita (de Vita and Flemming, 2001, p. 8). The theoretical goal of capacity building, from this perspective, is to enhance the ability of nonprofit organizations to meet the changing needs of society.

Together, then, a well-grounded theoretical framework and the practical efforts of foundations, umbrella organizations, nonprofit boards, and venture philanthropists, as well as public pressure, have pushed capacity building right up the management agenda. "A national infrastructure for capacity building is now taking shape" (de Vita and Flemming, 2001, p. 42). It includes a wide range of management support organizations, a variety of for-profit and nonprofit consulting firms, and increasingly, resources that can be downloaded from the World Wide Web.

Forces That Hinder Investment in Capacity

In the past, organizations were often tempted to spend as much money as possible on services and as little as possible on administration, and this is often still the case today. This paradigm is often supported by both foundations and government agencies who believe that their funding is most effective when it is spent on programs. Government contracts often provide a fixed percentage for overhead costs, and foundations have generally assumed that "other" sources of funding will pay for the central overhead required. Clearly, neither have typically seen the funding of capacity as a strategic investment aimed at strengthening organizations' ability to have long-term impact. Donors have also wanted their money to be spent directly on services and campaigns. Private donors are always acutely sensitive to nonprofit overhead costs and expect administration to be kept to a bare minimum. They do not want their funds spent on office overhead. Such desires are often fuelled by the organizations themselves. When desperate for funds, they promise that every cent donated will be spent on beneficiaries. Charity watchdog groups and the press provide a further disincentive to investment in organization infrastructure because they publicize ratios of administrative expenditure to program expenditure. Such figures imply that program expenditure is good and administrative expenditure is bad. The interests of board members and employees have also discouraged investment in the organization itself. People sit on boards or work for nonprofits primarily because they are interested in an organization's cause, not because they have an innate interest in building organization capacity.

There has therefore always been a real and acute tension between spending money on programs and investing in organization capacity. Short-term pressures to deliver services to people in desperate need or to campaign for pressing social and environmental issues can be powerful. As a result, the service and the organization "are considered to be competitors in a zero sum struggle for limited resources" (Letts, Ryan, and Grossman, 1999, p. 32).

So the pressure on organizations to spend as much of their funding as possible on services is intense, and it is complicated by the difficulty of separating out essential organization infrastructure from unnecessary administrative expenditure. "The difference between building an organization's capacity for success (muscle) and assembling a self-serving empire (fat) remains hard to distinguish" (Letts, Ryan, and Grossman, 1999, p. 32).

Lack of Capacity: A Stumbling Block to Effectiveness

Nevertheless, the intensive thinking about capacity building has contributed to an increasingly common view that capacity building is the crucial issue for organizations wanting to make a significant impact on the major social issues they exist to address. Lack of capacity is now seen by many as the bottleneck that thwarts the growth and development of nonprofit organizations and consequently their potential to have a greater impact. As Letts, Ryan, and Grossman (1999) put it: "The missing ingredient in the prevalent program-centered conception of social impact is organizational capacity. It is the capacity for strong performance in organizations—the ability to develop, sustain and improve the delivery of a mission—that provides the foundation for lasting social benefits" (pp. 3–4). Failure to attend to organizational and internal management issues is particularly acute in advocacy organizations. Focused as they often are on rapidly changing external agendas and staffed by people who are passionately committed to the cause, they often overlook many of the basic requirements of effective management. Many of them pay a high price in terms of poor staff retention; inefficient use of staff time, as people retreat into their own agendas; and underinvestment in technology that could give them greater efficiency and impact.

Foundations in particular now see lack of capacity as a bottleneck. As they began to pay more attention to evaluating the impact of their grants, it became clear that lack of organization capacity was a critical obstacle to achieving desired results. Evaluation after evaluation concluded that internal capacity was a key constraint. For example, the Boston Foundation's capacity building investments grew from a realization that many of the homeless and battered women's shelters that they were funding were failing in the first five years of operation because they were not building sustainable organization capacity. Associations representing various groups of organizations providing social care also now see lack of capacity as a stumbling block to effectiveness. In many fields, organizations have to be recognized by an accepted accrediting or standard-setting association, such as the Commission on Accreditation of Rehabilitation Facilities, to be eligible for government funding. They must demonstrate that they meet the association's requirements, and these increasingly include management standards.

Invest in Capacity Building

Despite the many disincentives, the case for significantly increased investment in organization and management has grown exponentially in recent years. Commitment to creating stronger organizations sprang from many sources. Public pressure has led board members and managers to begin asking questions about how they could increase the impact of their organizations. In the past a common response might have been to raise more funds. Although greater funding is clearly essential to increasing impact, organizations have learned that it is insufficient on its own. Leading organizations recognize that the organization itself can be a major barrier to achievement and that significant amounts of both attention and financial investment are justified to develop its effectiveness.

A further development has been the creation of the Alliance for Nonprofit Management, a professional association devoted to building the capacity of nonprofit organizations. Its members include management support organizations, management consultants and consulting firms, academic centers, policymakers, management assistance programs, and grantmakers, all concerned with "raising the bar on quality" as the tagline of the Alliance puts it. The capacity building movement gained further momentum with the growth of venture philanthropy in the mid-1990s (discussed further in Chapter Four). More often than not, venture philanthropists were highly successful businesspeople who had made their fortunes establishing and then selling businesses. They wanted to invest some of their money in social causes, and they knew from their business experience that building organization capacity was an essential ingredient of success. The venture philanthropy movement gave capacity building a major boost, and it also brought new funds to pay for it.

So from small beginnings the capacity building movement has now become a hot topic in the nonprofit sector. The best evidence of the rate at which it has grown comes from the Foundation Center, which reports that grants for "management development," "technical assistance," and "program evaluation" totaled $466 million in 2000 (Foundation Center, 2002, pp. 36–37). This is 16 percent up from the previous year's figures and up from $170 million in 1994 (Foundation Center, 1996, pp. 82-83). Although funding may fall from its peak following the decline of the stock market at the turn of the century, it is likely to remain above the levels of the mid-1990s.

As a result a new paradigm for organizational effectiveness has emerged:

A Fresh Paradigm for Effectiveness: Key Characteristics

- Making continuous strategic investment in the development of the organization itself, its people, and its relationships to give it the power to have greater impact

- Charging the full cost of programs to funders, and being comfortable about making surpluses

- Using unrestricted income and foundation grants to invest in the capacity of the organization itself

- Using unrestricted income to subsidize services only when there is a compelling case and a demonstrable connection with the organization's strategic priorities

Identify the Critical Elements of Organization Capacity

The term *capacity building* first emerged in the international development field, where it has been used extensively to describe the empowerment of communities, the recognition of human rights, and the development of the civil society sector. Concepts of management, governance, and organization have not, however, been part of that first definition of capacity building. The term was subsequently adopted by managers and theorists and applied to organizations operating in the United States. In its widest use, *capacity building* refers to strengthening organizations' internal systems and their external strategies. *Internal capacity* is concerned with how organizations manage their affairs to deliver their mission. *External capacity* is concerned with what organizations set out to achieve, how they fund their activities, with whom they work, and how they relate to other organizations.

The experience of leading organizations points to the conclusion that key elements to be considered in developing internal capacity include

- The mission

- The board

- Staff, volunteers, and other people involved with achieving the mission

- Management skills

- Physical infrastructure

- Technology

- Evaluation

The key elements in developing external capacity include

- Relationships with funders, partners, and stakeholders

- Identification of relevant high-value services

- Orchestration of creative campaigns for social change

- Creativity in identifying and exploiting new sources of funds and income generation opportunities

Identify Where to Begin Capacity Building

Some researchers have attempted to identify the elements of capacity most critical to organizational success. In theory every aspect of an organization would benefit from investment. Better plans, more staff training, improved financial management systems, and more powerful IT systems could all make an organization stronger. So where should capacity building start, and how much time and money should be invested in each aspect of capacity?

A Brookings Institution survey of 250 researchers and providers of management assistance in the United States highlighted leadership as the single most important ingredient of effective organizations, finding that it "is impossible to overstate the importance of the leader to the high performing organization. Leadership was seen as the number one, and almost only, place to begin the journey from poor performance to high" (Light, 2002, p. 50). This survey also identified the internal structures critical to high-performing organizations. Respondents most frequently mentioned that these organizations

- Exploit information technology (74 percent)

- Give staff the authority to do their jobs (66 percent)

- Have few barriers between organization units (54 percent)

- Stay flat, with few layers between the top and the bottom of the organization (51 percent)

Survey respondents also identified the critical internal management systems of high-performing organizations. These organizations

- Use the board (90 percent)

- Clarify responsibilities (77 percent)

- Plan for the future and have strategic plans in place (73 percent)

- Use data to make decisions, despite the difficulty of measuring performance (63 percent)

- Invest in training (52 percent)

- Have an accurate, fast accounting system (47 percent)

Respondents' answers to questions about external capacity suggested that high-performance organizations

- Collaborate through strategic alliances, sharing services and sharing information

- Make money by generating unrestricted income

- Diversify their funding base

- Measure the outcomes of what they achieve, and compare their performance to that of other organizations

Christine Letts and her Harvard colleagues William Ryan and Allen Grossman (1999) compared high-performing nonprofit organizations with high-performing businesses. They concluded that four areas are critical to capacity building:

1. *Quality processes:* activities that translate commitment to quality into results by helping organizations determine whether and how a program is satisfying clients. Strengthening these processes requires management and staff to identify practical and measurable ways to improve services.

2. *Product development:* activities that help organizations search for good ideas and turn them into services

3. *Benchmarking:* processes for comparing key aspects of performance with the performance of other organizations

4. *Human resource development:* processes for motivating people to advance the organization's specific objectives and mission and for managing the human resource function in a strategic way

William Ryan told me that he and his coauthors identified these four because "they fit in the middle of the spectrum between high-level strategic planning and specific program management." He found that "nonprofit managers are good at managing at either end of the spectrum, but they neglect critically important capacity development work in the middle of the spectrum."

The consulting firm of McKinsey & Company conducted case studies of thirteen nonprofit organizations that engaged in capacity building over a ten-year period. This research, conducted for Venture Philanthropy Partners, a nonprofit philanthropic investment organization, led to the creation of the Capacity Framework (Figure 1.1), which contains seven essential elements of nonprofit capacity (McKinsey & Company, 2001):

1. *Aspirations:* an organization's mission, vision, and overarching goals, which collectively articulate its common sense of purpose and direction

2. *Strategies:* the coherent set of actions and programs aimed at fulfilling the organization's overarching goals

3. *Organizational skills:* the sum of the organization's capabilities, including such things as performance measurement, planning, resource management, and external relationship building

Figure 1.1. McKinsey Capacity Framework.

Source: McKinsey & Company, 2001, p. 36.

4. *Human resources:* the collective capabilities, experiences, potential, and commitment of the organization's board, management team, staff, and volunteers

5. *Systems and infrastructure:* the organization's planning, decision-making, knowledge management, and administrative systems, as well as the physical and technological assets that support the organization

6. *Organizational structure:* the combination of governance, organization design, interfunctional coordination, and individual job descriptions that shapes the organization's legal and management structure

7. *Culture:* the connective tissue that binds the organization together, including shared values and practices, behavioral norms, and most important, the organization's orientation toward performance

The McKinsey researchers saw these elements as being related in a hierarchy. They also used this research to develop the Capacity Assessment Grid (see McKinsey & Company, 2001), which provides a model of excellence against which organizations can assess their capacity. It can also be used to identify areas of capacity requiring most attention.

More recently, building on work by Letts, Ryan, and Grossman (1999), Carl Sussman (2003) has suggested that organizations need three types of capacity:

1. *Programmatic capacity:* the ability to carry out primary value-creating activities

2. *Organization capacity:* the structures, functions, systems, procedures, and culture that promote order and predictability

3. *Adaptive capacity:* the quest for change in pursuit of improved performance, relevance, and impact

Adaptive capacity refers to responsiveness to changes in the external environment. Sussman (2003) argues that four qualities capture the essence of adaptive capacity:

1. *External focus:* the ability to respond to key changes in the external environment

2. *Network connectedness:* the extent to which an organization is linked formally and informally with other organizations

3. *Inquisitiveness:* the appetite for inquiry and the ability to initiate change

4. *Innovation:* the ability to embrace new services, improve existing services, and develop supporting structures and processes

Sussman argues that all three types of capacity need to be in balance—too much or too little of any one type leads to ineffectiveness, and insufficient adaptive capacity in particular endangers an organization's long-term future.

A somewhat different approach has been taken by some umbrella organizations that operate at the state level and that have established sets of standards for nonprofit performance (typically, these standards are published on the Internet). In some states funders are using these standards as criteria for determining whether nonprofit organizations qualify for receiving government money. The best-known examples are the standards published by the Maryland Association of Nonprofit Organizations (1998–2004) and the Minnesota Council of Nonprofits (1998).

So, essential elements of capacity have been identified, tools for assessing organization capacity have been developed, and there is some evidence to suggest which are the most critical. The challenge for managers and board members is therefore one of assessing their organization's existing capacity and making wise judgments about the components that most require development to increase organizational effectiveness.

Adopt a Systematic Approach to Capacity Building

Although there is much anecdotal evidence and commonly accepted wisdom that top-quality management and governance lead to better organization performance, there is less understanding of the types and duration of capacity building initiatives that really work. Indeed, "There appear to be multiple starting points for improvement, several general strategies for growth, and a menu of characteristics that nonprofits can draw upon as target destinations for building capacity" (Light, 2002, p. 37). Nevertheless, evidence about the ingredients of successful capacity building is growing rapidly. Research by Paul Light and Elizabeth Hubbard (2002) gathered data from eight funders who together spent $28 million on approximately 380 capacity building grants that financed over 500 projects (see Table 1.1).

Table 1.1. Types of Capacity Building Projects Analyzed by Light and Hubbard.

Type of Project	No.	%
Internal management systems		
Planning, strategic planning	104	21
Fundraising, financial management	71	14
Governance, board development	62	12
Organizational assessment	42	8
Technology planning, training, acquisition	35	7
Evaluation and other	17	3
Total	331	65
External relations		
Communications, marketing	33	7
Mergers, alliances, joint ventures	17	3
Mission	13	3
Strategy	8	2
Constituent relationships	7	1
Business venture, program development	3	1
Total	81	17
Leadership		
Executive director transitions	34	7
Executive leadership, management skills	14	3
Total	48	10
Internal structure		
Human resources, staff development	40	8
Structure, management issues	3	1
Total	43	9
TOTAL	503	101[a]

[a]Percentages add up to more than 100 percent owing to rounding.
Source: Light and Hubbard, 2002, p. 14. Reprinted with permission.

Light and Hubbard propose that four key elements determine the ultimate success of a capacity building project:

1. The desired outcome or goal of the capacity building activity
2. The change strategy selected to realize that goal
3. The champions guiding the effort
4. The time, energy, and money invested in the process

The first step when approaching capacity building is to recognize that these four elements are all interrelated (Figure 1.2). Although in theory the desired outcome should determine the change strategy, which informs who should champion the effort and how much time and money it requires, in practice all four elements are in a dynamic relationship. The resources available will affect the choice of outcome, and the champion may influence the choice of change strategy.

Figure 1.2. Elements of a Capacity Building Project.

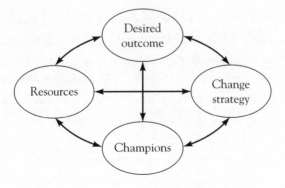

Source: Light and Hubbard, 2002, fig. 3. Reprinted with permission.

The Desired Outcomes

The desired outcomes of capacity building projects in this research fell into four categories:

1. *Improvements in internal management systems*, such as the strategic planning process, financial management systems, information systems, and performance management processes

2. *Improvements in external relationships*, such as collaborations with other organizations, fundraising, volunteer recruitment, changes in demand for a service, clarification of the mission, and marketing

3. *Improvements in leadership*, such as top-management and board skills, clarity of responsibilities, and the ability of the chief executive

4. *Improvements in internal structures*, such as management and governance structures, delegation, access to technology, and diversity among staff

(See Exhibit 1.1 for an example of identifying and accomplishing goals.)

The Change Strategy

The second of the four key elements of capacity building is the change strategy. Light and Hubbard (2002) comment that "discerning what kind of change strategy is likely to be most effective at any given time is a crucial skill for both nonprofit leaders and capacity building funders alike" (p. 7). And the approach organizations take to capacity building is seen as critical to its overall success. However, there is no straightforward methodology for moving from the analysis of the problem to the creation of an appropriate change strategy. Heterogeneity is a defining characteristic of the nonprofit sector, so it is hardly surprising to discover that it is difficult to generalize about effective intervention points and capacity

Exhibit 1.1. Building the Foundations for Growth: USA Child Care.

USA Child Care was established in 1995 by nationally known child-care professionals to be "a national voice for direct service providers who serve low and moderate income children and families." Initially this nonprofit developed a national campaign to increase child-care reimbursement rates, a training program for provider associations, and an information network. These were delivered through two separate organizations.

A review by the Conservation Company, a leading consultant to nonprofit organizations, identified that people were confused by the use of two organizations, resources were not being used efficiently, and the missions of both organizations were suffering. The Conservation Company planned a rigorous and systematic approach to strengthening the organization.

The first step in capacity building was to resolve the structural issue. At the same time, a new strategic plan was developed. The plans were crystallized at a weekend retreat. Each element of the strategy was then worked up in detail. For example, the strategy related to the merger identified what needed to be done, who would do it, when it would happen, and what it would cost.

USA Child Care's capacity was greatly enhanced when the merger of the two organizations was completed and new board committees were established. Board member Rick Hulefeld said, "We are much more focused now and have a real feeling for where we are going."

Source: Adapted from Alliance for Nonprofit Management, 2000.

building strategies. (One model, prioritizing human resource management, is described in Exhibit 1.2.)

The temptation in any analysis of capacity is to conclude that many components require attention and to attempt to address them all. However, organizations have limited capacity to build capacity. The constraints are usually senior management time and money. So the leadership has to make tough choices about the amount of

Exhibit 1.2. Citizen Schools Invests in Human Resources.

Citizen Schools is a Boston-based organization that seeks to educate children and strengthen community ties through improved after-school programs. Its program quality depends critically on the quality of the teaching staff and volunteers, which means human resources is at the top of this organization's capacity building priorities.

Citizen Schools was launched in 1995 by Ned Rimer and Eric Schwartz, two social entrepreneurs fresh from a successful personal experience teaching public school children first-aid and journalism. They had seen what difference they could make in the lives of children in a few short hours of their innovative after-school program, but at the time Boston offered parents few high-quality or affordable after-school options.

Schwartz and Rimer's model for tackling this problem was based around a cadre of "Citizen Teachers." These volunteers would help children between the ages of nine and fourteen develop skills in such areas as leadership, writing, public speaking, and using the scientific method. By framing these activities as "apprenticeships" and making them fun and educational, Schwartz and Rimer felt that Citizen Schools could meet an unserved need and at the same time improve Boston's poor educational testing results.

Citizen Schools quickly learned that a major challenge in the after-school sector was attracting and recruiting enough talented part-time teaching staff to populate the program. Schwartz and Rimer overcame this hurdle by creating an innovative employment model that relied on staff-sharing agreements with several leading Boston area nonprofits. Citizen Schools designed one- to two-year full-time positions, complete with benefits and professional development opportunities, and branded them as a prestigious "Fellows Program."

Citizen Schools then sought and secured corporate funding to underwrite the program. Under this program, each Fellow splits his or her time equally between Citizen Schools and another nonprofit organization. The Fellows now comprise more than one-third of the Citizen Schools staff, which has risen sharply from thirteen to its current level of eighty-nine.

Exhibit 1.2. Citizen Schools Invests in Human Resources, Cont'd.

Citizen Schools' overall investments in capacity building—including its focus on human resources—have been rewarded handsomely. On the financial front, it has leveraged its new strategic clarity and corporate and foundation partnerships into more than $8 million in additional funding. The program is reaching many more children, as well—from 560 in 1998 to more than 2,200 in 2003.

In terms of social impact, Citizen Schools can point to some very promising trends. In early tests, for example, children who have gone through Citizen Schools demonstrate significant improvements in writing skills. Furthermore, the product is in demand. There has been a large increase in the number of licensed after-school slots in Boston schools since 1995; much of this increase is attributable to Citizen Schools.

Source: Updated from McKinsey & Company, 2001, by New Profit Inc. Reprinted with permission.

capacity building that the organization can sustain and how to allocate limited but critical capacity building resources.

Managers acknowledge that sustainable development usually requires continuous effort over a period of time to change people's habits and behaviors and to create new ways of working. There is an ever-present danger of putting insufficient effort into building each component of capacity. Effort spread too thin over too many fronts may result in none being advanced in a significant and sustainable way. Yet nonprofits have a strong tendency to underestimate the time and funds required. The advice I received from Mary Ann Holohean, director of the Nonprofit Sector Advancement Fund at the capacity building Meyer Foundation, is to "make fewer, larger changes and take more time over them and make greater use of external support."

Additional strategic decisions concern the type of the intervention that is required and whether external assistance is needed to achieve the desired result. Although much management assistance is delivered by external consultants and trainers, there is growing evidence that peer-to-peer exchanges, such as networking, mentoring, and information sharing, also play an important role in capacity building.

The Champions

The third key element of a capacity building program is the need for a champion. One or more people have to have the capacity building initiative at the top of their agendas—planning the overall approach, driving the implementation timetable, and promoting the program to everyone affected. One of the reasons capacity building fails is the lack of a champion who has the skills, time, and resources to make a success of the initiative. All capacity building initiatives ultimately have to become embedded in the organization's culture—its way of doing things—and this requires the sustained effort and dedication that is best provided by a champion.

The Resources

The fourth key element is resources. Capacity building is supported largely by foundation grants combined with internal resources such as unrestricted income and surpluses from previous years. According to the Brookings Institution's Pathways to Nonprofit Effectiveness project, around one-third is supported by external funding, one-third by an organization's own resources, and one-third by a combination of external and internal resources. Research into a sample of funders with capacity building programs showed that *high*-resource funders spent an average of just under $200,000 per organization and *low*-resource funders spent an average of $27,500 per organization (Light and Hubbard, 2002).

One of the consequences of the larger and longer-term capacity building funding now offered is that funders tend to be in regular contact with recipients—often talking with them weekly. This provides both external pressure to maintain the momentum of the initiative and an ongoing source of advice and support.

Supportive Activities

To summarize, capacity builders need to clarify the desired outcomes of the initiative, develop an appropriate change strategy, appoint a leader who will be the initiative's champion, and ensure that the project is supported by significant resources. Nonprofits may seek assistance in conducting this systematic approach, and Exhibit 1.3 presents the principles followed by the most successful providers of such assistance.

Further insights come from the survey undertaken by McKinsey & Company (2001), which led the researchers to draw three conclusions about the overall approach to capacity building:

1. Resetting aspirations and strategy is often the first step in dramatically improving an organization's performance. The organizations that achieved the greatest increase in their capacity were those that created a new vision and a new strategy for the future. It is important to emphasize that a new aspiration or strategy can be transformative only when it is used to align the other aspects of organization capacity. If done thoroughly, this alignment process produces a tight institutional focus and a road-map for the organization to use with both internal and external audiences. These results help to keep everyone on track during the long and difficult process of building capacity.

2. A commitment to capacity building and project ownership among senior management is essential. Progress in effectively resetting aspirations and strategy, institutionalizing sound management processes, and improving systems to work at scale requires managerial ability as well as good leadership. In many cases in the organizations surveyed, the appointment of someone (often known as a chief operating officer) to take line management responsibility for a large proportion of the organization's internal affairs was key to ensuring that the organization worked efficiently and effectively.

**Exhibit 1.3. Principles of Successful
Capacity Building Assistance.**

Organizations seek assistance from many sources, including large for-profit consulting firms, for-profit and nonprofit consulting boutiques, solo practitioners, volunteer brokers, management support organizations, foundations, associations, and academic centers.

An intensive study of the most committed and successful providers by the Environmental Support Center and the nationally recognized nonprofit Innovation Network concluded that provider approaches could be boiled down to these nine principles:

1. *Every organization is capable of building its own capacity.* The most successful providers of capacity building carry a deep respect for the client's ability to build its own capacity and genuinely recognize that an organization is in charge of its own capacity building.

2. *Trust between the organization and the provider is essential.* Both parties must feel free to communicate openly, to ask for help beyond the usual, to risk disapproval, to listen, and to learn.

3. *Organizations must be ready for capacity building.* An organization should exhibit the following qualities:

   It is open to change and willing to question itself.

   It can clearly describe its mission.

   Its key members believe that capacity building will further the mission.

   It is prepared to commit the necessary time and resources to capacity building.

4. *Ongoing questioning means better answers.* The provider facilitates a climate in which questioning and feedback are encouraged.

5. *Team and peer learning are effective capacity building tools.* Working in pairs and having team learning experiences are good for capacity building.

6. *Capacity building should accommodate different learning styles.* Some people learn by doing and some by experimenting, some need to talk, some need to think, some are more visual and some more verbal—all need to be taken into account.

**Exhibit 1.3. Principles of Successful
Capacity Building Assistance, Cont'd.**

7. *Every organization has its own history and culture.* The better a provider's understanding of an organization's situation, the more powerful the capacity building.

8. *All people and all parts of an organization are interrelated.* No matter how specific the issue, it connects with the rest of the organization and must be dealt with in that way. Change has a far better chance of success when it involves people from many levels—staff, constituents, and board members.

9. *Capacity building takes time.* Intensive long-term training and apprenticeships prepare people to build organizations, and can take place in stages.

Source: Adapted from Fine, Kopf, and Thayer, 2002. Used with permission.

3. Patience is essential. The surveyed organizations found that almost everything about capacity building took longer and was more complicated than expected. Capacity building can feel like a never-ending process because improvements in one area place new demands on other areas. There are few quick fixes in capacity building.

Choose Among Four Strategies for Increasing Impact

Across America there is a widely held view that nonprofits have many well-tested ideas for tackling most of the social problems the nation faces. However, most nonprofits are local, small, and underfunded, and though valuable within their limited areas of operation, they are not having a significant nationwide impact on the fundamental problems they seek to address.

Considerable thought is being given to the different generic strategies these organizations can pursue to increase their impact. Although the thinking is at an early stage of development, particularly when compared to the business thinking on generic strategic options, some strands are emerging. They are pulled together here because each generic strategy has implications for the approaches organizations could take to capacity building.

The evidence from my research suggests that nonprofit organizations can pursue four fundamentally different strategies to increase their impact. They need to consider whether they wish to expand geographically or to increase the range of services offered. These two generic strategies combine to create four options that organizations with ambitions for expansion need to consider. They can

- Diversify

- Specialize

- Scale up

- Scale deep

These strategic options are related as illustrated in Figure 1.3.

Figure 1.3. Generic Strategies for Increasing Impact.

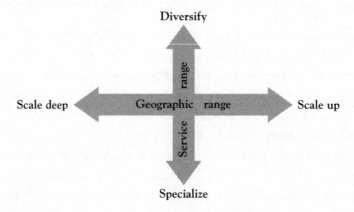

Diversification Strategy

Most nonprofits diversify, and they do so because they seek or are presented with new opportunities. They expand the range of services provided, and they offer services to related groups of people. For example, organizations that assist people with health problems diversify into research about the causes of the problem, and organizations that assist children diversify into similar services for young adults. Diversification is perhaps the most common strategy for increasing impact because it does not threaten existing services. It is often pursued incrementally and may not be a conscious strategy. Diversification enables organizations to exploit the *economies of scope* that arise from offering one group of people a range of services. It also enables them to attract additional resources, either through selling new services to purchasers or by appealing to different groups of donors. Diversification is an attractive strategy because it is generally funded by new resources and therefore avoids the need to make hard choices about the reallocation of existing resources. As a strategy it does not threaten the coalition of stakeholders that has been established to support current activities.

Many organizations begin by providing services and then diversify into campaigning for their cause because they recognize that their own efforts will always be small compared to those of government. They believe that they can get greater leverage in achieving their mission by campaigning for new legislation or to change government spending priorities.

Diversification does have significant drawbacks as a strategy. There is a danger that the organization will attempt to undertake an ever-wider range of activities and then find it does not have the capacity or the skills to provide effective management and support for everything it does. The lack of capacity often exhibits itself as ever-lengthening meeting agendas, incomplete projects, stressed staff, increased sickness among staff, and problems with staff retention.

Specialization Strategy

An alternative strategy is to specialize and become more focused on the organization's existing field of operation. This might involve enhancing existing services to meet the needs of service users better, or it could involve improving service quality. Letts, Ryan, and Grossman (1999) offer the example of the Vera Institute of Justice, an organization that designs and operates demonstration programs as a means of improving justice. It has conducted in-depth field research into the causes and dynamics of violence among youth. Instead of evaluating a specific program, the organization has been tracking, over several years, the lives of a select number of inner-city teenagers. It has worked in a focused way in its own area of specialization and delved deeper into the underlying issues that it exists to address. Sometimes a specialization strategy is a response to a diversification strategy that has become too broad. Organizations may add services, reach out to new groups, and then conclude that they do not have the capacity and the competence to manage this wide range of services. Alternatively, they may conclude that some services would be more successful if they were located in other organizations or if they were established as independent organizations. Such specialization enables an organization to concentrate its resources on a more limited number of people or services.

However, specialization also has its drawbacks. It can lead to loss of funding streams, as money is often linked directly to a service. It can also narrow the organization's potential donor base, as the remaining activities may appeal to fewer funders.

Scaling-Up Strategy

Scaling up is a generic strategy receiving much attention at present (and therefore explored more thoroughly here than the other approaches). It is a strategy for replicating successful approaches so they can benefit more people. The proponents of scaling up argue that the nonprofit sector could have greater impact if organizations spread successful methods of addressing social issues more widely around the country. They see economies of scale potentially resulting from more widespread application of the most effective models. "Few nonprofit organizations today have the scale and organizational ability to tackle the most challenging social problems effectively. Only 18 percent of nonprofits have a budget of $1 million or more. Most use their limited resources to market themselves to the same donor groups, to compete for the same foundation grants, to recruit the same people and ultimately to reach the same populations" (Meehan and Silverman, 2001, p. 14). So the potential for the sector as a whole to increase its impact is significant.

There are many examples of organizations that have successfully scaled up in the past, such as the Red Cross, Volunteers of America, and Big Brothers Big Sisters. Going to scale is therefore not an entirely new challenge. It was achieved by organizations that are now the backbone of the nonprofit sector because they had great ideas that resonated with people all over the country who grasped the opportunity to establish a service in their areas.

Harvard Business School researcher Jane Wei-Skillern asked a sample of managers why some nonprofits are reticent about going to scale. She concludes that

- Social entrepreneurs tend to focus on perfecting their ideas and tend not to think about the strategic alternatives for rolling out a program.

- People in nonprofits find it less exciting to act on other people's ideas than to create their own.

- Setting up a new program and *going to scale* require entirely different skills, and these distinct skills are seldom found in one person.

Scaling up has its critics. Some see it as a business perspective that is concerned only with efficiency and impact. They argue that

good ideas can be promulgated across the sector by publicizing successful programs and encouraging networking between organizations.
Dennis Derryck, a professor at New School University in New York,
argued to me that "neighborhoods are very specific, culturally, ethnically, and spiritually, so approaches to social problems have to be tailored to individual circumstances." Derryck also argued that great
social changes such as the granting of civil rights, the promotion of
women's rights, and actions to protect the environment have been
brought about by disparate groups of organizations that have remained
institutionally independent. His view is supported by two others I
interviewed: Michael Edwards, director of governance and civil society at the Ford Foundation, who says, "creating federations and
encouraging networking can be a more effective growth strategy," and
Roni Posner, executive director of the Alliance for Nonprofit Management, who says, "big is not always better in the nonprofit world."

One problem for organizations attempting to go to scale, according to Mary Ann Holohean, is that they find they are not embedded in the local community. Some of the best projects "grow out of
the community." She sees a big difference between a "community-
based" organization and a "community-occupying" organization.

Dees, Anderson, and Wei-Skillern (2002) looked at the ways
organizations scale up and identified three distinct approaches:

- Scaling up principles (by promoting an idea for others
  to follow)

- Scaling up specific programs (by working through affiliated organizations)

- Scaling up an entire organization (by creating an integrated national branch structure)

They argue that each has advantages and disadvantages. Promoting ideas can involve speaking at conferences, writing up experiences, publishing best-practice guidance, and employing a raft of

other approaches to interest other organizations in the idea or the service. Learning can be shared through networking. It is inexpensive, but it does not allow organizations to exploit economies of scale, and the scaling-up process cannot be managed in an integrated way.

Working with affiliated organizations allows for more varied approaches and more creativity in the way the service is scaled up. The service can be adapted more easily to suit local circumstances. Some nonprofits establish different levels of affiliates, ranging from setting up organizations that use the nonprofit's name and have a close relationship with it to giving an idea away to a separate organization and offering periodic support. (Exhibit 1.4 presents an affiliation case study.)

Most organizations examined in Jane Wei-Skillern's research wanted to scale up through branches. She explained to me her belief that social entrepreneurs want to "own" their creations and are reluctant to let go. They are concerned that other people will take their model but not deliver it to the same standards. Branch structures also allow best practice to be spread in a controlled way, supported by technical assistance and training. The appeal of branch structures is that they offer the greatest opportunity to create a brand and potentially a virtuous circle, in which a growing brand attracts more funds, which in turn further strengthens the brand. However, branches also require standards and a means of monitoring performance, so they are much more complex to establish.

A number of conclusions emerge from Wei-Skillern's research into scaling up. First, *replication* is about taking good ideas and modifying them to fit one's own circumstances. It is not about rote application of a good idea.

Second, when organizations scaled up, they learned more in a shorter time than organizations did that were undertaking an activity at one site. This is an important but underrecognized benefit of scaling up.

Exhibit 1.4. Women's World Banking:
Scaling Up Through Affiliates.

The Mission of Women's World Banking (WWB) is to expand the economic participation and power of low-income women by opening access to finance, information, and markets. WWB works toward achieving its goal in three ways:

- By providing and organizing support to affiliates who in turn offer direct services to low-income women

- By building learning and change networks comprising leading microfinance institutions and banks

- By working with policymakers to build financial systems that work for the poor majority

When Michaela Walsh founded WWB, she wanted to create a global organization with decisions made from the bottom up. Instead of creating a global institution, she established a network of affiliates—independent, country-based organizations with local boards.

At the end of 2002, the WWB had forty affiliates in thirty-four countries with over 400,000 active clients; the average loan was $415, the average repayment rate was 98.5%, and costs were 21 cents for every $1 lent.

This is how the organization built capacity through an affiliate model:

1979: Founder established the organization, using her own savings.

1981: First affiliates established in Colombia and Kenya.

1986: Requirements for becoming an affiliate established (small local capital fund, business plan consistent with WWB principles, board and management dominated by women).

1989: Training program established for affiliates (WWB grows to 10,000 clients).

1990: Affiliate management program launched in which affiliate presidents and executive directors critique each other's business plans with the aim of enhancing financial skills.

1994: Affiliate/Network Partnership Agreement approved. At the same global annual meeting, key performance indicators and standards were adopted. The partnership agreement process involves affiliate members, the global team, and neighboring affiliates in an annual review and strategic planning process (WWB grows to 100,000 clients).

Exhibit 1.4. Women's World Banking:
Scaling Up Through Affiliates, Cont'd.

1996: Global meeting agreed that one-third of the parent organization's funds be spent on serving existing affiliates, one-third on expanding the network and building broader networks, and one-third on policy work, knowledge building, and dissemination.

1997: Agreement made that the strategy to 2000 is to spend more on tailored services for affiliates, to disaffiliate nonperforming affiliates, and to give associate organizations access to WWB workshops and policy forums.

1998: Revised Partnership Agreement created by consensus, with affiliates establishing performance standards to be achieved by 2000.

1999: Program established to pilot innovations with leading affiliates, partly funded by WWB.

2001: Global Network for Banking Innovation in Microfinance launched, engaging leaders of mainstream financial institutions that are committed to microfinance as a profitable business opportunity.

2002: Capital fund used to back loan guarantees for affiliates exceeded $44 million.

According to Nancy Barry, president of WWB:

We have spent a lot of time and effort building this common culture. Through annual global or regional meetings, affiliate leaders from around the world have built our shared mission, vision, and value statements. These values include a belief that poor women are entrepreneurs, clients, and change agents—and should not be treated as passive beneficiaries of social services. They include a shared belief in business approaches to economic and social changes, with all affiliates expected to build sustainable, responsive services and institutions serving large numbers of poor women, not short-lived projects.

Our values include a belief in the power of self-determined organizations, bound by mutual accountability for results, rather than donor-driven approaches or top-down controls.

Source: Adapted from Austin and Harmeling, 1999. Copyright © 1999 by the President and Fellows of Harvard College. Harvard Business School case 9-300-050 by J.E. Austin was written as a basis for class discussion rather than to illustrate either effective or ineffective handling of an administrative situation. Reprinted by permission of Harvard Business School; all rights reserved.

Third, scaling up must be *demand pulled* by the local community, not *supply pushed* by a national organization. Sustainable organizations need local energy, supported by a peer-to-peer approach because nonprofit leaders learn best from each other.

Fourth, leaders need to be seen to be doing solid work in their community, not as working primarily to scale up their ideas. This finding is supported by Mary Ann Holohean: "Humility is required, and a nonhierarchical approach works best."

Finally, performance measurement is seen as a critical aspect of scaling up effectively. Managers need to be completely clear about how they will measure their success, and they must create transparency across the whole organization. This should involve a few simple, useful, and pragmatic measures.

Scaling-Deep Strategy

Organizations that pursue a strategy of scaling deep focus their activities in a limited geographic area and on a well-defined user group. They might aim to reach a higher percentage of their user group and enhance the effectiveness of their service. They can focus their attention on strengthening their local relationships and their local brand. "Scaling deep is about the 'best of breed' in your field" (Dees, Emerson, and Economy, 2002).

Scaling deep has the advantages of maintaining staff and board attention on limited and well-defined objectives and of concentrating resources. Compared to other strategies, it is less demanding of organization capacity. Management may be more straightforward and administrative overheads lower. However, scaling deep may not allow an organization to exploit economies of scale and may limit the pool of donors interested in supporting the organization.

Combined Strategies

Some organizations pursue more than one generic strategy at the same time—for example, attempting to diversify and scale up at the same time or attempting to specialize and scale deep at the

Figure 1.4. Different Strategy Combinations Make Different Demands on Organization Capacity.

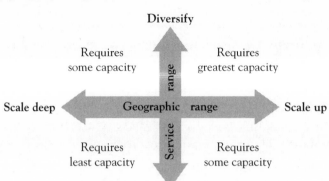

same time. Different combinations make different demands on organization capacity. Diversifying and scaling up is the most demanding, and specializing and scaling deep is considerably less so (see Figure 1.4).

Measure the Impact of Capacity Building

With all this interest in capacity building, people are also asking whether the results are worth the effort. Does better governance or better planning enhance organization performance? Indeed, as Light and Hubbard (2002) ask, "What are the measurable outcomes of a measurement outcome system?" Their answer is that there are at least three outcome levels:

- *Outputs:* which demonstrate whether the immediate objectives of the initiative have been met (such as a new system implemented or technology installed)

- *Organizational outcomes:* which show whether the initiative improved the functioning or performance of the organization (such as greater productivity or increased efficiency)

- *Mission impacts:* which establish whether the initiative resulted in the organization's achieving greater impact (such as more people housed or better-informed users)

In an ideal world, managers, board members, and funders would prefer to see mission impacts—and there is growing demand for such evidence. However, many capacity building initiatives are small compared to the overall size of the organization, so specific impacts may be hard to discern among all the other internal and external changes taking place simultaneously. As one funder said, "It would be the height of hubris to say that our $30,000 planning effort resulted in better client services in a $2.5 million direct service organization" (Light and Hubbard, 2002, p. 29).

Even though organizations need to take stock of the effectiveness of capacity building before and after each initiative and review whether that effort achieved the desired results, accuracy is not always easy, because of the tendency of those involved to inflate the perceived outcomes of initiatives to justify the time and effort invested. Light and Hubbard (2002) suggest a 360-degree survey of key stakeholders before and after the capacity building initiative to assess perceptions of outcomes against expectations. They go further to propose that if a number of organizations carried out such reviews, evidence of the impacts of different initiatives in organizations of varied sizes, ages, and types could be examined to determine which types of initiative are perceived to have the greatest impact.

Although demonstrating the success of capacity building is not easy, a number of studies of reengineering outcomes in the private sector suggest that an average success rate might be in the region of 25 to 50 percent. So a seemingly low success rate might be expected in the nonprofit sector as well. Nevertheless, there is a growing commitment to invest more effort into measuring the results of capacity building and an expectation that as organizations gather data the evidence base about the effectiveness of different approaches to capacity building will increase. Those organizations that contribute to that effort will be best placed to exploit the benefits and apply the learning that will inevitably emerge over the coming years.

Summary

Recognize Lack of Capacity as a Critical Constraint

- Government funders, private donors, and charity watchdogs unintentionally pressure organizations to underinvest in organization capacity.

- Lack of capacity is seen as the bottleneck that is constraining nonprofit organizations from having greater impact on the pressing social issues that the nation faces.

Invest in Capacity Building

- As interest in capacity building has grown exponentially, the case for significant investment in organization and management has grown also.

- A new paradigm of organizational effectiveness has emerged involving

  Making continuous strategic investment in the organization

  Charging funders the full cost of programs

  Using unrestricted income to invest in organization capacity

  Subsidizing services only when they have a demonstrable connection with the organization's strategic priorities.

Identify the Critical Elements of Organization Capacity

- Internal capacity building focuses on developing the mission, the board, staff and volunteers, management skills, physical infrastructure, technology, and evaluation.

- External capacity building is concerned with taking new initiatives, developing new strategies, and attracting new and more diversified income sources.

Adopt a Systematic Approach to Capacity Building

- The four key elements that shape the ultimate success of a capacity building project are

    The desired outcome

    The change strategy selected

    The champions guiding the effort

    The time, energy, and money invested in the process

- Most capacity building projects are concerned with strategic planning, fundraising and financial management, board development, communications, and marketing.

- Key ingredients of successful initiatives include new aspirations, commitment from senior management, and plenty of patience.

Choose Among Four Strategies for Increasing Impact

- There are four generic strategies for increasing impact: diversification, specialization, scaling up, and scaling deep.

- Diversification is the most common and least threatening to current activities but risks overstretching the organization's management capacity.

- Specialization involves making a greater effort with an existing group of users but can reduce access to funders and donors.

- Scaling up has the potential to increase organizational impact but there are dangers of not being properly connected to the local community.

- Scaling deep involves focusing on a geographic area but may not allow the organization to exploit economies of scale.

Measure the Impact of Capacity Building

- There are three levels of outcomes:

  The output of the initiative

  The impact on the organization

  The impact on the organization's mission

- Organizations need to take stock of the effectiveness of capacity building before and after each capacity building initiative.

Action Checklist

Developing organization capacity is an essential prerequisite for building a strong organization on secure foundations. Board members and managers who want their organizations to be delivering the greatest impact should

1. Recognize that they are responsible for ensuring that their organization makes significant investments in building its own capacity.

2. Use one of the lists of critical organization capacity elements in this chapter as a starting point for identifying the capacities their organization needs to have a greater impact.

3. Be rigorous in standing back and assessing which capacities are most critical for the next stage of their organization's development.

4. Prioritize capacity building initiatives, because organizations can cope with only a limited number at any one time.

5. Sequence capacity building initiatives, because some will be dependent on successful implementation of others.

6. Ensure that all capacity building initiatives have a clear strategy, a named leader, and sufficient resources to make a significant difference.

7. Make certain that success criteria are established before implementation begins and that evaluations are conducted systematically as the initiative progresses and following completion.

8. Be confident about charging the full costs of delivering services, including the cost of capital, and when possible allow for a modest surplus to fund future investment in initiatives such as capacity development.

2

Managing Performance

M ore than ever before, the public wants to know what non-profit organizations are accomplishing. Foundations, governments, and major donors want to know that their resources have achieved the desired results. They are less interested in what a funded organization did and more interested in the outcome and impact of the funding. The movement toward transparency and accountability in all walks of life means that nonprofit organizations reporting on the outcomes of their work will be regarded more highly, and therefore will receive more financial support, than those that do not report on outcomes.

As I mentioned earlier, although performance measurement seems easy in theory, it has been difficult in practice. As one chief executive commented in a survey, "Measuring mission success is like the Holy Grail for nonprofits—much sought after but never found" (Sawhill and Williamson, 2001, p. 379). The authors of the survey report comment, "Nonprofits simply have not been able to duplicate the crisp, straightforward way that businesses measure their performance" (p. 371). In an interview, Michael Cortes, director of the Institute for Nonprofit Organization Management at the University of San Francisco, concurred: "Performance management is in its early stages of development and is not a settled area yet." So did Paul Jansen, a director at McKinsey & Company, saying, "No one has cracked the code for performance metrics. We are in the evolutionary stage and the challenge is to get people to begin a journey that will take ten or more years."

Leaders in the nonprofit field acknowledge that performance management will become increasingly important as organizations strive to ensure all efforts are focused on achieving their objectives as efficiently as possible. However, they are also conscious that an organization's work may have a catalytic effect on a whole field and can be more important than its outputs or outcomes. Inevitably, it is much harder to ascribe causality for these wider impacts. "We know when we have played a role," Kim Smith, cofounder and CEO of the New Schools Venture Fund, told me, "but we don't know the extent of our contribution." Furthermore, there are concerns about the wider impact of performance management on the sector, because there "are few actionable assessment tools that measure impact at a community-wide level or can describe the impact of policy, research, advocacy and other efforts in tackling the more complex and intractable problems of society" (Global Leaders for Tomorrow, 2003, p. 5). Some fear that a relentless focus on outcomes will further dry up funds for organizations seeking to make constructive changes on a community-wide, issue-based, or systemic level (Global Leaders for Tomorrow, 2003).

Despite these acknowledged limitations, the next step, according to Alan Abramson, director of the Nonprofit Sector and Philanthropy program at the Aspen Institute, "is to move from measuring outcomes to managing impact." The key to managing impact is assembling information on the organization's outcomes and using it systematically in management and board decision making. Knowledge about performance can then be used in an active way to inform decisions that enhance organizations' effectiveness.

This chapter demonstrates that leading-edge nonprofit organizations:

- Grasp the opportunity to manage performance
- Recognize legitimate concerns
- Select measures that fit the organization's mission

- Use results to drive decisions at every level
- Embed performance management in the organization culture

Grasp the Opportunity to Manage Performance

Both organization history and current trends are driving the growing interest in performance management.

The Origins of Performance Management

Measuring performance in nonprofits has a long history, beginning with reporting on financial performance. People wanted to know how organizations spent their money. That was followed by measurement of outputs, because people wanted to know what organizations did with their funds. Interest in outputs can be traced to the late 1950s and the advent of the Great Society social programs of the 1960s, principally the model cities and the community action programs. In 1976, the United Way's program specification system defined 587 categories of human services and suggested measures for each. More recently, there has been much interest in setting standards and measuring quality to provide information about how well organizations are delivering their services. In the early 1980s, the idea of using key performance indicators became popular, particularly in public service organizations. Later, in the 1980s, accrediting bodies began requiring service providers to measure participant satisfaction.

Outcome measurement appears to follow naturally from these previous developments and addresses the question, What was achieved? It is viewed by many as the next brick in the wall of performance measurement and as a management approach that is here to stay. Distinctions among *inputs* (money and staff and volunteer time), *outputs* (the numbers of people served and campaigns run), *outcomes* (the results of the services for individuals), and *impacts* (the community-wide results of services and campaigns) are widely accepted. "Any scan of nonprofit publications, academic and trade journals and even mainstream media, reveals a popular fixation on results and accountability. Whatever the term—the message is the same: a demand for clear measurement of impact" (Global Leaders for Tomorrow, 2003, p. 8).

Interest in outcomes and impact took off in the early 1990s when the United Way of America made significant investments in developing outcome measurement tools and promoted them across the sector. In 1992, Harold Williams and Arthur Webb of the Rensselaerville Institute published a significant book, *Outcome Funding: A New Approach to Public Sector Grantmaking*, that added to the momentum. Many national organizations picked up these initiatives and encouraged and supported their regional and local chapters in taking steps to measure outcomes. By 1998, the American Cancer Society was providing training on outcome measurement for its local units, the American Foundation for the Blind annual leadership conference focused on outcomes, and the American Red Cross reported that 100 of its chapters were currently working on outcome measurement. In 2003, the United Way of America reported in detail on the outcome measurement activities of thirty-three national organizations. The report noted that many of these organizations had moved from helping chapters measure outcomes to helping them use outcome data and increase the effectiveness of their programs. As Elizabeth Boris, director of the Center on Nonprofits and Philanthropy at the Urban Institute told me, "Foundations, government, and United Ways have all come to the same views around the need to measure impact."

Most recently, the debate has moved from measuring outcomes to the use of data to manage performance. Implementation of performance management has been pushed particularly hard by venture philanthropists. They want to see numbers that demonstrate growth and effectiveness. They expect the organizations that they fund to produce reports similar to investment reports, with graphs and charts showing the numbers of people served and the outcomes of the services. They are driving the organizations they fund to make significant improvements to their performance management systems. However, William Ryan, Research Fellow at Harvard's

Hauser Center for Nonprofit Organizations, also told me that "there has been a backlash against the types of performance metrics foisted on organizations by the new philanthropists." The numbers are sometimes seen as simplistic and as failing to represent the subtleties and complexities of providing services to people who often have multiple problems that are not amenable to simple measures.

Forces Driving Organizations to Manage Performance

There are many external forces driving nonprofit organizations to develop performance management systems. First, there are growing demands for greater transparency and accountability. People increasingly expect nonprofits to be clear and honest about what they are doing and accountable for their achievements and failures. Some call for *radical transparency*, which would enable anyone to see precisely what a nonprofit is doing. According to Charles Lyons, chief executive of US Fund for UNICEF, "Radical transparency may be the key to improving performance."

Second, funders want to know what has been achieved with their money and, critically, are more willing to pay for the costs of gathering and reporting on performance. There is some skepticism about the value of "in-depth" evaluations, but a great deal of interest in low-cost systems that provide information that is good enough to demonstrate outcomes and inform future decision making.

Third, the widespread move to funding individuals who require state health and social services, rather than funding the suppliers, has emphasized results-oriented service delivery. Outcomes for individual participants are usually recorded and can be a requirement in care contracts. The availability of these data is encouraging organizations to assemble information on the overall performance of a service and use that information to gain insights into which actions achieve the desired results. In many parts of the sector, including child and family services, health care, rehabilitation, and home care, providers are required to meet standards established by accreditation agencies. Four of the leading accreditation organizations require evidence that organizations are measuring outcomes, and some specify the topics for which outcomes must be measured (United Way of America, 2003).

Fourth, the creation of GuideStar—the national database on non-profit organizations—has catalyzed some organizations to summarize their performance in an easily accessible way. All organizations included in the database have an opportunity to complete a *goals and results* section that asks them to summarize past achievements in one paragraph and to set out headline plans for the coming year. Because it is widely used, GuideStar is inevitably encouraging organizations to post information on achievements and future plans, although the performance data posted on the site at the time of this writing varied considerably in quality.

Finally, nonprofits are subject to continual attention from the members of the press, who are always ready to highlight wrong-doing. This feeds public cynicism about nonprofits, which is hard to counter without evidence of solid achievements. The vacuum of information about accomplishments leaves nonprofits wide open to criticism. Performance management offers an opportunity to create widespread understanding of long-term successes that buttress orga-nizations against such media challenges.

Although the demands for improved performance are primarily external, boards and managers recognize that performance man-agement is a powerful tool for keeping organizations focused on results. "Nonprofit board members have a well-known tendency to stray, to promote pet projects and initiatives, and nothing combats such hobbyism better than a clear, commonly agreed upon set of institutional measures" (Sawhill and Williamson, 2001).

Similarly managers find that the presence of performance met-rics helps to focus the efforts of their staff. They are also finding that good performance measures help in seeking grant funding.

Beyond the pragmatics, there is a compelling theoretical case for performance management. Resources are always limited, so organi-zations need to evaluate their work to understand which services deliver the best results. This information should inform resource allocation decisions that in the past have often been based more on well-crafted funding applications than on rigorously tested evidence of achievements. Funders can then invest more heavily in those programs proven to be effective and withdraw from those shown to be less effective.

A further strand in the theoretical case stems from the flow of funds to nonprofits. Unlike for-profit organizations, nonprofits do not have a built-in organizational reward system. When a for-profit is successful, its sales and profits increase, so successful organizations prosper and unsuccessful ones eventually fail. In the nonprofit world it is possible for an organization to be highly successful at fundraising and deliver poor services. Performance management is therefore the missing link that can connect results to future rewards, in the form of both new and extended funding. (Exhibit 2.1 displays the outcome measures used by an agency serving persons with disabilities.)

Current Measurement Activity

So, are organizations grasping the opportunity to manage performance more systematically? In 1997, a survey of outcome measurement suggested that "there has been an explosion of outcome measurement activity in recent years" (Newcomer, 1997, p. 245). In 1998, an INDEPENDENT SECTOR survey of 1,700 organizations found that 43 percent were collecting information on changes in client conditions or behaviors and 67 percent were routinely collecting information on clients' satisfaction with services (Wiener, Kirsch, and McCormack, 2001). More recently, Paul Light's 2002 survey of executive directors found that 92 percent reported an increased emphasis on outcome measurement and 79 percent reported that the increase was "a great deal" or "a fair amount."

It is clear that outcome measures are here to stay. Leading organizations are now focusing on implementing performance management systems that enable managers and boards to determine what the organization has accomplished and to keep staff attention on achieving the mission.

Exhibit 2.1. Measuring Outcomes: Toolworks.

Toolworks, a San Francisco–based agency providing services to increase economic and social opportunities for disabled people, makes extensive use of outcome measures. "We promote the measures when we are approaching funders," says Executive Director Donna Feingold. "We also use them to identify gaps in our services. For example, our community support services developed because our outcome follow-ups identified that although we had got people into work, they were lonely and had poor-quality home life."

The twelve outcome measures for Toolworks' 2000–2001 employment program come from seven separate sources:

Measure	Data Source	Goal	Outcome
Effectiveness			
No. of clients placed in new jobs	Placement reports	72	73
% earning $8 or more per hour	Placement reports	75%	67%
% maintaining job for 90 days or more	Placement reports	85%	84%
% securing subsidized housing	Case records	25%	30%
No. of new contracts secured	Contract files	10	12
Efficiency			
No. of clients with reduced reliance on public benefits	Case records	175	219
% placed within 90 days of intake	Placement reports	80%	74%
% receiving support from generic resources	Case records	50%	64%
% of employees maintaining an accident-free workplace	Claim reports	95%	91%
Satisfaction			
% of clients satisfied with the service	Satisfaction surveys	75%	76%
% of satisfied staff	Staff survey	75%	86%
% of satisfied referring agencies	Survey	75%	89%

A summary of all outcome measures is presented at the annual meeting, and the measures are reported regularly to staff.

Source: Data provided by Toolworks.

Recognize Legitimate Concerns

Although the case for performance management is strong and it is widely accepted that the move to measure outcomes and impacts has been valuable, nonprofits face significant challenges in implementing such systems. Research into performance management for foundations has demonstrated that as measurement moves away from outcomes at the level of the funded organization and toward policy change, fewer models or systems exist for measuring impact (Figure 2.1). Recent research into outcome measurement in nonprofits came to a similar conclusion: "Leaders of nonprofit organizations face a particular bind in responding to the demands for results-based accountability. If they focus only on the project-level outcomes over which they have the most control or for which indicators are readily available, they risk default on the larger question of accountability to publicly valued goals. On the other hand, if they try to demonstrate the impact of their particular projects on community-wide outcomes, they risk taking credit inappropriately or shouldering the blame for indicators beyond their control" (Campbell, 2002, p. 243).

Figure 2.1. Levels of Outcome Measurement for Foundations.

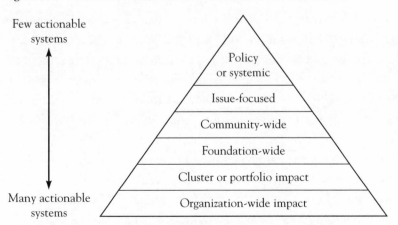

Source: Global Leaders for Tomorrow, 2003, p. 63. Reprinted with permission.

Practitioners also recognize that measurement is comparatively easy in some parts of the nonprofit world and much more difficult in others. Preventive work is frequently held up as one of the problem areas. For example, measuring how many of the teenagers who participated in a teen sexual health program did not get pregnant is only possible when they are tracked over a long time, and even then it is virtually impossible to link the program directly with the results. In circumstances such as this, intermediate indicators may be seen as more valuable. For example, measuring changes in people's attitudes before and after a service is delivered can provide valuable information to preventive program providers.

Some activities are amenable to quantitative measurement, and outcomes of other activities are more qualitative. The outcome of an employment program can be measured relatively easily in terms of the number of people obtaining employment of the type desired and staying in those jobs for a stated period. The outcomes of a counseling service are inherently less easy to measure because they are dependent on the quality of the interaction between people holding confidential discussions. "People are aware of the dangers of relying on numbers alone," according to Audrey Alvarado, executive director of the National Council of Nonprofit Associations, a network of state and regional associations representing 17,000 nonprofits throughout the country. "The challenge is to articulate achievements in ways people can understand—and this requires a combination of numbers and case studies."

The challenge of balancing quantitative and qualitative measures is reflected in evidence about the types of organizations that are most likely to measure outcomes. A joint INDEPENDENT SECTOR and Urban Institute study found that organizations involved in employment training, vocational rehabilitation, home health care, and nursing home care were more likely to track outcomes related to clients' conditions (Morley, Vinson, and Harty, 2001). In these areas it is often the case that reporting is required by external agencies, including funders and accreditation organizations such as the

Joint Commission on Accreditation of Healthcare Organizations, the Commission on Accreditation of Rehabilitation Facilities, and the Council on Accreditation. However, in other fields, such as youth work, mental health, and services for elderly people, it can be much more difficult to define outcomes, and accreditation organizations are less likely to require them. Organizations in these fields are consequently more likely to rely on qualitative reports of achievements than on quantitative measures of outcomes.

Other challenges are recognized and taken into account in the development of performance management systems. They include

- The risk that performance management could disadvantage areas of work that are less easily measured

- The danger that staff might be encouraged to target services where successful outcomes are more likely rather than areas of greatest need

- An excessive interest in short-term results at the expense of the long-term sustainability of initiatives—a particular concern among those nonprofit organizations where desired change may take many years or even decades.

Organizations must also cope with the challenge of establishing the primary purpose of a performance management system. As Peter Shiras, senior vice president of INDEPENDENT SECTOR, said, "There is a difference between what organizations need from measurement (honest, critical appraisal that feeds into organizations' learning) and what they need to give funders (evidence of success to get more money)." (Exhibit 2.2 describes how one organization deals with some of these challenges.)

Nonprofits also have concerns about the resource implications of improving performance management. Some approaches are expensive, and managers are acutely aware of the danger of spending time

Exhibit 2.2. Preventing Performance from Distorting Priorities: Children's Institute International.

Children's Institute International provides a home visiting service. Management and staff recognized that the "best outcome" for individuals varies. In most cases, keeping young people out of foster care is a desired outcome, but in a few cases, foster care might be the best option.

To overcome the problem this might cause if outcomes were measured simply in terms of avoiding foster care, they take a two-level approach. They conduct individual assessments on all their children, using standard child psychology development measures. In addition they establish goals for each child and family and assess individual achievement of the agreed goals. They use a goal attainment scale to measure the percentage of children achieving the stated goals and assimilate this data to produce program-level results. They benchmark their results against similar programs delivered by other organizations.

According to chief executive Mary Emmons, "A strong organization culture is required to avoid creaming the easy cases. Our aim is to help the most difficult cases that we are capable of assisting. We do turn down some families because their problems are too complex for our skills and resources. Even with this boundary, we recognize that very difficult cases do make heavy use of resources, so we top up state funding for these cases with donor income."

Source: Information provided by Children's Institute International.

and money on a performance system that ultimately never quite measures achievement of the organization's mission and may not deliver value concomitant with the cost of implementation. "Start-up costs are high and it is difficult to access resources to develop performance management systems," according to Alan Abramson of the Aspen Institute. There are many reports of expensive evaluations that do not turn out to be useful. The key, according to Abramson, is to "find low-cost ways of collecting and using data." Once the organization has succeeded in collecting data in usable forms, ways have to be found to make effective use of this information. "The big challenge is to incorporate measuring into everyday activities and then to adjust what the organization is doing when the measurements suggest change is necessary," says Abramson (also see Exhibit 2.3).

**Exhibit 2.3. Performance Management in Action:
Some Practical Advice.**

The United Way offers valuable advice about having realistic objectives when establishing performance management systems:

- "Requiring program managers to set outcome targets before they have at least a year of baseline outcome data is counterproductive. Programs with no experience in outcome measurement generally have no basis for setting an appropriate target, and their targets will likely be little more than guesses.

- "Fund allocators do not yet have enough experience with outcome measurement to judge whether a particular level of achieved performance is good, bad or in between.

- "Comparing seemingly similar programs to reward those with the 'best' outcomes is tempting but misguided. Even 'similar' programs have meaningful differences in mission, target audience, geographic location, staffing, service methodology and funding level.

- "In judging outcome findings, the best comparison for a program is itself: Is the program improving? Is it learning from earlier outcome findings, making adjustments, and having better results?

- "Despite the hope of many fund allocators, outcome findings will not make the allocation decision easier. Decisions about where to direct resources will remain complex and value based, and funding decisions always will need to consider more than outcome performance."

Source: Plantz, Greenway, and Hendricks, 1999, pp. 7–10. Copyright © John Wiley & Sons, Inc. Reprinted with permission of John Wiley & Sons, Inc.

Despite the many challenges, there is no doubt that performance management will become an essential part of management activity for most organizations. "There are no ultimate answers in performance metrics," Stephanie Lowell, nonprofit practice manager at McKinsey & Company in Boston, told me. "But having metrics does focus an organization on what it should be achieving. Understanding how a nonprofit service affects people in its client group is a valuable discipline." So although evaluation data are valuable when they are used as aids to decision making, they are not substitutes for good judgment. (Exhibit 2.4 presents another case study of getting started with performance management.)

Select Measures That Fit the Organization's Mission

According to the survey carried out jointly by INDEPENDENT SECTOR and the Urban Institute, nonprofit organizations are collecting information on two types of outcomes. First, they are examining *service outcomes* through measures of service quality or of user perceptions. The key question these measures address is whether users were satisfied with the service. Organizations ask participants how they rated the each aspect of a service such as its quality, timeliness, responsiveness, and staff attitudes. Second, organizations are gathering information on *end outcomes* through measures of the user actions or changed conditions that result from delivery of the service. They are capturing the numbers and percentages of people who exhibit the changes that the program was designed to achieve. A majority of the organizations in this survey collected both types of indicator (Morley, Vinson, and Harty, 2001).

Research by McKinsey & Company (Sawhill and Williamson, 2001) concluded that organizations have three options, which can be used in combination, for measuring their success in achieving their mission. First, they can *define their mission narrowly enough that progress can be measured directly*. The example of Goodwill Industries

Exhibit 2.4. Launching a Performance Management Initiative: Boys & Girls Clubs of Boston.

Boys & Girls Clubs of Boston is an $11 million organization that exists to help boys and girls, generally living in disadvantaged circumstances, develop the qualities needed to become responsible citizens and leaders. The organization provides activities and support services designed to assist in the educational, emotional, physical, and social development of six- to eighteen-year-olds, and it serves 8,000 children in the Boston area.

Management and staff decided to undertake a significant initiative to develop a performance management system and culture. As they had little information on service users, the initiative began by modernizing the membership database. This involved changing enrollment forms to collect more information and developing a balanced scorecard of outcome indicators. These methods were pilot-tested with a sample of clubs enthusiastic about the initiative. The challenge then was to take the initiative to scale and involve all the clubs.

Linda Whitlock, the chief executive, assembled a team of line managers to lead the project and also involved a board member with particular expertise in outcome measures. She decided that she would lead the initiative personally to ensure it was seen as a priority by everyone.

The organization raised $300,000 from foundations to finance implementation of the initiative. It formed a partnership with a university and began a long-term longitudinal study to attempt to measure the overall impact of club experience on people's lives. This study will measure the impact of the clubs on children's educational, emotional, social, and moral development.

"We have an obligation to know what impact we are having," said Linda Whitlock. "I have systematically built this initiative to ensure that it is sustainable—forever! It will enable us to differentiate ourselves significantly from other organizations seeking funds to do similar work."

Source: Information provided by Boys & Girls Clubs of Boston.

is frequently cited. Its mission is to help disabled people by providing job training and employment services, and with an income of over $1,600 million per annum, it is the country's seventh largest nonprofit. It measures the number of people served, the number finding employment, and the salaries that these employees earn. Second, through research, organizations can *demonstrate a direct connection between their service and the desired results*. JumpStart Coalition, a nonprofit dedicated to improving the educational outcomes of poor children, is an example. It takes the lowest achievers in the Head Start program and provides them with a basic literacy skills program. Academically robust studies have demonstrated that children who attend this program at the age of four have better educational outcomes throughout primary school. The number of children attending this program is therefore a good measure of JumpStart's achievement of its mission. Third, organizations can *develop micro-level goals that imply success on a grander scale*. The Nature Conservancy, for example, has a grand mission to increase global biodiversity—which it cannot measure. But its main activity is to purchase and protect important sites, and it is currently responsible for over 11.5 million acres of land. It measures the health of biodiversity at its own sites by evaluating the condition of plants and animals it is trying to save and tracks efforts to counter the most critical threats to environmental health. (Exhibit 2.5 offers further examples of useful outcome measures.)

For many nonprofits, following up service users three, six, twelve, and more months after the service has been provided is seen as important because the outcome of the service may not show immediately (see, for example, Exhibit 2.6). Though difficult in cases where it is hard to keep track of recipients (as it is in homeless services, for example), follow-ups can provide high-quality information about outcomes. Clearly, however, data gathering becomes increasingly difficult and expensive as the time between the delivery of the service and the follow-up grows.

Exhibit 2.5. Examples of Outcome Measures.

- Number and percentage of vocational rehabilitation participants placed in employment who retained their job for 90 and 150 days
- Number and percentage of youth service participants who went on to attend 2- or 4-year college courses
- Number and percentage of Alzheimer's clients with improvements or no change in walking steadily, self-feeding, interacting with others
- Number and percentage of mental health clients placed in less restrictive settings
- Number and percentage of people screened for drugs who show a decreased amount of substances 3, 6, and 12 months after a drug treatment program
- Number and percentage of clients who retained housing in which they were placed 3, 6, and 12 months after leaving the program
- Pounds of material recovered and recycled by environmental programs

Source: Morley, Vinson, and Harty, 2001. Reprinted with permission.

Another aspect of choosing performance indicators is the need to capture the unique features of nonprofit activity. These might include

- Reaching underserved populations
- Providing opportunities for volunteering and citizen participation
- Bringing about change through advocacy work
- Providing opportunities for spiritual activity

Exhibit 2.6. Individual and Family Tracking and Evaluation Tool: Asian Neighborhood Design.

Asian Neighborhood Design (AND) has worked for over 20 years in the San Francisco Bay Area, sponsoring a variety of programs to help individuals and families get out of poverty. They use a Tracking and Evaluation Tool with many of their clients.

Each project participant, with an AND support person, crafts a personal self-sufficiency plan. Staff track the new participant's status in each of seven categories—from "income/assets" to "personal attributes"—with a score of −2, −1, +1, or +2. A score of −2 represents a high risk or crisis situation, while a +2 represents a strong, stable situation. At regular intervals they meet with their AND support person and assess their progress in each of the seven categories.

The tool is not only used for tracking and evaluation. It also guides the discussion between the AND support person and the participant, and it helps the participant to develop and carry through the self-sufficiency plan.

The tool helps AND evaluate how a participant is progressing and how long AND can continue to support the participant. The idea assumes that a person needs several strong supports to be considered self-sufficient and can handle no more than one or two risk areas at the same time.

This evaluation tool focuses on outcomes—on changes in people's lives that may be partly due to AND and other programs. It involves no expectation of precise measurement, and there is (intentionally) a large element of judgment in the numbers it yields. Nevertheless (and this is critically important to the value of the tool), large score differences, such as between a total score of −8 for one participant and +5 for another, should reflect easily recognizable differences in levels of self-sufficiency.

	Income/ Assets	Education/ Skills	Housing/ Food	Safety/ Environment	Human Service	Relationships	Personal Attributes
Major life issue:							
Assets:							
+2							
+1							
Barriers:							
−1							
−2							
TOTAL							

Source: Global Leaders for Tomorrow, 2003. Reprinted with permission.

A comprehensive performance management system will capture data on any special dimensions of nonprofit activity as well as the more obvious benefits to service users. "Agencies should tap many perspectives when identifying program outcomes. Program volunteers, current and past participants (and perhaps family members), persons such as teachers and employers, and other agencies can point out important outcomes" (Plantz, Greenway, and Hendricks, 1999, p. 7). (Exhibit 2.7 describes using outcome data to measure *social return*, the benefits beyond those that accrue to the individual.)

However, this should be balanced with the need to keep performance measures simple. As James Austin, chair of Harvard Business School's Social Enterprise Initiative, said to me, "The key issue is not ever-greater focus on the technicality of output measures or of ascribing causality. It is more important to identify meaningful measures and discover how to integrate them into management systems."

The importance of agreeing on measures with funders before work begins must also be stressed. Leading organizations ensure that they have explicit agreements with their funders about both the measures and the targets. This allows performance assessment to focus the organization on learning for the future rather than on retrospective debates about what the measures should have been (also see Exhibit 2.8).

Finally, the desire to learn from experience and continuously improve should be balanced against the need to keep some consistency from year to year so that trends can be measured and achievements celebrated.

Use Results to Drive Decisions at Every Level

Two broad approaches to measuring performance are emerging from the initiatives taken to date. The first and most common is a results-based approach that quantifies outcomes in relation to inputs, activities, and outputs. These can be reported on a balanced scorecard or a corporate dashboard. The second is comparative and uses

Exhibit 2.7. Social Return on Investment: REDF.

REDF (formerly the Roberts Enterprise Development Fund) is a venture philanthropy fund that invests in social enterprises. Investors want the enterprises that they support to be financially viable and, more important, to create significant social benefit. Investors therefore want to calculate the financial returns and social impact of each investment to verify that it has generated ample combined financial and social returns.

In the business world, methods for calculating financial returns are well understood and are based on discounted cash-flow analysis, taking the cash flows that the enterprise is expected to generate over coming years and discounting their value to allow for the fact that cash coming in next year is worth less than cash coming in now.

The significant breakthrough that REDF has made is to calculate social returns in a similar way. To value social returns, it calculates the reduction in Social Security payments and the reduction in the use of community clinics, mental health treatment, hospital emergency rooms, legal services, prison services, substance abuse treatment, and other public services that will result from employing disadvantaged people. REDF then discounts these values in the same way that businesses discount future cash flows.

As REDF's focus is employing people in social enterprises, it also adds in the value of the taxes that previously non-tax-paying employees will pay. Together these two amounts are a proxy for social value.

To create a total picture of the value of a social enterprise, REDF adds the financial value of the enterprise with its social value to create a *blended value*. REDF has calculated the financial and social returns of the eleven investments that it has made. These reports are well worth reading.

Industrial Maintenance Engineers: An Example of Calculating Social Return on Investment

Industrial Maintenance Engineers (IME) is a social enterprise that exists to provide professional cleaning services delivered by people with psychiatric disabilities, ex-offenders, and people with a history of substance abuse. It provides janitorial services for thirty-eight buildings, and is expected to have sales of $1.4 million by 2004. It employed seventy-seven people at the start of 2000.

Exhibit 2.7. Social Return on Investment: REDF, Cont'd.

Social Purpose Results (per target employee)	1999
Public savings	$23,531
New taxes paid by employees	$890
Wage improvement of each employee	$5,931
Financial improvement (wage improvement less reduced Social Security)	$3,594

At the time of its 2000 report on IME, REDF had invested just over $300,000 in the enterprise. The financial value of the enterprise was $477,000, and the social purpose value (over the lifetime of the enterprise) was a mighty $58 million, primarily because the overwhelming majority of employees were people who before employment had been heavily dependent on Social Security and a range of public services.

In 2003, IME won a substantial new contract, in part because it was able to demonstrate to the public sector contractor that from seventeen to twenty-eight months after hire, 71 percent of its recruits were still employed.

Source: Adapted from REDF, 2000.

benchmarks to review performance against the performance of similar organizations or services. These approaches can be applied simultaneously.

Approach	Reported In
Results-oriented	Balanced scorecards
	Corporate dashboards
Comparison-oriented	Benchmarking reports

The results-based approach is rooted in the well-established idea that inputs of resources support activities that lead to service or policy outputs, which in turn produce the desired outcomes. When this model is applied to nonprofit organizations, outputs are about the programs the organizations deliver, and outcomes are about the benefits to participants.

There is a widespread view that a nonprofit's choice of what to measure needs to be rooted in a theory of social change. The first step, according to Alan Abramson, is for an organization "to be clear about the underlying model of change that the organization is attempting to achieve. It can then use performance measurement to test whether the resources applied are having the desired effect."

The chain of relationships between activities, outputs, and outcomes is referred to as the *logic* or *theory* of how a program brings about benefits to its participants. The United Way talks of a series of "if-then" relationships and gives the example of pregnancy programs:

- If a program provides prenatal counseling to pregnant teens, then the teens have increased knowledge of good prenatal care.

- If the teens have increased knowledge of good prenatal care, then this leads to changed behavior: the teens eat the proper foods, take a prenatal vitamin each day and avoid cigarettes, alcohol and other drugs.

- If the teens follow these practices, then the result is that the teens deliver healthy newborns [Morley, Vinson, and Harty, 2001, p. 3].

The Balanced Scorecard

Some organizations have adopted the idea of the *balanced scorecard*, originally developed by Robert Kaplan and David Norton (1996) for use in the private sector. This assessment method is based on the notion that traditional corporate sector financial measures capture only past performance and that it is more important to measure the drivers of future performance. The aim is to measure performance on a range of dimensions, each chosen because it will assist the organization to achieve its overall mission. In the original balanced

Exhibit 2.8. Some Lessons for Funders.

The United Way offers this experience-based advice to funders who are encouraging the organizations they fund to develop outcome measures:

- "Funders . . . will play a key role in the nonprofit sector's move to a focus on outcomes. To be most constructive, funders should view their role as helping each program develop the outcome measurement approach that provides the most useful information for that program. To the extent that funders impose outcomes, measures, or timetables that do not align with agencies' efforts, they impede successful implementation.

- "Funders serve their own best interests by helping agencies develop capacity for outcome measurement.

- "Local funders can collaborate with each other very effectively to support agency efforts. They can, for example, pool resources to underwrite training and technical assistance. They also can agree on outcome measurement terminology, methodology and implementation timetables. Common application and reporting forms go even further in clarifying expectations and reducing the burden of paperwork on local agencies.

- "Funders can help agencies by providing an outside perspective on the reasonableness of agencies' outcome measurement plans and working collaboratively to help improve the proposed approach. Funders should accept outcomes, indicators and measurement methods established by relevant national organizations and accrediting bodies unless they fail to meet essential criteria.

- "As funders add outcome data as a reporting requirement, they should . . . drop existing reporting requirements that do not match this focus. If benefits for people are the critical emphasis, then some reports designed to monitor internal processes (for example, quarterly cash flow statements, detailed line-item budgets, salary information for specific staff, staffing structures, minutes of board meetings, internal policy and procedure manuals) should be eliminated. This action also helps offset the added burden for agencies of collecting and reporting outcome data."

Source: Plantz, Greenway, and Hendricks, 1999. Copyright © John Wiley & Sons, Inc. Reprinted with permission of John Wiley & Sons, Inc.

scorecard, Kaplan and Norton proposed that businesses should measure their performance by tracking dimensions of performance concerned with customers, learning and growth within the organization, and internal business processes as well as financial performance. So the balanced scorecard focuses managers on both outcomes and the health of the organization that is producing the outcomes.

Kaplan and Norton's ideas have been widely implemented in the for-profit world. For the nonprofit sector, Kaplan (2001) has added a fifth dimension of *social impact,* to put the organization's mission at the heart of the scorecard. Some nonprofit organizations have followed the model precisely. Others have taken the general principle of measuring performance using a range of indicators grouped into four or five dimensions but have adjusted the dimensions to suit their circumstances (see, for example, Table 2.1).

According to Kaplan (2001), use of "the balanced scorecard has enabled nonprofit organizations to bridge the gap between vague mission and strategy statements and day-to-day operational actions. It has facilitated a process by which an organization can achieve strategic focus, avoiding the pathology of attempting to be everything to everyone. The measurement system has shifted the focus from programs and initiatives to the outcomes the initiatives and programs are supposed to accomplish" (p. 369). The balanced scorecard approach acknowledges that aggregating performance data is often not appropriate in the nonprofit world. "The key benefit of the balanced scorecard," as Jeff Bradach, managing partner of Bridgespan Group, a consulting firm to nonprofits, said to me, "is that it helps to organize data. Operating data is very important and having it well organized enables effective accountability."

Some of the performance measures used in the balanced scorecard are concerned with tracking internal performance. This reflects a compelling argument Harvard Business School professor Allen Grossman made to me: "There is evidence that if nonprofit organizations have good plans, quality assurance systems, measurement systems, and mechanisms for improving performance, then they will have better delivery of their service."

New Profit Inc., a venture philanthropy group, requires the organizations it funds to prepare balanced scorecards. It reports the following traits among those organizations (Global Leaders for Tomorrow, 2003, p. 56):

- "The management team will talk more about strategy and less about tactics.

- "Staff of the organization know and understand the strategy and how their job fits into it.

- "Organizations develop the capability to refresh and create their own scorecards.

- "Evaluation becomes more integrated with and embedded in the organization's operations."

Just as some managers and consultants counsel against attempts to make performance indicators unrealistically scientific, some also take the view that it is more important to have a workable scorecard than to strive after the perfect scorecard. "The precise categories of what to measure on the scorecard are not the critical issue," according to Allen Grossman. "The point is to understand the drivers of performance and get the board and staff to discuss these drivers. They need to go beyond fundraising and good governance to get insights into the ecology of how nonprofits function."

Some organizations are taking the balanced scorecard approach one step further, in line with Kaplan and Norton's (2000) proposal that organizations should use their key performance indicators to create a *strategy map* that helps managers see the connections between each of the drivers of performance and the intended results. A strategy map builds on the work many organizations have already done on strategic planning. Strategic plans establish organizations' missions, objectives, and the overall strategies for achieving a mission. Strategy maps take this one step further. They attempt to reduce the strategy to its essential elements and to show how the organization will deliver the desired mission (Figure 2.2).

Table 2.1. Citizen Schools 2001 Balanced Scorecard.

Aspect	Objectives	Measures and Goals
Social impact	A. Deliver a superior quality program that educates children and strengthens community by building skills (writing, data analysis, and oral presentation), access, leadership, and community connections.	1. Student impact rating of 4.0 or higher on a 5-point scale (composite of up to 10 key questions from various stakeholders). 2. 75% (or more) of students at campuses focusing on writing (currently 9 of 11) will increase by one rubric level their writing skills during the academic year. 75% (or more) of all students will improve their oral presentation skills (data from both rubrics and staff assessments). *Stretch goal:* Greater than 80%.
Financial	B. Receive $7.5 million in cash or commitments toward four-year, $25 million campaign.	3. Reach the $7.5 million goal by end of year. *Stretch goal:* Greater than $8.5 million. *Stretch goal 2:* Nonfoundation funding increases (minimum of >10% versus growth targets) faster than expenses between 2000–2001.
	C. Stay within 2001 budget.	4. Post 5%+ surplus and stay within budget of $4.8 million.
Customer	D. *Students:* Expand student demand and enrollment.	5. Increase student enrollment from 1,248 in FY2000 to 1,530 (±5%). *Stretch goal:* Demand grows significantly as evidenced by ⅔ of campuses with a waitlist of 10% or more enrollment for fall 2001 program.
	E. *Citizen teachers:* Provide outstanding volunteer experience and thereby increase pool of volunteers.	6. 85% or more of CTs surveyed indicate they would (a) return and teach a future apprenticeship, (b) refer a friend to teach an apprenticeship, and (c) rate the experience as 4.0 or greater on its positive impact on the volunteer.

F. *Training partners:* Deliver high-quality, high-impact training to first-year CS partners.	7. 4.0 (or better) rating of quality and impact of training by executive directors and participating staff from 2+ partners.
Operations G. Develop more precise evaluation instruments for measuring program impact.	8. Complete the following: Hire external evaluator for three-year evaluation, revise constituent surveys, and develop strong measurement tools in all key outcome areas.
H. Set stage for national leverage of CS Model.	9. *Publishing:* Document and internally publish Version 1.0 CS Best Practices.
	10. *Policy:* Four meetings with local officials, four with state/national officials, and favorable coverage in five media outlets.
I. Deepen school partnerships.	11. Eight of twelve campus directors and eight of twelve school principals (or primary school liaisons) rate the following components of the partnership as 4.0 or greater: (a) academic alignment, (b) enrollment demand, and (c) community engagement.
J. Consistently implement action plan.	12. Successfully accomplish 75% or more of action plan goals within one quarter of goal. *Stretch goal:* 85% or more of action plan.

Note: Table notes with additional detail have been omitted.
Source: Citizen Schools and New Profit Inc. Printed with permission.

Figure 2.2. Strategy Map for a Venture Philanthropist–Funded Organization.

New Leaders for New Schools aims to improve the performance of state schools by recruiting, training, placing, and supporting a new generation of outstanding school principals. The organization trains and places school principals in urban schools. It plans to place 500 school principals by 2010. In 2002 it expected that 30,000 children will have enhanced educational prospects following the appointment of its highly trained school leaders. Its $2 million start-up funding was generated by seed funding from three venture philanthropy organizations: Boston-based New Profit Inc., San Francisco-based New Schools Venture Fund, and the Los Angeles-based Broad Foundation. Its strategy map and the associated performance indicators are evolving. At the time of writing it was as follows. It is somewhat overwhelming at first glance as it reduces the organization's strategy and performance to one diagram. It is easiest to read it from the bottom upward.

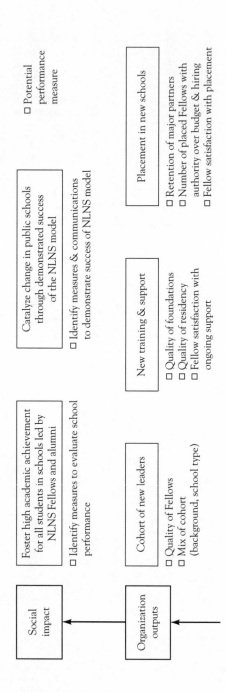

□ Potential
  performance
  measure

Social
impact

Organization
outputs

Foster high academic achievement
for all students in schools led by
NLNS Fellows and alumni

□ Identify measures to evaluate school
  performance

Cohort of new leaders

□ Quality of Fellows
□ Mix of cohort
  (background, school type)

Catalyze change in public schools
through demonstrated success
of the NLNS model

□ Identify measures & communications
  to demonstrate success of NLNS model

New training & support

□ Quality of foundations
□ Quality of residency
□ Fellow satisfaction with
  ongoing support

Placement in new schools

□ Retention of major partners
□ Number of placed Fellows with
  authority over budget & hiring
□ Fellow satisfaction with placement

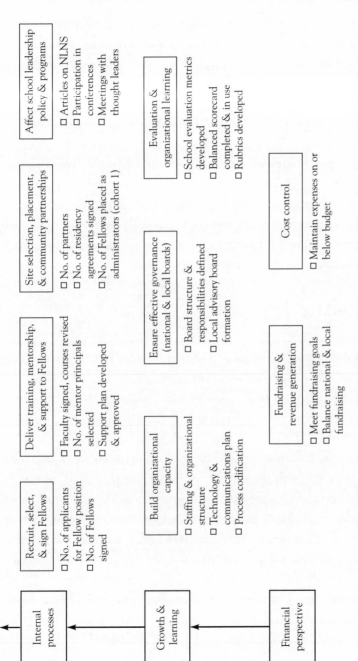

The diagram shows a balanced scorecard strategy map with four perspectives arranged vertically on the left: Internal processes, Growth & learning, and Financial perspective, with arrows flowing upward.

Internal processes row boxes:

Recruit, select, & sign Fellows
- No. of applicants for Fellow position
- No. of Fellows signed

Deliver training, mentorship, & support to Fellows
- Faculty signed, courses revised
- No. of mentor principals selected
- Support plan developed & approved

Site selection, placement, & community partnerships
- No. of partners
- No. of residency agreements signed
- No. of Fellows placed as administrators (cohort 1)

Affect school leadership policy & programs
- Articles on NLNS
- Participation in conferences
- Meetings with thought leaders

Growth & learning row boxes:

Build organizational capacity
- Staffing & organizational structure
- Technology & communications plan
- Process codification

Ensure effective governance (national & local boards)
- Board structure & responsibilities defined
- Local advisory board formation

Evaluation & organizational learning
- School evaluation metrics developed
- Balanced scorecard completed & in use
- Rubrics developed

Financial perspective row boxes:

Fundraising & revenue generation
- Meet fundraising goals
- Balance national & local fundraising

Cost control
- Maintain expenses on or below budget

Source: Information provided by New Leaders for New Schools; strategy map simplified from a map provided by New Profit Inc. Reprinted with permission.

The Corporate Dashboard

One of the dangers faced by managers who use performance information is that they may be quickly overwhelmed with data. To overcome this, a number of organizations have implemented a *corporate dashboard*—a limited number of key indicators that can be read, like a car dashboard, at a glance and that give an overview of the organization's performance. The dashboard contains data on the key outcomes the organization is achieving. It is typically produced quarterly and distributed to board and staff and sometimes to external funders as well. The concept of the dashboard reflects the notion that a "single outcome indicator seldom provides a sufficiently comprehensive perspective on an organization's outcomes" (Morley, Vinson, and Harty, 2001) and that a range of measures is needed to get an accurate overview (see Exhibit 2.9).

Benchmarking

Some organizations are using benchmarking not only to gain a tighter understanding of their own performance but also to compare their performance with that of other organizations. Benchmarking has particular appeal to nonprofit organizations because it builds on their tradition of cooperation, which reflects underlying missions that transcend the roles of individual organizations.

There are a number of approaches to benchmarking. Some organizations allow others to visit and discover their differences in processes and results. Some organizations conduct *study tours* with each other or in small groups. Some engage in more formal benchmarking that involves systematic data collection across a range of organizations to compare performance, and some form *clubs* to learn collaboratively about methods of driving improvements.

According to Letts, Ryan, and Grossman (1999), "Benchmarking is an organizational learning process that bridges the gap between great ideas and great performance" (p. 86). They argue that

Exhibit 2.9. Dashboard Indicators: Jewish Vocational Service.

Founded in 1973, Jewish Vocational Service (JVS) San Francisco is a nonsectarian organization that, as its mission statement says, links "employers and individuals together to achieve their employment goals by providing the skills necessary for success in today's workplace." Ten years ago JVS established a sophisticated client database, and seven years ago it began building a performance culture. The organization has over one hundred performance indicators, covering all aspects of its work. These have been boiled down to the twelve that are most closely aligned with JVS corporate strategy. These twelve form the JVS corporate dashboard, which is derived from a balanced scorecard approach to measuring performance and employs the four performance headings also used on the JVS strategy map.

The dashboard is updated quarterly (no more than thirty working days after the end of the quarter) and sent to all staff twice a year with a commentary from the chief executive. The dashboard results are a key input for the annual operating planning process and are also reported half-yearly to the board along with bullet points summarizing progress in achieving annual goals. Board meetings are scheduled to coincide with publication of the dashboard. Data from the performance system are also used in personal performance reviews and in the salary-setting process. A performance measurement committee of volunteers meets three to four times a year to help refine measurement tools and analyze performance. This committee consists of experts from the foundation sector and veterans of the McKinsey and Bain consulting practices, who bring corporate expertise and fresh eyes to their tools and the performance outcomes.

In the future, JVS San Francisco is planning to link client service usage data with its contract invoicing system and to introduce a barcode swipe system so that attendance data is input by their clients. "Creating an integrated performance system enabled us to respond efficiently to the differing requirements of our funders," said Executive Director Abby Snay. "It also enabled us to provide key information for managing the organization more effectively."

Exhibit 2.9. Dashboard Indicators: Jewish Vocational Service, Cont'd.

JVS San Francisco Quarterly Dashboard: Year-End Results

	2000/01 Performance	Target	2001/02 Performance
Adults and youth with challenges to employment			
No. of job placements secured	740	814	705
% of students completing skill-building programs	76%	85%	81%
% of students demonstrating gains in pre/post tests	86%	92%	90%
% of clients placed in full-time/benefited positions	36%	40%	34%
Average wage at placement	$11.47	$12.45	$11.95
% of available program capacity filled	93%	95%	91%
% stakeholder satisfaction with services	90%	95%	94%
Building organization capacity			
Capital funds generated	$0.84m	$3.78m	$1.01m
No. of courses certified	1	2	0
Learning and growth			
Average staff turnover	24%	23%	27%
Finance			
Total fee-based revenue	$ 46k		$84k
Contribution of unrestricted revenue	$530k		$480k

Abby Snay admits the dashboard is not yet perfect, and the organization is planning further improvements based on its experience and feedback from its stakeholders.

Source: Information and table provided by Jewish Vocational Service San Francisco.

organizations should invest time and resources in benchmarking because "nonprofits must maximize the value of what they do with the resources they use. A learning process like benchmarking enables them to measure and improve value. . . . For most nonprofit professionals a process like benchmarking enables them to increase the organization's problem solving capacity" (p. 96).

"We are due for a wave of interest in benchmarking," according to McKinsey's Paul Jansen. "It usually starts with industrial tourism. This develops into a desire to collect meaningful measures, and often a fight over which numbers are the most pertinent. Only after it has gone through these two stages do opportunities for real insight emerge—when organizations understand the various practices that lie behind differences in performance."

Creating and maintaining the momentum for benchmarking is not easy because it can seem far removed from the organization's mission. Letts, Ryan, and Grossman (1999) argue that the "burden of developing a compelling case for benchmarking falls to the leaders of a nonprofit. They must be willing to risk exposing their organization's strengths and weaknesses . . . to define their organizational learning needs . . . and present their case to funders and staff" (pp. 101–102).

Embed Performance Management in the Organization Culture

By themselves, measures do not deliver performance improvements. Results are achieved by putting performance at the heart of management. This requires actions by the board, senior management, and service managers.

Action to Take

At the board level, some organizations give the program committee responsibility for performance management. The Urban League, the influential organization that assists African Americans to secure economic self-reliance, power, and civil rights, has a board committee on programs and affiliates whose main purpose is to monitor performance. It reviews each program every year and is chaired by the board's senior vice chair. The Urban League also has an annual board retreat that monitors the organization's performance. Similarly, Big Brothers Big Sisters of Long Island has a program committee of the board that monitors the outcome evaluations of the individuals the organization serves and of the organization as a whole. Jewish Vocational Service adopts a slightly different approach. It has a board committee dedicated specifically to performance measurement. This committee meets quarterly to review the results and to refine the performance management system. Other boards take the approach of combining the strategy and performance functions, so one board committee oversees the development of both the strategic plan and the performance management system.

Continuous support from the chief executive and senior management is seen as essential to maintaining the momentum of a process that takes years rather than months to implement. Children's Institute International, for example, discovered that it needed to create two promotion routes if staff were to achieve the required performance focus. "Two different types of people are needed to enhance performance," said chief executive Mary Emmons in an interview. "One has the professional skill set and the other the managerial perspective. So we created the two routes and then invested heavily in training on topics such as finance and contract compliance to give program managers the tools they needed to manage performance. We also invested heavily in IT so they had the information they needed to manage performance." Many organizations stress the importance of stories in bringing the performance system to life. Each of the REDF social return on investment reports, for example, contains an employee highlight that tells how one person's life was transformed by the social enterprise.

The key point to learn is that creating a performance management system and culture requires sustained effort over many years. It also needs significant resources in both money and staff time. To overcome the challenges and implement successful performance management systems, organizations have found that they need to explain the rationale for putting resources into such systems and to address people's legitimate concerns. This is a topic that benefits from extensive discussion before new initiatives are launched. In practical terms it is usually necessary create a project, appoint a project leader, and establish clear and realistic objectives. The project team should report to senior management, and it should involve line management at every opportunity. Its final objective should be to embed the arrangements into the organization's culture so the team itself can disband, having completed its work.

The Lessons of Performance Management

So what has been learned by organizations that have set out to embed performance management in their organization culture? The most common point made by interviewees was that this undertaking will lead organizations to be more modest in their aspirations and to simplify their activities. Virginia Hodgkinson, professor at the Center for the Study of Voluntary Organizations and Service at Georgetown University, said that "performance management does lead to reassessment of goals and to clearer separation of long- and short-term goals."

"Efforts to improve performance will lead organizations to simplify," according to Harvard's Allen Grossman. "Having impact requires focus, and unfortunately, nonprofits use the veil of the nobility of their cause to justify a wide range of activities. This is unlikely to lead to optimum performance." Alan Abramson of the Aspen Institute gave a similar message, "Performance management will lead organizations and foundations to simplify what they are attempting to achieve and be more modest in their aspirations. This is a necessary change because there is often a significant mismatch between organizations' aspirations and their resources."

The McKinsey research reviewed earlier found that the existence of a system of measures helps to establish a culture of accountability. "For years, the independent sector has gotten a free ride in this regard; very few donors or boards ever held management accountable for results and on the rare occasions when they did, it took a long time to gather the necessary evidence to act. Performance measures . . . vastly simplify that process for boards, senior managers and program managers alike" (Sawhill and Williamson, 2001, p. 385).

Finally, experienced commentators stress simplicity. "Focus on practical, pragmatic measures, avoid perfection and don't be academic," according to Mary Ann Holohean, director of the Nonprofit Sector Advancement Fund at the Meyer Foundation. "Keep it simple, accessible, computerizable, and efficient," advises Elizabeth Boris of the influential Urban Institute in Washington.

Summary

Grasp the Opportunity to Manage Performance

- Demands for greater transparency, clearer accountability, and sharper focus on achieving objectives are leading organizations to put greater effort into performance management.

- Performance information helps funders invest in programs proven to be effective and withdraw from programs that are less effective. It is the link that should connect current results with future funding.

- Organizations are integrating outcome information into corporate performance management systems and using it in decision making.

Recognize Legitimate Concerns

- Measuring performance is easier

  At the level of individual organizations
  For some types of services
  In some sectors

- Organizations need to be aware of the dangers of focusing only on measurable outcomes, accepting only easy cases, and taking a short-term view.

- Performance management must be adapted to suit the circumstances and to balance quantitative and qualitative outcomes.

- Organizations need to use existing data, focus on low-cost ways of generating new data, and ensure that the results are incorporated into everyday decision making.

Select Measures That Fit the Organization's Mission

- Organizations are collecting information on service outcomes and end outcomes.

- Mission success can be measured by defining the mission narrowly, using research to demonstrate the connection between services and the desired results, and developing micro-level goals that imply success on a wider scale.

- Following up on users six, nine, and twelve months after a service has been delivered is important because the outcome of many nonprofit activities may not show for many months.

- The unique features of nonprofit activity, such as reaching underserved populations, providing opportunities for citizen participation, and bringing about change with advocacy work, also need to be captured.

- The desire to learn from experience and continuously improve should be balanced by the need to maintain consistency from year to year.

Use Performance Results to Drive Decisions at Every Level

- The two approaches to performance management are results based and comparison based.

- Leading organizations clarify the logic or theory of change that underpins high performance.

- The balanced scorecard and the corporate dashboard are two common methods of summarizing corporate performance.

- The different approaches to benchmarking build on the sector's tradition of collaboration. Benchmarking is a systematic learning process. It requires consistent top-management support to ensure that it delivers long-term impact.

Embed Performance Management in the Organization Culture

- Leading organizations make a board committee responsible for monitoring performance and overseeing improvements to the performance management system.

- Chief executives and senior managers act on the results of the performance management system.

- Performance management leads organizations to simplify their objectives, focus their activities, and be more accountable.

- Introducing performance management requires a project team with a leader, sufficient resources to sustain the initiative over the long term, and a brief to embed the process into line management activities.

Action Checklist

Effective performance management is going to become even more important as organizations strive to raise more funds and have a greater impact. Easy in theory, it requires continuous effort in practice to develop a system that delivers high value to board members, managers, and other stakeholders but is also easy to administer. Board members and managers who want to increase the effectiveness of their organization's performance management system should

1. Anticipate that demands from funders, donors, and other stakeholders for outcome-oriented performance information will grow dramatically over the coming years.

2. Identify the performance information the organization already collects.

3. Set targets for improving the performance management system.

4. Establish a board committee that has overall responsibility for strengthening the performance management system and ensuring that the board acts on the results of that system.

5. Allocate responsibility for enhancing the performance management system to a senior manager, and ensure that he or she has the power and resources to deliver performance improvement programs.

6. Continuously strive to collect performance information that tracks the achievement of the organization's mission as closely as possible.

7. Ensure that these data are presented regularly to the board and management and used to take actions to strengthen program delivery.

8. Embed a culture of measuring performance in all levels of the organization, so everyone demands good-quality information and uses it to drive performance improvements.

3

Creating Strategic Alliances

Nonprofit organizations form strategic alliances because they believe that they can achieve their missions more effectively through collaborations with other organizations. In fact there has always been a high level of interdependence among nonprofits—they have joined together to form umbrella bodies, professional associations, purchasing clubs, insurance cooperatives, and advocacy organizations to further their interests. Indeed, the first Amherst H. Wilder Foundation publication to promote collaboration appeared in 1915.

From the mid- to late 1970s, pressure from funders stimulated this interest in collaboration. Many states encouraged the development of collaborative networks to address welfare, poverty, and employment issues. According to the Wilder publication *Collaboration: What Makes It Work,* "autonomy and 'going it alone' are frowned upon in complex systems such as mental health, services for the handicapped and youth employment" (Mattessich, Murray-Close, and Monsey, 2001, p. 3). Toward the end of the 1980s, interest in mergers began to grow as funders became concerned about duplication of services and the effectiveness of organizations that lacked critical mass. However, with some notable exceptions, many *mergers* turned out to be *takeovers* of struggling organizations by stronger ones. Although there was a strong case for mergers, sufficiently strong external pressures seldom existed to overcome organizations' fear of loss of autonomy and independence. Since the 1990s, there has been a growing interest in partnerships as organizations have frequently come to realize that they lack the skills and resources to address increasingly complex social problems. They have recognized that combining resources can create programs with greater impact, integrating back-office functions can increase efficiency, and introducing ideas and knowledge from other sectors can transform an organization's perspectives on social issues.

Strategic alliances are therefore increasingly common. A survey of a random sample of 400 nonprofits discovered that 24 percent had experience with strategic restructuring. They reported that it had enabled them to cut costs (through volume buying and sharing employees), hire more experienced staff, and provide staff with improved compensation and greater career opportunities (La Piana and Kohm, 2003). Further evidence of interest in alliances comes from the Mandel Center for Nonprofit Organizations in its book *Nonprofit Strategic Alliances Case Studies: Lessons from the Trenches* (Yankey, McClellan, and Jacobus, 2001). In short, strategic partnerships are now seen as having great potential to enhance the effectiveness of the nonprofit sector. "The twenty-first century will be the age of alliances," declares James Austin in the first sentence of his groundbreaking book *The Collaboration Challenge* (2000).

Managers have also come to realize that there are many different types of alliances, ranging from total independence of the organizations involved to a full merger (Exhibit 3.1). These relationships are seen to exist on a continuum with a low level of commitment and a small loss of autonomy at one end and a high level of engagement and considerable integration at the other. Exploring the intermediate relationships is more common than entering into the complications of mergers, with all their associated structural, legal, and personnel challenges.

It is widely acknowledged that managing partnerships is even more challenging than managing single organizations. The preparatory stage demands thorough research to establish the capacity and stability of each organization to the satisfaction of the others. Relationships take time to establish, and dedication is required to ensure success. As Mary Pearl, executive director of the Wildlife Trust explained to me, "the return in terms of impact has to be much greater than the time the organization has to invest in establishing the partnership."

This chapter demonstrates that leading-edge organizations

- Establish strategic alliances to increase impact

- Choose alliance types that suit the circumstances

- Create alliances with the corporate sector

- Build alliances on trustworthy relationships

- Merge to build strategic capacity

Establish Strategic Alliances to Increase Impact

The dramatic growth in strategic alliances is being driven by organizations' desire to

- Increase mission impact

- Exploit economies of scale

- Achieve cost savings

- Attain critical mass

- Respond to mounting competition

Increase Mission Impact

Greater impact can often now be achieved only by organizations combining their skills and resources. The case for collaboration is that the most complex problems society faces cannot be tackled by any one organization acting alone. Issues of poor educational

Exhibit 3.1. Terms Used for Organizational Relationships.

Many different terms are used to describe organizations working together, and there is no universal agreement on their definitions. The following is a guide to a number of these terms as they are used in this book.

The terms **strategic alliance** and **collaboration** refer to a significant long-term relationship between two or more organizations that share resources to achieve their missions more effectively.

Words used interchangeably with *strategic alliance* and *collaboration* are **partnership** and **coalition.**

Strategic restructuring occurs when two or more independent organizations reorganize themselves to establish an ongoing relationship either to increase the administrative efficiency or to further the mission of one or more of the participating organizations.

The results of all these activities include the following:

Administrative consolidation: an alliance that involves sharing, exchanging, or contracting administrative functions.

Joint program or project: an alliance that involves launching and managing one or more programs or projects to further participating organizations' missions.

Management service organization: an organization formed to further the administrative efficiency of two or more other organizations.

Joint venture: an organization formed to further the administrative or service aims of two or more other organizations; the partners share the governance of the new organization.

Group structure: an organization newly formed, or an existing organization designated as *parent*, that governs the functions of a number of other organizations, the *subsidiaries*.

Merged organizations: two or more organizations that combine their assets under one corporate structure.

Source: Connolly and York, 2002. Reprinted with the permission of TCC Group (formerly known as The Conservation Company).

achievement, drug misuse, crime, and poverty are inherently complex and interrelated and are often best addressed by agencies working in an integrated way. Also, as Mattessich, Murray-Close, and Monsey (2001) point out: "In her highly regarded 1989 book, *Collaborating*, Barbara Gray notes that the quality of results often increases when a problem is addressed through interagency collaboration. This happens because the organizations working jointly are likely to do a broader, more comprehensive analysis of the issues and opportunities. They also have complementary resources that diversify their capability to accomplish tasks" (p. 4).

Strategic alliances are often created to improve the quality and range of services offered. This can involve

- Joint bids for contracts for the provision of a human service

- Joint ventures in fundraising, where two or more organizations working together can raise more funds than they can separately

- Creation of a *one-stop shop*, bringing services together in one building or one delivery system

In 1999, researchers at La Piana Associates and the Chapin Hall Center for Children at the University of Chicago carried out a survey of 192 organizations with recent experience in strategic restructuring. They found that organizations more often restructured to improve the quality and range of what they do and the efficiency with which they do it than to meet any immediate threats of closure or pressure from funders (Kohm, La Piana, and Gowdy, 2000). The most common benefits that respondents to this survey reported were increased collaborations on programs with partner organizations, increased services, increased administrative capacity and quality, and increased market share.

Exploit Economies of Scale

Strategic alliances are also created to exploit economies of scale: for example, a local service might wish to *scale up* to provide the service at a regional or national level. This change allows overhead costs to be spread over a larger number of service users and thus reduces the overhead unit costs. For example, Citizen Schools, an organization that offers after-school support for underprivileged children, knows that it needs to increase the number of schools it runs to cover the organization's central overhead costs. The organization has made a detailed analysis of the cost structures of different growth strategies and knows that it will need new partners to achieve the required economies of scale.

Achieve Cost Savings

Another reason for forming an alliance is to achieve cost savings. There are opportunities to reduce both program and core administration costs. Paul Jansen, a director at McKinsey & Company, reminds organizations that "they have to consider the size of the prize." He told me that "administration costs are around 10 percent of total costs, but program costs can be around 70 to 80 percent of total costs. So if economies can be found in delivering programs the potential prize is much larger."

To address administration costs, some nonprofits are coming together to share administrative systems and are forming management service organizations. This can save back-office costs by combining the provision of finance systems, information technology, and human resource services. According to James Austin (2000), "Many nonprofits will be propelled into austerity alliances . . . to eliminate duplicative costs and excess capacity through shared facilities, services or activities (p. 9)." However, strategic restructuring expert David La Piana cautioned that "although cost reduction is a major motivator, cost savings are seldom a short-term outcome of mergers and consolidations."

Attain Critical Mass

Organizations are also creating strategic alliances to give themselves critical mass. The nonprofit sector includes many small organizations that survive on minimal resources and huge individual commitment. There are many opportunities for them to combine management and governance and create fewer units with greater capacity to compete for funds and deliver greater impact. McKinsey's Paul Jansen believes that "organizations with incomes of less than $500k per year are too small to have any economies of scale or economies of skill. They need to restructure to create critical mass."

National organizations with branch and chapter structures have led the way in persuading smaller branches to merge and create critical mass. The United Way of Greater Los Angeles, for example, merged thirty-nine branches into one, leading to a significant increase in effectiveness. "Alliances are the way forward for lobbying work," Anita Aaron, executive director of LightHouse for the Blind and Visually Impaired, said in an interview. "Most organizations cannot afford a separate lobbying function, but we can all contribute toward the creation of larger and more effective organizations that specialize in lobbying."

Larger organizations are able to build more widely recognized brands. This makes fundraising easier and also enables the organization to attract high-caliber staff. Larger nonprofits are also able to afford more thorough and wide-ranging evaluations of their work and are therefore better positioned to demonstrate their achievements.

Respond to Mounting Competition

Many nonprofits are considering a fundamental change in organization structure because of the economic pressures of increased competition from other nonprofits and from businesses. "Competition from for-profits is driving nonprofits to form partnerships," according to Peter Manzo, executive director of the Center for Nonprofit Management in Los Angeles. He gave me the example of thirteen child-care organizations in Los Angeles that came together because of competition from for-profit organizations. His point is confirmed by a survey that reports that "[c]ompetition is a key factor in strategic restructuring. Organizations are attempting to temper competition by cooperating or merging" (Kohm, La Piana, and Gowdy, 2000, p. 2).

The growth of strategic alliances can be seen as a natural development within the sector. "Strategic restructuring is natural as the nonprofit sector matures," according to David La Piana (1998). "When a business's restructuring is successful, its stock value rises dramatically. When a nonprofit's restructuring is successful, its ability to fulfil its social mission rises dramatically" (p. 5).

The Role of Funders

Funders have a particularly delicate role in restructuring. On the one hand they are uniquely positioned to require organizations that should form strategic alliances to restructure and increase their impact. No other external stakeholder holds the power needed to force this change. Organizations are being driven to form alliances by funders who are "frustrated with overlapping programs, service gaps, turf battles and lack of coordination" (La Piana, 1998, p. 3). On the other hand funders may push organizations into inappropriate and unwanted relationships. "The past decade has included 'collaboration mania' among some people who set policy and offer funding. Unfortunately, it has also become a nostrum among some nonprofit organizations desperate to attempt anything to survive in a challenging environment" (Mattessich, Murray-Close, and Monsey, 2001, p. 34).

Views on the proper role of funders in encouraging restructuring are divided, between those who believe funders should not force collaboration on grantees and those who argue that they are the only stakeholders with the power to drive change. "Many experts maintain that funders should not drive the move to restructure because their grantees will be less likely to 'own' the process and the results. However, others thought that unless nonprofit organizations

were pushed, they would resist even considering strategic restructuring, let alone implementing it" (Connolly and York, 2002, p. 7).
Some nonprofit managers point out somewhat wryly that many
foundations find it easier to require funded organizations to form
alliances than to form partnerships with other foundations. Even
foundations that make the funding of alliances a priority appear less
enthusiastic about forming alliances themselves. The critics argue
that the advantages funders would receive from forming strategic
alliances might be as great as the advantages their funded nonprofits get from their alliances.

Choose Alliance Types That Suit the Circumstances

As discussed earlier, there is a range of alliance types, each of which
fits different circumstances (Figure 3.1). The lowest level of joint
working involves cooperation and coordination agreements. These
allow organizations to share information and sometimes plans, refer
service users to each other, and avoid unnecessary competition. Such

Figure 3.1. Continuum of Types of Strategic Alliances.

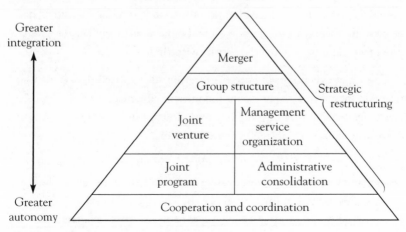

Source: Based on ideas from Arsenault, 1998, and La Piana, 1998.

arrangements can be short term and often depend on personal relationships between people in the cooperating organizations. They are
not strategic alliances and do not involve strategic restructuring. All
the other types of collaboration are longer term, involve significant
resources, and usually require a legal agreement to formalize the relationship or the establishment of new legal entities. (The five types
of alliances that occupy the center of Figure 3.1 will be discussed
here. Mergers are examined in the final section of the chapter.)

Joint Programs

The relationship that is most prevalent and carries the lowest risk is
the joint program. These relationships are often time limited and
may take the form of a contractual agreement. They allow two or
more organizations to work together without affecting their ultimate
autonomy (Exhibit 3.2). They often involve service delivery and
fundraising activity. In joint programming both parties contribute

---

Exhibit 3.2. Joint Programming: Century Health.

Century Health, an Ohio-based community health center, decided to
work with Open Arms, a domestic violence and rape crisis service, to
provide a domestic violence offenders program. Community leaders had
decided that the town of Findlay should have a visitation center where
offenders could have supervised visits with their children.

The chief executives of both organizations recognized that Century
needed Open Arms' expertise with domestic violence and that Open
Arms needed Century's experience with drug misuse, because 80 percent
of the offenders had substance abuse problems.

Century Health is responsible for Harmony House, the visitation
center, and Open Arms is responsible for the offenders program. The
two chief executives jointly supervise the manager, a member of
Century's staff. No funds are exchanged between the two agencies.

Source: Kohm, La Piana, and Gowdy, 2000. Reproduced with permission from
Chapin Hall Center for Children.

Figure 3.2. Joint Program Delivered by Management.

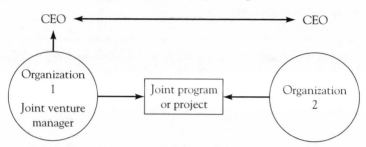

staff and resources, the joint venture is the responsibility of a manager in one of the organizations (Figure 3.2), and oversight is provided by the chief executives of both organizations.

Administrative Consolidations

A similarly low-risk option is to consolidate back-office activity. For example, one organization might sell spare capacity such as computer space or excess financial or human resource management capacity to another. Administrative consolidation might be an intermediate step before creating a management service organization or merging (Exhibit 3.3). These arrangements are established through joint operating agreements.

Joint Ventures

Jane Arsenault says in her excellent book *Forging Nonprofit Alliances* that nonprofits most commonly create joint ventures for

- *Knowledge sharing*: where organizations recognize that each has a distinctive competency, innovative approach, or specialized knowledge that if shared will contribute to higher-quality service outcomes for both

- *Market access*: where organizations can reach a new user group or extend their geographic reach

- *New product or program development*: where development costs can be shared between organizations

Exhibit 3.3. Sharing Back-Office Services in Rhode Island: Self Help and New Visions.

Self Help and New Visions are two social service agencies providing substance-abuse programs, food banks, homeless shelters, health clinics, and child care in Rhode Island. When the executive director of New Visions retired, the executive director of Self Help was appointed to lead both organizations. Together, the two organizations employ 275 people and have a combined budget of $15 million.

They remained separate because it was important to maintain their identities, which were linked to the communities each one served. However, they did sign an agreement to create a joint human resource department. In addition they saved money by purchasing health insurance, telephone services, and medical supplies together.

After five years they considered continuing their agreement indefinitely. The opportunity to seek new funding from a source that favored larger organizations persuaded them to consider a merger, despite misgivings among clients and staff.

Source: Adapted from Whelan, 2002. Reprinted with the permission of The Chronicle of Philanthropy, http://philanthropy.com.

There are two types of joint ventures, one controlled by a legal agreement and the other by the establishment of a separate organization. In both cases the partners separate the joint venture from ongoing operations. Both types are appropriate where neither organization currently has the required skills, where the joint venture requires a culture different from the partner organizations' cultures, or where the joint venture is physically separated from the partners.

In the arrangement controlled by a legal agreement, a joint oversight group is established consisting of members of the partner organizations. The joint venture manager reports to this group. This model gives the manager a great degree of autonomy and therefore requires all parties to have a high level of confidence in the manager's skills. A system for rotating the people who serve as oversight group chair is common in this arrangement. An example of this type of arrangement is four organizations in San Francisco that created a fifth group to carry out client assessments for all of them (Figure 3.3). In the arrangement where the joint venture is a separately incorporated organization with its own board, each partner has an agreed number of seats on that board and the constitution of the joint venture can be changed only with the agreement of the partners (Figure 3.4). This model is appropriate where there are significant financial or liability risks.

The desire of some governmental authorities to reduce the number of providers with whom they contract has given joint ventures a significant boost, because nonprofits can combine together to bid as one organization. That organization can then manage the contract, allowing the partners to focus on the provision of the service. This arrangement enables the partners to incorporate greater management capacity into the service without distorting their own sensitive administrative cost ratios (Exhibit 3.4).

Figure 3.3. Joint Venture Governed by a Joint Oversight Group.

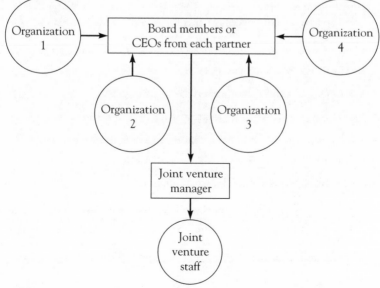

Figure 3.4. Separately Incorporated Joint Venture.

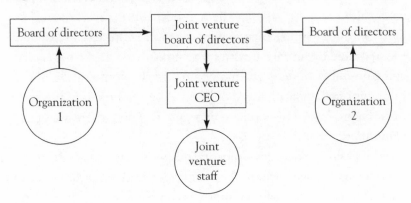

Exhibit 3.4. Homeless Development Initiative.

A group of agencies worked together with the City of San Francisco to use a Defense Department site to provide services for homeless people. They established a joint venture to provide housing, employment, and economic development services.

According to Donna Feingold, chief executive of Toolworks, one of the agency partners, the success of this joint venture depended on

- Having an overarching goal that was greater than the objectives of the individual agencies
- Keeping focused on the mission
- Developing good working relationships between the partners
- Paying attention to what was communicated and how it was communicated
- Accepting give-and-take between agencies

The greatest challenge was working with the city authority, as it was a key funder and its culture was different from that of the other partners.

Source: Interview with Donna Feingold, executive director of Toolworks.

Management Service Organizations

Management service organizations, known as MSOs, are another form of strategic alliance. Nonprofits are establishing MSOs because some management and administrative services can be provided more efficiently in groups of organizations than in separate organizations.

There are two types of MSO. The first is a partnership between a number of organizations that come together to create a separate body to provide all the partners with one or more services (Exhibit 3.5). This MSO may be a for-profit or a tax-exempt organization (as the IRS has relaxed the rules on the status of MSOs that service nonprofit organizations). The second type is an entity created within an existing nonprofit to sell excess capacity in some of the nonprofit's administrative services to other nonprofits. It is known as a *wholly-owned* MSO.

MSOs typically provide such services as (Arsenault, 1998):

- *Personnel management:* recruitment, staff training, purchasing of benefits, payroll, and legal compliance

- *Facilities management:* lease management, building maintenance, provision and servicing of equipment

- *Financial services:* fully integrated financial systems, invoicing, management and financial accounts, group purchasing

- *Fundraising:* raising funds jointly for all partners or for each organization individually

- *Planning:* data analysis, supporting planning committees

- *Contracts management:* for leases and equipment

- *Marketing:* market analysis, developing communication strategies, design and production of print

Exhibit 3.5. Establishing an MSO: Partners for Community.

Partners for Community (PfC) is an MSO in Massachusetts with two founding partners and three affiliate organizations. It was established by two social service–providing organizations that were struggling to cover their overhead costs as cost-of-living expenses rose faster than income from government grants and contracts.

PfC provides financial, human resource, information, technology, facility, procurement, and organization development services. The idea of starting an MSO emerged after discussions clarified that a merger would jeopardize existing contracts and that neither organization wanted to lose the reputation associated with its name.

The first savings came when the two organizations moved into one building. Later a language center, a small community development corporation, and an employment training center contracted to have PfC provide their administration. A key decision was the appointment of a chief operating officer. He oversaw the transfer of all the original partners' financial information to one accounting program and re-organized the flow of work so that financial staff worked according to function rather than agency. "Improving our information technology was reason enough for us to come together," claimed one of the original partners. "Economies of scale really make sense in this area."

Source: Kohm, La Piana, and Gowdy, 2000. Reproduced with the permission of Chapin Hall Center for Children.

- *Quality assurance:* establishment of quality standards, monitoring, management information system support, improvement efforts and outcome studies

Although MSOs may provide back-office services more effi-ciently, they nevertheless have their own challenges. "The greatest challenge in the wholly owned MSO is to engender a sense of cus-tomer service in the staff on the front line" (Arsenault, 1998, p. 60). Joseph Haggerty, president of United Way of Greater Los Angeles concurred, telling me that "the problem with MSOs is that they lack a charitable mission." Wholly owned MSOs may also allow servicing the parent organization to take priority over meeting the needs of the often smaller purchasers of the MSO's services.

Group Structures

Group structures allow a number of separate organizations to operate under the umbrella of one *parent* organization (Figure 3.5). They are appropriate when the subsidiaries all have different activities but want to be part of one organization. Subsidiaries may be offered different degrees of autonomy, depending on whether the parent wishes to exercise tight control or to give them freedom to pursue their own activities within agreed boundaries.

Some organizations registered as charitable and religious organizations (501[c][3] organizations) are creating social welfare subsidiaries with a different tax status (501[c][4] organizations) so that the subsidiaries can carry out lobbying activities without risking regulatory interventions when their expenditure on lobbying exceeds the legal limits for charitable and religious organizations. Some organizations are creating subsidiaries to offset risks or potential liabilities: for example, those arising from trading activities. Yet others are establishing social welfare subsidiaries when regulations require that a majority of a service provider's board members be service users

Figure 3.5. Group Structure.

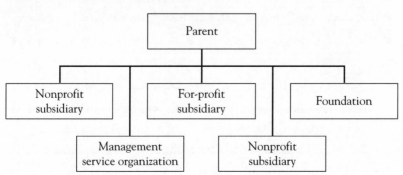

and the parent organization believes that this requirement is not appropriate for its own circumstances.

Group structures are becoming more popular as organizations become larger and more complex and want to divide their activities into more discrete units, each with its own governing board. These structures are undoubtedly complex to manage and govern, but they do provide significant opportunities for exploiting economies of scale. Those services most effectively provided by a central source, such as finance, IT, and property management, can be delivered by the parent organization, and those that are best provided by the subsidiaries can be located within those subsidiaries. The group structure also separates the strategic role of the parent— such as deciding what services the group as a whole should provide—from the operational role of each subsidiary, primarily the provision of a distinct service. It also may produce greater accountability, as the parent can nurture its subsidiaries and hold them to account for achieving agreed objectives (Exhibit 3.6).

Create Alliances with the Corporate Sector

Nonprofit organizations are also forming a wide range of successful partnerships with for-profit organizations. These relationships came to particular prominence in the early 1980s with the often-cited example of American Express's promise to help finance the renovation of the Statue of Liberty by donating one cent for every AMEX credit card transaction and two dollars for every new card issued. A 1996 article in the *Harvard Business Review* reported that

> since American Express's pioneering ventures, the number of alliances between nonprofit and for-profit organizations has skyrocketed. Avon, American Airlines, Ocean Spray, Polaroid, Ramada International Hotels, Arm & Hammer, Wal-Mart Stores and many other corporations have joined forces with national nonprofit institutions

Exhibit 3.6. Group Structure: PHMC and the Bridge.

The Bridge is a substance abuse treatment center whose budget grew to $2 million by the early 1990s. Following retirement of key staff and loss of a key contract, it ran into financial difficulties. It recognized that survival depended on finding a partner, so it investigated several options for its future. PHMC is a nonprofit public health organization that provides health and human services in the Delaware Valley. It had grown to a budget of $15 million.

Negotiations between the two organizations led to the conclusion that even though there was a good fit between their services, the relationship would have to be a parent-subsidiary model. This would protect PHMC from the financial liabilities of The Bridge and the risks associated with running a residential drug treatment program.

PHMC is the sole subsidiary of The Bridge and selects its own board. The first PHMC board included both PHMC representatives and people who had previously served on The Bridge's board. PHMC is contracted to provide finance, marketing, human resource, information system, and program development functions. The integration was not easy because there were cultural differences between the two organizations, some staff layoffs were unavoidable, and staff benefits were reduced. However, The Bridge now gives PHMC a wider range of services and a stronger reputation for supporting underserved populations, and The Bridge has benefited from PHMC's many services, including a fundraising campaign that raised over $200,000.

Source: Adapted from Vnenchak and Weiss, n.d.

such as the American Red Cross, the YMCA, the American Heart Association, and the Nature Conservancy as well as local agencies tackling problems in their communities. Today, it is unusual to go into a supermarket, fast-food restaurant, or drugstore without encountering posters and other promotional materials for a social program cosponsored by one or more private sector organizations [Andreasen, 1996, p. 115].

Today relationships between nonprofits and for-profits are big business. Although the total value of these relationships is impossible to calculate, *Giving USA 2003* reports that corporate philanthropy totaled almost $12 billion, representing just over 5 percent of contributions (AAFRC Trust for Philanthropy, 2003). Corporate sponsorships generated a further $700 million.

Businesses now recognize the value of creating strong relationships with the nonprofit sector. Business for Social Responsibility has made the following observations:

Corporate community involvement can:

- *Increase employee morale, retention, attendance, and performance.* Boston College's Center for Corporate Citizenship found that 84 percent of employees felt that a company's image in the community is important; 54 percent felt that it was very important. The study found that "the more an employee knows about the company's programs, the more likely he or she will be loyal and positive about the company."

- *Develop employee skills.* The business benefits of employee community involvement help to develop a variety of competencies, including teamwork, planning and implementation, communication, project management, listening skills and customer focus.

- *Enhance company reputation.* Americans think most favorably of companies that focus their philanthropic efforts on donating products and encouraging employee volunteering in the community.

- *Attract investors.* More than 12.5 percent of investment in U.S. companies is screened for social factors such as community investment. U.S. assets in socially screened portfolios rose to $2.6 trillion in 1999 from $639 billion in 1995.

- *Increase customer goodwill and loyalty.* A 1997 Cone/
  Roper study found that 76 percent of consumers
  would switch their purchases to a retail store associated with a good cause.

- *Improve relationships with the community.* Many companies find that community involvement can open
  new markets, reduce local regulatory obstacles, provide access to the local political process, generate
  positive media coverage and increase company or
  brand awareness within the community [Business
  for Social Responsibility, 2001–2004].

Many businesses are therefore seeking to establish longer-term
and more strategic relationships with nonprofit organizations. In
his book *The Collaboration Challenge,* James Austin (2000) presented a continuum of relationships between nonprofits and for-
profits (Table 3.1). These relationships begin with a *philanthropic
stage,* in which the company is a charitable donor. The resources
may be significant to the nonprofit but are not strategically significant to the company. When the philanthropic stage is successful,
the relationship moves to the *transactional stage.* This is a more
active relationship in which both parties expect more significant
benefits. Activities may include cause-related marketing, event
sponsorship, product certification, licensing agreements, and employee volunteering. Many relationships between nonprofits and
for-profits begin at this stage. Nonprofit organizations that have
leading-edge relationships have reached the *integrative stage.* In
these cases missions, people, and activities are increasingly integrated. The relationship becomes more deeply embedded in both
organizations' corporate strategies and the resources involved are
progressively more significant.

Austin (2000) also reports that a particular benefit of these relationships is the opportunities that they create for partners to learn

Table 3.1. The Collaboration Continuum.

Relationship Stage	Philanthropic	Transactional	Integrative	
Level of engagement	Low	↑	↑	↑	High
Importance to mission	Peripheral	↑	↑	↑	Strategic
Magnitude of resources	Small	↑	↑	↑	Big
Scope of activities	Narrow	↑	↑	↑	Broad
Interaction level	Infrequent	↑	↑	↑	Intensive
Managerial complexity	Simple	↑	↑	↑	Complex
Strategic value	Modest	↑	↑	↑	Major

Source: Austin, J.E. *The Collaboration Challenge: How Nonprofits and Businesses Succeed Through Strategic Alliances.* San Francisco: Jossey-Bass, 2000, p. 35. Copyright © 2000 John Wiley & Sons, Inc. Reprinted with the permission of John Wiley & Sons, Inc.

from each other: "Cross-sector partnering was distinctive because the participants in such alliances were likely to have noticeably different performance measures, competitive dynamics, organization cultures, decision-making styles, personnel competencies, professional languages, incentive and motivational structures, and emotional content" (p. 14).

These relationships frequently develop organically over a period of years. Children's Institute International has a strategic alliance with the management consulting firm Accenture. The institute benefits by having a mentor for the chief executive and receiving assistance with strategic planning and with marketing, all of which has made a significant contribution to building the organization's management capacity. Accenture benefits by being able to show that it has contributed to the Los Angeles community and by receiving opportunities for its staff to work on projects that they feel are important. The success of this relationship has been recognized at the National Philanthropy Day Awards. More recently, Children's Institute International and a for-profit partner have successfully bid for a contract to deliver mental health services. The for-profit organization will deliver the high-end psychiatric work in hospitals, and the institute will deliver a range of associated community services. This commitment is currently small, but it is further evidence of the opportunities for private and nonprofit organizations to work together in strategic alliances.

So, the connections between businesses and nonprofits are moving on from the traditional philanthropic model to a more sophisticated set of relationships that deliver quantifiable benefits to both parties. People at the frontiers of these relationships report that the greatest challenge is meshing the cultures of the corporate and nonprofit sectors. For-profit organizations move faster and have clearer lines of accountability. Nonprofit organizations take a consultative approach and have multiple stakeholders to consider (Exhibit 3.7).

Exhibit 3.7. A Nonprofit and For-Profit Alliance: KaBOOM!

Since 1995, KaBOOM! has been motivating communities nationwide to create healthy play opportunities for young people. KaBOOM! works with businesses, foundations, civic groups and individuals to *lead* volunteer-driven, community-built playground and skatepark projects; *seed* change in communities through training programs, challenge grants, publications, and free on-line Project Planner™ services; and *advocate* for young people's right to play. KaBOOM! has created more than 700 new playgrounds and skateparks and renovated more than 1,300 others. In addition, ESKAL8, the national skatepark program powered by KaBOOM!, was introduced in 2003 to meet the growing demand for places for young people to safely skateboard, BMX bike, and in-line skate.

The majority of the $30 million investment KaBOOM! has spear-headed has come from innovative partnerships with corporations, including Home Depot, Sprint, Stride Rite, Ben and Jerry's Homemade, Snapple Beverages, Computer Associates, the Madison Square Garden Cheering for Children Foundation, and Fairytale Brownies.

Chief executive and cofounder Darell Hammond says, "One of the lessons we've learned is to pick the right partners. We jokingly say that we start our best partnerships by dating our sponsors. We invite potential partners to see us in action at a playground or skatepark construction day or presenting at one of our training conferences. Then we ask if we can meet to learn of their intentions. We hear what motivates them and, as with any honest courting couple, we tell them everything about us that we can."

He advises for-profits and nonprofits to be curious about each other: "I think that in our rush to raise funds and meet business goals, organizations fail to learn enough about each other to ensure that their missions and goals match. Our most powerful sustainable project results come when we are able to build a relationship between a company and a community that is driven by a shared vision, shared power, shared resources, shared responsibility, and shared accountability."

Source: Adapted from INDEPENDENT SECTOR, n.d. Printed with permission.

Build Alliances on Trustworthy Relationships

Managing strategic alliances presents special challenges because there are always two or more sets of staff, managers, and board members involved. Research into 192 strategic restructurings found that the higher-level integrations required in joint ventures and management service organizations presented more challenges than the less demanding alliances of joint programs and administrative consolidations (Kohm, La Piana, and Gowdy, 2000). The most common challenges the researchers identified were

- Managing conflicting organizational cultures

- Adjusting staff to new roles and positions

- Allaying concerns about loss of autonomy

- Building trust among organizations

Most actions needed to deliver a successful strategic alliance are ultimately concerned with building and maintaining trustworthy relationships between the partners. "Increasing trust is the key and should be an explicit objective," Michael Cortes, director of the Institute for Nonprofit Organization Management at the University of San Francisco, told me. Thus organizations need to reflect on some essential prerequisites before establishing or joining a strategic alliance (also see Exhibit 3.8):

- None of the partners should be in a crisis of any form, because the pressures will inevitably spill over into the alliance.

- Partners should have spare organization capacity to meet the demands of the alliance or the resources to create new capacity.

Exhibit 3.8. Alliance Lessons from Practical Experience.

United Ways are often catalysts in creating and supporting strategic alliances. The United Way of Greater Los Angeles has considerable experience with negotiating its own alliances as well as catalyzing others. Chief executive Joseph Haggerty recommends the following:

- Involve the chief executive from the start.

- Make a member of the permanent staff responsible for negotiating the agreement, and appoint a board member to provide oversight.

- Ensure that there will be continuity of staff in partner agencies.

- Expect all parties to deliver on their commitments.

- Encourage board members to visit the partnership in action.

- Limit the number of strategic alliances that the organization develops.

- Recognize that alliances will increase administrative overheads.

- Be tough in turning down offers for alliances if they are not appropriate or consistent with the organization's values.

- Base all alliances on written agreements.

Source: Interview with Joseph Haggerty, president of United Way of Greater Los Angeles.

- There should be good relations between the board members and managers of all the organizations that will be part of the alliance.

- Organizations committed to working in partnerships should have a strategic plan that emphasizes partnerships.

In addition, according to Donna Feingold, chief executive of Toolworks, "Managers need to understand that sometimes they are collaborating and sometimes they are competing with the very same organizations."

Organizations that meet the prerequisites and are considering an alliance should also attend to these seven essential attributes of successful alliances:

1. *Shared values.* To be successful in an alliance the organizations need to hold a shared set of values about the cause they are championing and about ways of working together. These values will influence the way the parties approach the alliance and how they work together.

2. *Leadership.* Partnerships require champions in each of the participating organizations, and these individuals need to take direct responsibility for achieving the partnership goals. Partnerships also require the unequivocal support of the leaders of the participating organizations. Boys & Girls Clubs of Boston, for example, appointed a vice president with responsibility for partnerships (a post on the senior management team) to ensure that alliances are given senior management attention.

3. *Clarity of mission and strategy.* Strategic alliances need a compelling mission, realistic objectives, and a clear strategy for achieving them. "Each partnership needs to have great clarity over its goals, achievable objectives with win-win opportunities for both organizations," as Linda Whitlock, chief executive of Boys & Girls Clubs of Boston, told me.

4. *Board commitment.* The boards of all participating organizations need to be strongly committed to the partnership and willing to support it through the good times and the difficult times. Bill Tyman, chief executive of Big Brothers Big Sisters of Long Island, told me that for some alliances he establishes a subcommittee with members drawn from both boards and both staffs. For others he goes even further—each partner has a seat on the other's board. To ensure that each organization has an overview of the partner organization, board minutes are circulated to partners. He also requires that counterparts

(board members, CEOs, managers, and staff) meet each other frequently to encourage good personal relationships.

5. *Sufficient resources.* To be successful, strategic alliances need proper resources, and management needs great honesty and realism about the financial commitments each organization will have to make to the partnership and the staff and management time that will be required. When it comes to demonstrating how the resources have been applied, the financial reports need to be tailored to the needs of the partnership rather than simply following the standard reporting formats of the participating organizations.

6. *Open and honest communications.* Managers need to recognize that many different stakeholders, such as funders, board and committee members, staff, chapters and volunteers, may be affected by a strategic alliance. Each group requires regular and thorough communication. Formal communications should be supported by plenty of informal communications, ideally at board, senior management, and staff levels. Sharing information across two or more organizations to keep staff, managers, and board members of all organizations in touch with progress and problems requires even more effort and attention than communication within an organization, itself no small challenge.

7. *Good faith negotiations.* Organizations should explicitly commit to good faith negotiations when the alliance is being established. David La Piana has learned much from the many alliance discussions he has facilitated. He now sets three ground rules for organizations that are discussing the establishment of an alliance:

There should be no material changes in the partnership proposition.

Negotiators must be named, and there should be no changes during negotiations.

There must be no negotiations with other external parties.

These rules should not changed unless all partners agree to the change beforehand. La Piana also recommends establishing an open list of the issues being worked on and communicating updates regularly to negotiators and other stakeholders so they can see the progress and the status of each issue at a glance.

These seven attributes create the foundation for trustworthy relationships between the partners. They enable all parties to admit failures when things go wrong and to celebrate success frequently when milestones and objectives are achieved (also see Exhibit 3.9).

Thomas Backer and Alex Norman (2000) have a particular eye for the people issues in creating strategic alliances. They say, "Few partnerships are created with appropriate attention to the behavioral and management science that has accumulated over the last few years—both about how to create partnerships or collaborations and about how to sustain them over time" (p. 39). They see the biggest problem as unrealistic expectations (also see Exhibit 3.10). When I interviewed Thomas Backer, president of the Human Interaction Research Institute, he recommended that leaders start by thinking about how the partnership will assist the other partners, not their own organization: "Seeing the situation from other people's perspectives is invariably helpful."

Merge to Build Strategic Capacity

Although there are no official statistics, mergers are much less prevalent than other forms of strategic alliance. Nevertheless there is significant merger activity (see, for example, Exhibit 3.11) and a growing interest in mergers as a strategy to strengthen nonprofit organizations' strategic capacity, and nonprofit "leaders generally agree that the sector is witnessing a dramatic increase in the frequency with which mergers are being considered and executed" (La Piana, 2000, p. 1). Newspapers are mentioning mergers more

Exhibit 3.9. Factors Influencing Alliance Success.

The Amherst H. Wilder Foundation recently updated its authoritative review of the research into what it calls *collaborations*. In this research the ten most frequently mentioned factors that contribute to the success of strategic alliances were

1. **Mutual respect, understanding, and trust**—for the culture and the limitations of members

2. **Sufficient funds, staff, materials, and time**

3. **An appropriate cross-section of members**—representing each segment of the community affected by the collaboration

4. **Multiple layers of participation**—board, management, and staff

5. **Members who see collaboration as in their self-interest**—advantages exceed loss of autonomy

6. **Development of clear roles and policy guidelines,** and an understanding of how members discharge their responsibilities

7. **Open and frequent communication**

8. **Shared vision**

9. **Skilled leadership**—by an individual with organizational and interpersonal leadership skills, who carries out the role with fairness and is granted legitimacy by the collaborative partners

10. **History of collaboration in the community**—with members understanding their expectations of each other.

The authors of the study emphasized that the frequency with which factors were mentioned did not necessarily equate with their impact on the success of the collaboration, but it did give an indication of their importance.

Source: From *Collaboration: What Makes It Work, 2nd Edition,* by Paul Mattessich, Marta Murray-Close, and Barbara Monsey, 2001, pp. 8–10. Copyright 2001 Amherst H. Wilder Foundation. Used with permission.

Exhibit 3.10. Dealing with Autonomy and Self-Interest.

Autonomy is a precious attribute for many nonprofit organizations, and self-interest cannot be ignored.

According to Florence Green:

> Successful collaboration involves some degree of letting go of personal ego and the needs of individual organizations to meet the larger agenda of collaboration. It is essential that all of the players know what they or their organizations are willing to invest, what they are willing to give up and what they simply cannot compromise on.

According to David La Piana, in his highly successful BoardSource publication *Beyond Collaboration*:

> **Self-interest** is neither inappropriate nor unethical in a nonprofit context. It is a legitimate and major issue in strategic restructuring negotiations. The challenge is to identify and address participants' legitimate self-interest concerns so that they do not move underground to reemerge as sabotage.

> **Autonomy** and independence are much cherished rewards in a sector where compensation is not a primary motivator. Most impasses encountered in the course of strategic restructuring efforts can be traced to inadequate attention having been accorded to this emotional and potentially explosive issue. One way to defuse this potent issue is to ask the proponents of autonomy to detail their concerns and fears. Without interruption, argument or rebuttal—indeed with great and sympathetic care—they should be encouraged to articulate their worst fears for their organization, for their constituency and for themselves. Subsequent thorough discussion of each concern can result in compromises, cleared-up misunderstandings, and well-informed agreements to disagree. Equally important, these discussions will reveal the motivations of the parties and thereby begin to build mutual trust, an essential foundation for a successful outcome in any strategic restructuring process.

Sources: Green, 2001; La Piana, 1998.

Exhibit 3.11. Merger Activity: Volunteers of America.

Volunteers of America (VOA) is a national, spiritually based human services organization with over 11,000 staff and income exceeding $500 million per year. It assists over 1 million people and benefits from the efforts of over 40,000 volunteers.

Over recent years it has been approached by a number of local agencies that wished to form alliances with Volunteers of America. Twelve have successfully merged with it, and VOA national president Charles Gould told me that "there will be more in the future. Although economics drives some organizations to seek mergers, we are actively pursuing [mergers]. They get the advantage of joining the Volunteers of America brand, and we achieve economies of scale and greater promotion of the brand."

Source: Interview with Charles Gould, national president of Volunteers of America.

frequently, and surveys of chief executives demonstrate much enthusiasm for mergers, though most say other organizations should merge and not their own. Moreover, "The consensus among people studying mergers seems to be that economic conditions are driving the sector toward a shake-out and consolidation. Factors include the growth of the nonprofit sector, competition with businesses and other nonprofits, devolution, welfare reform, upward pressure on salaries, and the realization by a growing number of nonprofit managers that mergers are viable options" (La Piana, 2000, p. 1).

All this is occurring despite evidence that many business mergers do not deliver the anticipated immediate benefits. La Piana (2000) points out that

> The real benefits of a merger are not short term and tactical but medium to long term and strategic:

- Better market positioning

- A larger market share

- A higher public profile

- Greater political influence

- More strategic fundraising

- A larger staff allowing greater specialization of functions and the provision of more service

- The creation of a continuum of services under unified control

- Better economies of scale [p. 4].

Paul Jansen of McKinsey sees additional advantages: "The strategic benefit is that scale allows organizations to hire better quality managers and that is the key. In my experience mergers also allow organizations to transfer best practice both in programs and in management."

Although strategic mergers are espoused, they are comparatively rare. Mergers of last resort are much more common. "Merger or consolidation is seldom the first thought of leaders of a troubled organization; instead they deplete reserves, even restricted endowments, live in expectation of the next grant, defer facilities upkeep, and reduce services and salaries; in short, they hang on and hope for a miracle" (La Piana, 1998, p. 10).

Types of Organizations Merging

Mergers are most prevalent in the mental health, substance abuse, child welfare, and homeless fields, and the typical pattern is *strong joins weak*, in what amounts to more of a takeover than a merger. As organizations take a more strategic approach, some are merging with their competitors. Others are responding to donor pressures (Table 3.2). An increasingly significant area of activity is the acquisition of

Table 3.2. Typology of Mergers.

Type	Merger of	Aims	Example	Comment
Horizontal	Organizations in the same field	Economies of scale Increased service reach	Homeless organizations Hospices	Common for larger bodies to "take over" ailing agencies
Vertical	Organizations offering sequential services	Continuity of relationships with users	Hospital and home care agency Infant and toddler center and a preschool	Frequently implemented with parent corporation model
Conglomerate	Organizations in unrelated fields	Diversify income sources Economies of management	Group homes for adult developmentally disabled and a school for behaviorally disordered children	Not common and not thought to yield significant benefits
Concentric	Organizations in related fields, but not competitive	Satisfy users with multiple needs Create new service opportunities	Drug misuse agency and mental health agency	Used to integrate services into a one-stop shop

Source: Based on Arsenault, J. *Forging Nonprofit Alliances: A Comprehensive Guide to Enhancing Your Mission Through Joint Ventures and Partnerships, Management Service Organizations, Parent Corporations, and Mergers.* San Francisco: Jossey-Bass, 1998, pp. 84–86. Copyright © 1998 John Wiley & Sons, Inc. Reprinted with the permission of John Wiley & Sons, Inc.

nonprofits by for-profits. Private hospitals in particular have been buying nonprofits. Nursing homes, home health agencies, and child welfare, substance abuse, and mental health organizations are also being acquired, with the income from these sales being used to create endowments and so transform the original nonprofit into a grant-giving foundation.

Steps in a Successful Merger

The key to a successful merger is to build trust and confidence. Most mergers involve partners who not only know each other but who often have a history of poor relationships. Thomas Backer, president of the Human Interaction Research Institute, recommends making "an assumption that people are not really friends at the start of the process."

Four essential steps contribute to a successful merger:

1. *Define the prize,* the vision of a merged organization assisting more people, mounting stronger campaigns, and providing better-quality and more integrated services. The prize should become the touchstone that everyone can hold onto when negotiations become difficult.

2. *Establish a process and a time scale for negotiations.* David La Piana told me that "time scale is important. It should be neither too long nor too short. The ideal is four to six months." He recommends that organizations "identify all the issues that might arise at the first meeting and then agree which ones need to be solved before the merger can proceed." The proposed process should anticipate that there will be difficulties and should therefore include a mechanism for resolving the biggest obstacles. He sets out detailed advice for each stage of the merger process in *The Nonprofit Mergers Workbook* (La Piana, 2000).

3. *Address the biggest obstacles early on.* Two areas that commonly present difficulties are the name of the merged organization and who should fill the key roles of chair and chief executive. Inability to agree on any major point can bring the whole process to a grinding halt. Difficult issues need to be raised early in the process, but not before good personal relationships have been established.

4. *Recognize that cultural integration is the greatest challenge.* "There is ample evidence that a significant reason why mergers fail is the inability of the two organizations to integrate at a cultural level" (Arsenault, 1998, p. 88). People bring their own organization culture to the negotiating table and expect others to share their point of view, not realizing that their organization's beliefs and norms are different from the prospective partner's. A failure to deal with difficult and sensitive issues, particularly those concerned with redundancies, relocation, and redefined jobs, often means that these issues will emerge as problems years after the formal completion of the merger. Experts refer to *unconsummated* mergers, where the organizations have legally merged but the people have not integrated. They also caution that mergers have a remarkable ability to re-create within themselves the very problems that they were established to solve.

Even when these steps are followed, experience shows that it is easy to underestimate the time and effort required to bring a merger to a successful conclusion. Whelan (2000), for example, reports that "[c]harity leaders and consultants say they now realize just how much time, care and attention to the people involved with both organizations are required to make [partnership] efforts successful."

———————

Summary

Establish Strategic Alliances to Increase Impact

- Leading organizations are seeing opportunities for increasing impact that can be exploited only by combining their skills and resources.

- Strategic alliances enable organizations to improve the quality and range of their services, exploit economies of scale, and create critical mass.

- Funders are uniquely positioned to encourage, and sometimes require, organizations to collaborate, but they need to ensure that the process is fully owned by the participants.

Choose Alliance Types That Suit the Circumstances

- Organizations are establishing different types of strategic alliances, which sit on a continuum with cooperation and coordination at one end, strategic alliances in the middle, and mergers at the other end.

- Joint ventures, management service organizations, and group structures can all contribute to increasing impact.

Create Alliances with the Corporate Sector

- Nonprofit organizations are forming a wide range of successful partnerships with for-profit organizations.

- Relationships exist at three levels—the philanthropic stage, the transactional stage, and the integrative stage.

- Connections between businesses and nonprofits are moving from traditional philanthropy toward transactional and integrative relationships.

- Alliances present learning opportunities because partners' cultures, decision-making styles, and performance measures are different.

Build Alliances on Trustworthy Relationships

- Managing strategic alliances presents challenges of integrating conflicting cultures, adjusting staff to new roles, and allaying concerns about loss of autonomy.

- The seven essential attributes are shared values, strong leadership, clarity of mission and strategy, board commitment, sufficient resources, open communications, and good faith negotiations.

Merge to Build Strategic Capacity

- Most mergers are driven by economic conditions, but some organizations are merging to strengthen their market position and public profile, extend their political influence, and increase strategic fundraising.

- The four steps in a successful merger are to define the prize, establish a process and time scale, address the biggest obstacles early on, and recognize that cultural integration is the greatest challenge.

Action Checklist for Strategic Alliances

Nonprofit organizations will increasingly work across organization boundaries. The skills required to make partnerships successful will need to become deeply embedded in organizations' cultures and ways of working. Board members and managers who want to strengthen their organization's strategic alliances should

1. Regularly review their organization's position in the context of other organizations operating in the same or related fields.

2. Create a short list of organizations with similar missions, with similar user groups, or in similar geographic areas.

3. Review whether their organization's mission might be achieved more effectively or efficiently by forming new strategic alliances.

4. Make an assessment of the type of alliance that will have the greatest impact on their organization's mission.

5. Ensure that both the board and senior management are truly committed to the formation of strategic alliances.

6. Engage in open, informative conversations with potential partners.

7. Acknowledge that alliances always involve the loss of some autonomy in return for greater mission impact.

8. Recognize that the benefits must significantly outweigh the time invested in the alliance.

9. Manage alliances tightly, and ensure thorough and ongoing communication between partners' boards, managers, and staff.

Action Checklist for Corporate Sector Alliances

Forming strategic alliances with corporate sector organizations can yield big benefits to both parties. Nonprofit board members and managers who want strengthen their organization's corporate sector alliances should

1. Be creative with ideas for establishing win-win strategic alliances with corporations. Ensure that all board members and senior managers continuously seek new opportunities.

2. Keep new alliances in people's minds by reporting on the success of existing alliances. Hold periodic brainstorming sessions to generate new ideas.

3. Remember that existing contacts will be the easiest way into a corporation, so board members have a valuable role to play.

4. Review opportunities from the partner's perspective; be clear about the benefits they would achieve from the alliance.

5. Recognize that all alliances need to be tightly managed; appoint someone to take lead responsibility for each alliance.

6. Remember that continuous, open, and honest communication is critical for the long-term success of a relationship.

7. Focus on a smaller number of high-value relationships rather than a larger number of low-value ones.

8. If a relationship has run its course, be honest—celebrate the achievements, and bring it to a conclusion.

4

Exploiting Changing Patterns of Funding

The financing of nonprofit activity has changed significantly over recent years, and it will change further over the coming years. Leading-edge nonprofit organizations have spotted these changes and are grasping new opportunities to finance their growth and development.

Nonprofits receive 38 percent of their income from private payments for services. Models for managing these income streams broadly follow the theory and practices that are well established in the business community. Organizations compete for customers and charge prices that sometimes cover full costs and sometimes require a charitable subsidy. Either way, the laws of supply and demand prevail and conventional business management theory is most salient. Nonprofits receive a further 31 percent from government grants and contracts and 20 percent from private funders, including individual contributors, foundations, and corporate donors (INDEPENDENT SECTOR and Urban Institute, 2002). These latter sources of funds are the unique feature of the nonprofit sector, because the providers of this funding are not the beneficiaries of the services. Business theory often does not help.

This chapter is about the fundamental shifts in the sources of financing, or capital, that are unique to the nonprofit sector and that together account for just over half its income. Sources of nonprofit financing have diversified dramatically over the last ten or so years. In the past the main sources of private funding were grants, direct-mail solicitations, bequests, and annual fundraising campaigns. Today sources include program-related investments, venture philanthropy, community development finance institutions, loans, bonds, equity investments, and a range of other financial instruments. Although they represent a small proportion of total funding, each is a significant development. In addition to finding new sources of financing, nonprofits are dealing with the striking changes taking place in the organized funding community. Foundations are showing a growing interest in the effectiveness and impact of the organizations that they fund. The establishment of Grantmakers for Effective Organizations in 1997, as an affinity group of the Council on Foundations, epitomizes funders' growing interest in capacity building and organizational impact.

Some foundations and high-net-worth donors have started to provide funded organizations with a much higher level of support and in return expect greater accountability for achieving results. This is known as *high-engagement* philanthropy. Venture philanthropists have taken this tactic even further, translating for-profit venture capital approaches into approaches for the nonprofit world and demonstrating how an even higher level of engagement can work. Although these approaches are still small scale and controversial, their effects are challenging conventional thinking across much of the sector.

This chapter demonstrates that leading-edge organizations

- Take advantage of fundamental trends in finance sources

- Expect more demanding funders

- Capitalize on new funding sources

Take Advantage of Fundamental Trends in Finance Sources

A brief overview of the financing of nonprofits shows that private funding has grown dramatically in real terms in the last thirty years, from $21 billion in 1970 to $211 billion in 2001. Growth has been particularly rapid in the last ten years, with income from private funding more than doubling in this period (Figure 4.1). Individuals provided three-quarters of these funds in donations and a further 7.5 percent in bequests (Figure 4.2). Their generosity has grown during this period, rising, in constant dollars, from $327 per capita in 1970 to $511 in 1998 (the latest year for which figures were available), "fueled by a booming technology industry that was fast producing

Figure 4.1. How Much Is Given to Nonprofits?

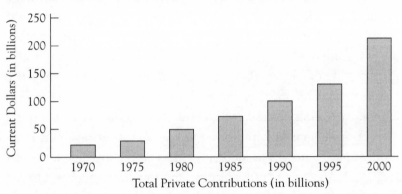

Sources: Data from AAFRC Trust for Philanthropy, 2002; INDEPENDENT SEC-
TOR and Urban Institute, 2002.

Figure 4.2. Who Gives to Nonprofits?

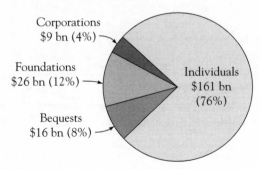

Source: Data from INDEPENDENT SECTOR and Urban Institute, *The New Nonprofit Almanac and Desk Reference: The Essential Facts and Figures for Managers, Researchers, and Volunteers.* San Francisco: Jossey-Bass, 2002. Copyright © 2002 John
Wiley & Sons, Inc. Reprinted with the permission of John Wiley & Sons, Inc.

new multimillionaires" (INDEPENDENT SECTOR and Urban Institute, 2002). This growth reflects increasing personal income. Giving by the nation as a whole has varied between 1.6 percent and 1.9 percent of personal income during this thirty-year period, and in 1998, stood at a high of 1.9 percent. So even though people are giving more, they are not giving a significantly higher percentage of their income.

The Nonprofit Capital Market

Within this overall pattern of considerable expansion, both the range and the number of organizations offering funds to nonprofit organizations are growing rapidly. The number of organizations seeking financing is growing just as fast. As a result academics are beginning to talk about a market for nonprofit financing, known as the *nonprofit capital market*, or the *nonprofit funding market*. This concept mirrors such business world structures as the business capital market, stock markets, and other financial institutions. The nonprofit capital market has many providers and many recipients and includes both primary providers and intermediaries such as United Way agencies and community foundations (Figure 4.3).

This powerful idea is beginning to shape thinking about sector funding, though the name *capital market* is slightly misleading because the notions of *capital* and *revenue* are not yet as clearly delineated in the nonprofit sector as they are in the business world.

Figure 4.3   The Nonprofit Capital Market.

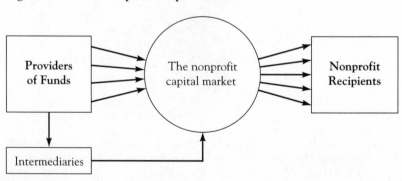

Experts argue that the nonprofit capital market is immature compared to the market for business capital. Feedback from recipients to providers is poor, so funders do not know which types of investments have greater social impact and which are less effective. Few performance metrics are used across the sector, so it is difficult for funders to compare the impact of their different *investments*. And funding bodies are highly fragmented, which also makes knowledge about what works best hard to obtain. Some analysts therefore envision a more rational, segmented, and thus more efficient and responsive nonprofit capital market (Ryan, 2001).

Experts further believe that changes are taking place that could have a significant impact on the recipients of funds. Jed Emerson (1999) of Stanford University says, "The nonprofit capital market is not a static organism, but is dynamic, with new players entering, old players exiting and new approaches to philanthropic strategies coming into play" (p. 200). He makes a case for organized restructuring of the nonprofit capital market: "The major challenge confronting the nonprofit capital market is that of how to organize itself more effectively so that one investment may build upon the next to maximize both the efficient use of charitable resources and the added value of various charitable investments" (p. 210).

In the more immediate future, the most significant changes that nonprofit organizations must consider include

- A greater concentration of wealth among a small number of high-net-worth donors

- Significant potential growth in bequests

- Further increases in noncash donations

A Greater Concentration of Wealth Among Certain Donors

People who are earning money and therefore paying taxes give larger sums than nonearners. The average charitable contribution of tax filers was $3,163 in 1998. This has grown from $2,138 per

person in 1986, a constant dollar increase of 45 percent (INDEPEN-
DENT SECTOR and Urban Institute, 2002). The more people earn,
the more they are likely to give. The American Association of
Fund-Raising Counsel estimates that a massive one-third of all individual donations comes from the wealthiest 1 percent of households
(AAFRC Trust for Philanthropy, 2002). This means the potential
rewards from identifying high-level donors, capturing and maintaining their interest, and retaining their contributions are considerable. Fundraising will therefore become more targeted, and based
on building more individualized relationships with donors. Furthermore, these are the very donors who will make the greatest
demands on the recipients. They are already asking questions about
the effects that their donations are having, and they will want more
evidence of impact in the future.

Significant Potential Growth in Bequests

Although bequests account for a small proportion of giving at present, researchers have calculated that over the next fifty-five years
an extraordinary $73 trillion will be transferred between genera-
tions (Havens and Schervish, 1999). This wealth has been accumulated through people's propensity to save, strong long-term stock
market performance, and increasing housing prices. Its ownership
is concentrated among a very small proportion of the population,
with 1 percent of households controlling 40 percent of the nation's
wealth (Salamon, 1999). The evidence of the 1980s is that people
with substantial wealth are more likely to establish foundations and
give some of their money away before they die than to bequeath it
for distribution after their deaths (a third of all existing U.S. foundations were established in the 1980s). Assuming that donors continue to bequeath the same proportion of their income to charity
as they do today, intergenerational wealth transfer will produce an
extra $11.5 trillion for the nonprofit sector over the next fifty-five
years (Havens and Schervish, 1999).

As a result some Americans are talking of a possible "golden age of philanthropy," producing significant additional unrestricted funding for nonprofit organizations. Even the least optimistic scenario for intergenerational wealth transfer suggests that $41 trillion will pass down over the next fifty-five years, generating $6 trillion for charities. The exact figure has been the subject of much debate, particularly following falls in the stock market, but the original researchers have published a robust rebuttal of the challenges (Havens and Schervish, 2003). Whether or not such a golden age materializes, the opportunity for organizations to capture the interest of this group of donors and significantly increase their own income from bequests is potentially enormous.

Further Increases in Noncash Donations

The nature of personal giving has also changed over the last ten years. In addition to financial gifts, noncash donations have increased significantly (Figure 4.4). From 1987 to 1997 (the last year for which figures are available), noncash donations increased from 12 percent to 28 percent of gifts. These noncash gifts include property, jewelry, stocks, works of art, cars, and food (from the food industry) among

Figure 4.4. Increases in Noncash Donations.

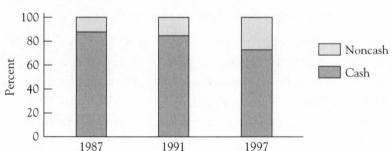

Source: INDEPENDENT SECTOR and Urban Institute, *The New Nonprofit Almanac and Desk Reference: The Essential Facts and Figures for Managers, Researchers, and Volunteers.* San Francisco: Jossey-Bass, 2002, p. 65. Copyright © 2002 John Wiley & Sons, Inc. Reprinted with the permission of John Wiley & Sons, Inc.

other items. Those nonprofits that organize to collect unwanted cars, obtain goods for recycling, accept jewelry, and take stocks and shares as donations will be better placed to exploit these opportunities.

Expect More Demanding Funders

The current trend is undoubtedly for funders to become more engaged with the organizations that they support. They are recognizing the power that they have and the responsibility associated with that power. Despite criticism of top-down approaches to accountability, the strong trend is toward funders' demanding evidence of the impact of the programs and organizations that they finance at the same time as they are offering greater support to those organizations.

Leading organizations are therefore learning to

- Expect fewer, larger, and more strategic grants

- Engage in more partnerships

- Provide greater accountability

- Share more learning across the sector   ·

Expect Fewer, Larger, and More Strategic Grants

Funders are realizing that the scope of their previous goals far exceeded the available resources. They are therefore attempting to establish more realistic objectives for their programs. Under pressure to demonstrate results, foundations in particular are likely to continue focusing their funding so they can more easily measure their impact.

Some foundations are replacing the traditional funding sectors—such as arts, youth, environment, and human services—with cross-sector programs—such as efforts to reduce poverty—that traverse the traditional functional boundaries. Some foundations are also taking the initiative, asking for proposals for programs that will enable them to achieve particular strategic objectives. The current volume of these focused approaches has led the Foundation Center to publish the *RFP Bulletin*, a weekly listing of requests for proposals that circulates these RFPs among fund-seeking nonprofits.

Together these trends are leading funders to offer fewer, larger, and more strategic grants. This in turn is driving grant seekers to present larger, more strategic responses. However, this proactive approach has been the subject of some criticism, particularly from people working on the front lines. They believe that they know what is best for their communities and resent the arrogance of funders who define how social problems should be solved and focus their funding on explicit social objectives. "Locality differences are very important in the U.S.," Rikki Abzug, assistant professor at the Milano Graduate School of Management and Urban Policy in New York, said to me. "Neighborhoods are very specific culturally, ethnically, and spiritually." She cited the positive example of the Casey Foundation program on strengthening families, which asks nonprofit organizations what they think is most needed in their communities. So, despite the general trend toward having fewer, longer-term, and more encompassing relationships with grantees, some foundations have made an explicit decision to be responsive to grant seekers' requests and to continue distributing a large number of small community grants.

Engage in More Partnerships

Funders are encouraging grant seekers to work in partnership both with each other and with funders themselves. They are also encouraging applications from partnerships and from consortia of organizations. As a result some applicants are creating alliances to jointly seek funds that are then distributed to member organizations. Some funders are also forming partnerships and consortia with other funders to increase the resources available for a particular issue.

Some funders see themselves in long-term partnerships with grant recipients. Mary Ann Holohean, director of the Nonprofit

Sector Advancement Fund at the Meyer Foundation, told me that the foundation offers "organizations a menu of support including advice, loans, and advances to cover cash-flow difficulties as well as grants. Our relationship does not mean we will give them funds every year, but we will stay in partnership with them."

Provide Greater Accountability

In the past nonprofits' public accountability has been light, centered on receipt of permission to operate from the Internal Revenue Service and submission of an annual tax return (IRS Form 990). This began to change following a small number of high-profile charity scandals in the 1990s, involving such organizations as the United Way of America and New Era Philanthropy. As Kevin Kearns (1996) describes it, "Nonprofits have (until recently) lived a relatively charmed existence in an unregulated environment" (p. 1). However, this has changed over the last ten years. Periods of general lack of interest in public policy on nonprofits have tended to be interrupted by sudden explosions of scrutiny, usually following major scandals. As a result, says Kearns, "The debate on accountability in the nonprofit sector has emerged from the chambers of legislatures and the courts and entered the living rooms of citizens across the country" (p. 26). The issue of nonprofit effectiveness has also become a matter of public policy. "The question increasingly being raised by communities, scholars, the media, governments and politicians is whether the impact achieved by foundations . . . is sufficient to justify continuation of their privileged and protected status" (Prager, 1999).

The most dramatic response to these challenges has been the rapid growth and influence of Grantmakers for Effective Organizations. Established in 1997, this association now has 340 foundation members, including many of the largest and most influential foundations and regional associations of grantmakers. It draws over 550 people to its biannual conferences and is dedicated to promoting learning and encouraging dialogue among funders working in the field of organizational effectiveness.

"Related to the growing demand for greater accountability in philanthropy is the increased attention being given to program assessment and evaluation. Talk among foundation boards and staff these days is all about outcomes and how to measure them" (Prager, 1999). Funding for evaluation of the impact of individual grants and of grantmaking programs is increasingly seen as an integral part of a grant. The greatest attention is being paid to ongoing evaluations that are "good enough" to demonstrate results, rather than to large-scale, postproject evaluations that are often seen as expensive and not offering good value for money. This, however, is creating some anxiety. "There is the fear that the resulting preoccupation with measurable outcomes and objective evidence may prevent foundations from taking on the kinds of big issues they are so well positioned to address. Further, there is concern that foundations may be misleading themselves and others by attempting to apply scientific evaluation to areas that, by their very nature, are complex, ambiguous, and ever changing" (Prager, 1999).

Nevertheless the overall trend is clear. Organizations will be expected to build evaluation and impact assessment into their project proposals, and funders will want to see and publish the results achieved with their funding. Foundations in particular will be paying greater attention to assessing the overall impact of their funding programs and the extent to which they are achieving overall foundation objectives (Exhibit 4.1).

Share More Learning Across the Sector

Public pressure is also driving foundations to improve their communications. There is a growing feeling that in return for the tax breaks that foundations receive, they have a duty to report in an open, accessible, and meaningful way on how they have spent their money and what it has achieved.

Finally, there is an emerging view that evaluation should be less concerned with how well one grant has or has not been used and more concerned with the opportunity for organizations and funders

Exhibit 4.1. Paying Attention to Results:
Youth Development at the Edna McConnell Clark Foundation.

The Edna McConnell Clark Foundation decided to focus its funding on helping to strengthen youth development organizations. It adopted a new approach to grantmaking, which it called *institution and field building*.

The heart of the process is a comprehensive, multistage process used to identify promising organizations, assess their overall capabilities, and invest in those best positioned to benefit from the McConnell Clark approach. Typically the relationship involves

- **Identifying** organizations by scanning various communities for successful organizations that meet predetermined criteria

- **Due diligence** work through which the foundation studies the organization's program models, leadership and management, financial strength, and internal performance measurement systems

- **Business planning** to specify the steps the organization will take to achieve its growth

- **Investment,** with substantial multiyear funding linked to agreements about the goals the organization says it will reach and for which it will be held accountable

- **Performance tracking and evaluation** to monitor achievements and develop the organization's capacity to evaluate its work and improve its operations

Cash investment in each organization ranges from $1 million to $5 million for up to five years. Nonfinancial support includes professional and technical assistance, help with communications, and introductions to other funders. Once work has begun, a foundation portfolio manager—a senior staff member responsible for managing relationships with grant recipients—maintains contact with the organization, reviews its performance, and provides ongoing support and assistance.

Source: Information from Edna McConnell Clark Foundation, 2004a, 2004b.

to learn from each other. Consequently, some funders are requiring nonprofits working on similar issues to have more contact with each other. Other funders are taking the initiative by bringing organizations together to share experiences. In this way everyone can learn more about what works and what does not work, and can use this knowledge to increase future effectiveness. Organizations that integrate shared learning opportunities into their funding applications are therefore more likely to be successful than those that ignore this significant trend. (Exhibit 4.2 sums up some features of foundation programs that make a difference.)

Capitalize on New Funding Sources

The traditional reliance nonprofits have on income from donors, government, and the sale of services is slowly changing. New sources of funds have become available over the last few years. Although small in proportion to the sector's total income, each presents new opportunities and challenges for nonprofit managers. How significant each will become in the future is hard to predict.

Some suggest that nonprofits could follow a business model here. Businesses select from a range of sources of finance: banks for low-risk and low-return funding, the equity market for medium-risk funding and higher returns, and venture capitalists for high-risk incubation of new ideas. Similarly, it is argued, nonprofits should look to a range of financial instruments, selecting the one that best suits their requirements or that offers nontraditional types of funding.

The most interesting nontraditional sources of funds are

- Program-related investment

- High-engagement funders

- Venture philanthropy

**Exhibit 4.2. Characteristics of an
Effective Foundation Program.**

Research into the views of foundation leaders and observers of
philanthropy, commissioned by Grantmakers in Health, produced a
seminal review of the trends and tensions inherent in grantmaking.
After examining responses to the question, "What are the characteristics of foundation programs that have really had an impact?" the
report author advanced the view that an effective foundation program
is one characterized by

Coherent sense of purpose—a clear understanding of intent and
expectations articulated up front

Focus—targeting a specific societal issue, problem, or need that has
been identified by the foundation as compelling as well as consistent
with its mission, values, and priorities

Thorough knowledge of the field—basing action on an in-depth
knowledge of the issue, problem or need being addressed

Clear theory of change—selecting an implementation strategy on
the basis of a clearly articulated change theory and process judged
to be the most effective one for achieving intended outcomes

Strategic deployment of resources—mobilizing and deploying all
the resources available to the foundation so as to increase the like-
lihood of success and to attract and leverage the participation and
resources of other partners

Timeliness and duration—maximizing the potential for success by
taking into account the realities of the environment in which the
program will be operating and the readiness of actors to act; sticking
with a program for sufficient time to make a real difference

Interaction with key constituencies—involving key constituencies
from the initial conceptualization through implementation and
evaluation

Mobilization of communities—drawing, building on, and strengthening the capacity of communities to solve their own problems

Communications—including communication strategies and tools as
integral elements of every program undertaken

**Exhibit 4.2. Characteristics of an
Effective Foundation Program, Cont'd.**

Active program management—adopting a program management
style that emphasizes working with participants in foundation initiatives in such a way as to increase the effectiveness of each element
of the initiative and the degree to which those elements add up to
a productive whole

Staffing—building a staff of program officers who view their jobs as
working in partnership with grant recipients and others to develop
and implement programs directed toward the achievement of foundation goals and expectations; creating an organizational environment conducive to their creativity and productivity

Source: Prager, 1999, pp. 6–7. Reprinted with the permission of Grantmakers In
Health, www.gih.org.

Program-Related Investment

Traditionally, foundations have used the interest or gains on their
investments to finance their grantmaking programs. More recently,
some foundations have begun investing a small proportion of their
capital in nonprofit organizations in the form of loans. So instead
of investing all their capital in mainstream financial institutions,
they invest some in the organizations they wish to assist. These
investments are an alternative to grants and are known as *program-
related investments*, or PRIs.

The value of these loans grew dramatically in the late 1990s as a
result of the stock market boom. In 2001, $233 million was lent to
nonprofit organizations in new program-related investments.
Despite the tough economic environment, the number of PRI
providers continued to grow and stood at 225 organizations in 2001,
according to the Foundation Center. Loans in the largest category
(37 percent) were for community development and housing, including housing development, neighborhood revitalization in urban
centers, and small business promotion in rural communities. A further 19 percent were investments in health and education projects

(Renz, 2003). Most PRI funding is used to support organizations through direct loans and loan guarantees and to capitalize development banks and venture funds. A small proportion enables nonprofits to acquire or improve property used for charitable purposes.

Just under 200 foundations provide PRIs. Two-thirds of their loans were for more than $100,000, and 16 percent were for more than $1 million. Many of the recipients are financial intermediaries that in turn lend money to development and housing agencies, job-training agencies, community organizations, arts groups, and other borrowers. These intermediaries include loan funds, credit unions, development banks, microenterprise funds, and venture capital funds. Half the funding made available financed capital projects (Renz, 2003).

The case for greater program-related investment is based partly on the needs of nonprofit organizations for different types of finance, and partly on a growing unease that the overwhelming majority of foundations' capital is invested to produce maximum financial benefit for the foundation as opposed to bringing wider social benefits. A small percentage of foundations do use ethical criteria to guide their investment strategies. However, most do not, and these may inadvertently be investing in businesses that are directly or indirectly linked to the very problems that the same foundations' grant recipients are trying to solve. So some foundations have decided that they can better achieve their social mission by investing their capital in social projects, even if this means accepting a lower rate of return. Indeed, some commentators argue that foundations should be paying much greater attention to the 95 percent of their assets that is not paid out each year, than to the 5 percent that is paid out. At present most staff and board effort is focused on grant-making. This limits staff and board attention to around 5 percent of foundation resources. Emerson (2002), for example, argues that by "not engaging in total foundation asset management we are consistently missing the point of philanthropy, which is not grantmaking itself, but the application of precious resources to support the creation of a more whole, just and peaceful world."

For any foundation the balance between maximizing long-term return on funds and using those funds for immediate impact on major need is hard to get right. But the availability of PRIs does mean that some of the capital required by nonprofit organizations can be financed by loans, thus releasing hard-won donations and retained earnings to be used for other investments or program activities.

High-Engagement Funders

A small number of funders have begun to require a much higher level of accountability from grant recipients, and in return these funders offer grantees a higher level of support. Some of these are new funders and some are existing foundations that have decided to take a high-engagement approach. The assumption behind high-engagement funding is that enhancing organization performance is critical to achieving social goals. "Among all the options available to them as grant-makers—funding research, dissemination of best practice, training and education for professionals . . . high engagement funders conclude that improving the work of a given number of particular nonprofit organizations will be the best means of achieving their social goals" (Letts and Ryan, 2003, p. 26).

High-engagement philanthropy is "a combination of three elements—a range of informal and formal assistance that we call "strategy coaching," the use of reliable money, and attention to alignment of funder and grantee interests. Standing alone, each of these is a common feature of grant making. Together, they constitute a distinctive grant-making approach" (Letts and Ryan, 2003, p. 28). The aim is to create a more open and trusting relationship, with the funded organization reporting both on achievements and on problems.

Strategy coaching aims to help organizations develop robust strategies and in particular to support them in developing "business plans" that identify relatively short-term goals and establish how those goals will be achieved. The highly engaged funder acts as a sounding board, offering judgment and insight. The funder also expects to see strategy converted into action and takes a keen interest in the nonprofit's results. In return the funder offers long-term and flexible support for grant recipients, which can include training and consulting to support activities such as financial management, marketing, and fundraising. Although high-engagement funding is more expensive for the funder, these costs are treated not as grant administration costs but as investments designed to help the nonprofit achieve greater impact. High-engagement funding also places demands on the grantmaking organization itself because of the high level of skill and experience demanded from that organization's staff. This may require the grantmaker to raise its own game and recruit or develop the required skills.

The result of this approach is that funders are making long-term investments in organizations, rather than providing one-off grants for individual programs or projects. Nonprofits appreciate this approach, though with some caveats. One authoritative review of the impact of high-engagement philanthropy concluded that grant recipients valued the high-engagement approach but preferred the freedom to select the management support they required rather than accepting the funders' chosen suppliers (Letts and Ryan, 2003).

Venture Philanthropy

Venture philanthropy is a particular type of high-engagement philanthropy. It is modeled on the success of venture capitalists who invest in a portfolio of businesses, monitor their performance closely, provide frequent assistance, help them to raise further funds, and have a defined exit point, often five to seven years after making the initial investment. The resources for venture philanthropy tend to come from successful businesspeople who wish to become involved in the nonprofits they finance and to hold these nonprofits accountable for performance.

Venture philanthropy starts from the principle that this type of funding is an *investment* and not a grant. The funders are committed to the organization's objectives and usually want to back the organization as a whole. They want to see rapid organization growth, and they want to ensure that the organization develops its overall capacity as well as its programs. Venture philanthropists believe they can achieve the greatest impact by offering a combination of multiyear funding, strategic coaching, assistance in building organization capacity, and access to local networks of businesspeople and funders. Most important, they expect tight accountability from the organizations in which they invest. They see themselves as entering a true partnership that depends on openness and trust. They share the risk of things going wrong and the satisfaction of seeing real achievements.

Two disparate trends created the conditions in which venture philanthropy could thrive. First, nonprofit organizations became increasingly aware of their need for entrepreneurial skills and for more unrestricted funding to invest in their own organizations. Second, the unprecedented wealth creation in the late 1990s produced a significant number of people with both a desire to put something back into the community and the time and the resources to realize their intentions.

Coming from the business world, venture philanthropists have the mind-set of investors. They want to see a *social return* on their investment, and they are often keen to get to the *root cause* of an issue. In an interview, Kelly Fitzsimmons, cofounder and managing director of New Profit Inc., a Boston-based venture philanthropy organization, told me that "investors want to raise the bar of investment results. Our investors believe that these results are achieved by the compounding effect of good investment choices, high standards, good management and tight accountability" (Exhibit 4.3).

Although venture philanthropy has gained a high public profile, it is new, and the scale of the funding is still tiny. There are forty-two venture philanthropy funds in the United States, and their total capital is estimated to be just over $400 million. Two-thirds of these

Exhibit 4.3. A Venture Philanthropy Fund: New Profit Inc.

New Profit Inc. (NPI) is a venture philanthropy fund whose goal is to achieve large-scale social change by investing in and partnering with a select group of innovative, high-performing nonprofit organizations. It supports social entrepreneurs in bringing their organizations to larger scale by providing them with significant, performance-based growth capital as well as intellectual capital in the form of strategy consulting, growth planning assistance, management support, and network access.

Established in 1998, NPI has raised capital of over $15 million and secured a further $10 million for the organizations in its portfolio. Its forty-five investors put up a minimum of $100,000 each over four years, and in return they participate in the investors' network, help to select recipients, and offer expertise to recipients through mentoring and strategy advice. NPI produces biannual reports to update investors on the progress of each recipient against agreed performance measures for organization growth and social impact. It has nine staff and an annual operating budget of $870,000, not including grants to its nonprofit portfolio.

NPI funds eight organizations with four-year grants ranging from $500,000 to $2 million in intellectual and financial capital. Seven of the eight are in the education field, and each receives on average 1,000 hours of staff time per year. They are

BELL (Building Educated Leaders for Life), which operates after-school programs in disadvantaged communities for minority students aged eight to eleven to promote academic proficiency

Citizen Schools, which engages students aged nine to fourteen through fun, challenging, hands-on out-of-school apprenticeships with a focus on academic gains

JumpStart, which delivers an early childhood literacy program, working one-to-one with at-risk urban preschoolers and using a research-backed curriculum

New Leaders for New Schools, which recruits, trains, places, and supports a new generation of outstanding school principals in urban state schools

Exhibit 4.3. A Venture Philanthropy Fund: New Profit Inc., Cont'd.

Teach for America, which offers recent outstanding and diverse college graduates opportunities to teach for two years in schools with insufficient resources

Working Today, which is working toward the day when independent workers have access to a full safety net of affordable, portable benefits, workplace rights, and legal protection

College Summit, which reaches low-income high school students with a program that doubles their rate of enrollment in college

Computers for Youth, which provides computers and training to students aged nine to fourteen (and their families) to teach computer literacy and engage them in learning.

NPI has a strategic partnership with the Monitor Group, the international consulting firm. Monitor does not charge for most of this strategic consulting because the work gives its staff interesting and challenging personal development opportunities. Monitor wants to leverage its expertise for the benefit of NPI's portfolio organizations and the larger field of philanthropy.

NPI's output and results are impressive. The annual average revenue growth among its portfolio of organizations was 28 percent since its inception, compared to about 3 percent per year for the average U.S. youth development organization. The number of people served by NPI's organizations is growing by rates varying from 20 to 30 percent per year for the older and larger organizations to over 300 percent per year for the smaller and newer organizations, with an overall average of 35 percent annual growth since 1999.

According to Kelly Fitzsimmons, one of the cofounders, "The greatest challenge has been attracting senior and talented people to work alongside the entrepreneur who is driving the enterprise."

Source: Information from New Profit Inc.

organizations were incorporated after January 1999. They exist in eighteen states, the majority being in California (eleven), New York (six), and Texas (four) (Community Wealth Ventures, 2002). In 2001, they made grants of $50 million, significant new money but representing less than 0.2 percent of all grants made by foundations. However, nonmonetary support is an important element of their offer, and fifteen of the forty-two estimate that their noncash support is of greater value than their financial support. For example, Social Venture Partners, a Seattle-based fund on which organizations in twenty-one other locations have modeled themselves, invests 500 to 600 hours of partner time in each recipient organization (Community Wealth Ventures, 2002).

Venture philanthropists invest more in youth and education than any other field, with eighteen of the forty-two focused on this area; perhaps this focus is linked to venture philanthropists' general desire to get to the root of social problems. Although some make grants in the $25,000 to $75,000 range, seven invest $1 million or more in each recipient organization. Most grants run for between four and seven years. The most common criterion for selecting recipients is strong leadership, reflecting venture philanthropists' belief in investing in individuals with the personal attributes and skills required to achieve the desired social impact (see, for example, Exhibit 4.4).

The 2002 annual review prepared by Community Wealth Ventures showed that the forty-two venture philanthropy organizations identified

- Have an average of 3.4 staff

- Measure outcomes using social return on investment and the balanced scorecard

- Are interested in measures that track the performance of the organization itself as well as impact on the community

Exhibit 4.4. A Recipient Case Study: Citizen Schools.

Citizen Schools was founded in 1994 to provide a network of after-school and summer educational programs. The programs are based on an apprenticeship model of rigorous hands-on learning that unites volunteer adults with children nine to fourteen years old. Citizen Schools believe that out-of-school time represents the greatest untapped opportunity for improving children's education and strengthening communities. In 1999, it was serving 900 children and won a competitive bid to receive financial and strategic support from New Profit Inc. This support

- Tightened the organization's *theory of change* (at the individual and field levels) and strengthened its evaluation system

- Provided CEO coaching and facilitation for the leadership team and board meetings

- Created a balanced scorecard as a simple quarterly action-planning tool

- Developed detailed costing and financial models for scaling up the service

Since NPI became involved, Citizen Schools has grown to serve 2,200 children (as of 2003). Its funding base has grown from $1.8 million to $6.6 million, and the Citizen Schools University has been launched to replicate the model across the country.

According to founder Eric Schwartz, "The clarity of our vision, tightness of our action plan and power of our evaluation metrics are demonstrably greater. More importantly, we're building the capacity to continue to grow, improve, and creatively impact the field. [New Profit Inc.] provided $3.7 million towards our $25 million four-year growth plan—less than 20 percent of the total but vitally important to our momentum and ultimate success. [This support] has worked for us—big time. We've more than doubled in size while improving quality and starting to replicate nationally. We're serving twice as many children and serving them better. Venture philanthropists have brought us tough-minded concentration on results."

Source: Information from New Profit Inc.

The role and potential of venture philanthropy is one of the more controversial topics in the nonprofit sector at present. Given its relatively small size, it has generated a remarkable quantity of heated debate. The case for both venture philanthropy and high-engagement funding is that each of them

- Responds to flaws in the current funding arrangements

- Provides a new approach to philanthropy that appeals to people who are not attracted by traditional grant-making and who bring new resources to the sector

- Offers *core funding*, which organizations say they desperately need

- Provides a range of nonfinancial support such as coaching and technical assistance

- Supplies flexible funding

- Demands accountability, an approach often lacking in the nonprofit sector

Beyond that, it is clear from the requests these funders receive from nonprofits that there is simply a big demand for this type of investment (Etchart and Davis, 2002). Furthermore, venture philanthropy "should be an attractive alternative to both sides of the political spectrum," says Wendy Kopp, founder of Teach for America. "For conservatives we're bringing private sector and entrepreneurial approaches to public problems. For liberals we're all about social change and improving the welfare of the least privileged people" (Hunt, 2000).

The case against the venture philanthropy approach is most powerfully articulated by Bruce Sievers (2001), former chief executive of the Haas Foundation. He argues that there are four assumptions underlying venture capitalism that become deeply problematic when applied to philanthropy. First, venture capitalism depends on a single bottom-line test of success, whereas "Nonprofit activity has a complex and intangible range of aims that often elude simple classification and measurement." Second, venture philanthropy is based on the assumption of *going to scale*—replicating services at regional, national, or even international levels. This should lead to economies of scale, but nonprofits exist to meet highly differentiated social needs, to fill niches not satisfied by the public sector. Third, venture capitalists are actively engaged in the management of the enterprises they finance and so seek high levels of control. But nonprofit organizations are independent and have to maintain a balance of power between a range of stakeholders. An overly intrusive investor can threaten this independence. Fourth, venture capitalists always have an *exit strategy*, a route for getting their capital repaid. Venture philanthropists argue that they aim to help their organizations achieve financial self-sufficiency and that will release them from their commitments, but in the nonprofit situation this means either increasing income from fees for services or replacing venture philanthropy funding with money from government, foundations, or other donors.

Additionally, some commentators argue that venture philanthropy is a spin-off from the dot-com bubble that has now burst and that there will be no further significant inflows of new money. There is already some evidence for this view; existing venture philanthropy organizations reported difficulties finding new donors when the economy stopped growing in 2001.

The debate is best summed up by Eric Schwartz (2002), the founder of Citizen Schools. He says, "Venture philanthropy is too often cloaked in a blanket of for-profit superiority that lacks historical perspective and discounts what is most challenging about the nonprofit sector—the sector's focus on changing outcomes for the hardest-to-reach children and adults. However, most people agree with its substance—grantmaking that is long term, linked to performance, and combined with strategic noncash assistance—but many people object to the symbolism of venture philanthropy" (p. 15).

Despite the criticisms, many, including people I interviewed, believe that venture philanthropy will become a permanent feature of nonprofit funding. "It is here to stay," James Austin, chair of the

Social Enterprise Initiative at the Harvard Business School, told me. "There will be unprecedented wealth transfer between generations over the coming years. Although its impact is limited at present, it is all part of the growing heterogeneity of social enterprise." Virginia Hodgkinson, founding director of the Center for the Study of Voluntary Organizations and Service at Georgetown University, agreed: "It is not going to go away because there is a new breed of people who want a hands-on involvement in their philanthropy."

Some venture philanthropists now think that they were insufficiently sensitive to the culture of the sector and did not acknowledge its existing achievements. Mario Morino (2002), a leading figure in the field and cofounder of the $32 million fund Venture Philanthropy Partners, says that "one of the budding venture philanthropist's mistakes is that we don't listen. Some of us impose our point of view on others instead of paying attention to what's going on around us" (p. 2).

There is also an emerging view that venture philanthropy and high-engagement funding were both overhyped in the early stages of their development. As a Community Wealth Ventures report (2002) commented: "A few years ago, the concepts of venture philanthropy and high engagement grantmaking were over-inflated with airy promises to transform philanthropy as we know it. Today we can see that their progress towards that promise is real but not yet revolutionary."

Yet high-engagement funding and venture philanthropy have clearly had a major impact on the way people think about large-gift philanthropy and have provoked foundations to think about different approaches to grantmaking (Exhibit 4.5). Indeed, Julie Rogers (2002), president of the Meyer Foundation, says that "the challenge now is to widen the circle so that high-engagement strategies define how philanthropy is done for years to come" (p. 13).

So the approach is here to stay. Those organizations that wish to seek this type of finance, and are willing to gear up to its requirements, will no doubt benefit, particularly when the economy returns to

**Exhibit 4.5. Reflections on Five Years
of Venture Philanthropy Implementation.**

REDF (formerly the Roberts Enterprise Development Fund),
launched in 1997, believes that five guiding principles have emerged
as best practices in building productive partnerships with the nonprofit
organizations in its portfolio:

Clarity. We sign a detailed memorandum of understanding that
sets out REDF's expectations of the agency and the relationship,
and what the nonprofit can expect from REDF. It is reviewed every
year. Organizations appreciate the clarity of its contents and the
fact that everything is documented.

Communication. We conduct a semi-annual assessment (of each
other) and hold a monthly venture committee meeting with each
funded organization involving REDF's managing director and business analyst and the nonprofit chief executive, chief finance officer
and business manager. This increased communication is essential in
building more productive working relationships.

Customization. We tailor support to suit each organization's requirements from a menu that includes hands-on assistance in planning,
help with recruitment, networking, technology support and social
outcomes assessment.

Collaboration. We build strong positive relationships where problems
can be openly discussed and outcomes can be reviewed together
rather than imposed by the funder.

Consistency. We avoid communicating inconsistent messages.
This involves weekly portfolio review meetings with all REDF
staff to discuss the status of organizations, the messages to be con-
veyed and who will convey them.

Source: Based on Tuan, 2002a, 2002b. www.allavida.org/alliance. Used with
permission.

faster growth and more businesspeople make their fortunes who then want to make a significant contribution to the community.

Summary

Take Advantage of Fundamental Trends in Finance Sources

- Sources of financing are diversifying and now include program-related investments, venture philanthropy, community development finance institutions, loans, bonds, and equity investments.

- Traditional sources of financing have grown dramatically in real terms. Private contributions to nonprofit organizations have grown by 340 percent over the last twenty years, and government funding has grown by 195 percent.

- Changes in traditional sources of funding are likely to include

    A greater concentration of wealth among a small number of donors

    Significant potential growth in bequests

    Further increases in noncash donations

- Commentators are beginning to conceive of a *nonprofit capital market*. They see this market as being inefficient and needing reform.

Expect More Demanding Funders

- Funders are becoming much more involved with the organizations they finance, expecting clearer evidence of results and offering greater support.

- Leading organizations are expecting to

  Receive fewer, larger, and more strategic grants

  Engage in more partnerships, and provide greater accountability

  Share more learning across the sector

- The characteristics of an effective funder include a coherent purpose, focus, a knowledge of the field, a theory of change, strategic resource deployment, a long-term commitment, and active program management.

Capitalize on New Funding Sources

- Leading organizations look to a range of different financial instruments to fund different types of capital and revenue requirements.

- Program-related investment provides new capital funds to nonprofits and allows foundations to invest their resources in their mission.

- A new breed of high-engagement funders is taking new approaches to philanthropy and combining funding with strategic coaching, practical support, and demands for accountability.

- Although still small in size and controversial, venture philanthropy has had a significant impact on the sector. Funders are offering a combination of multiyear funding, strategic coaching, and other assistance to build organization capacity. They agree on ambitious targets with funded organizations and also have tough accountability requirements.

Action Checklist

The traditional patterns of funding nonprofit organizations have started to change and will alter much more significantly over the coming years. Board members and managers who want to exploit changing patterns of nonprofit funding should

1. Acknowledge that many funders will increasingly want a smaller number of longer-term, more strategic relationships with greater accountability for the impact of the funding.

2. Invest greater resources in seeking bequests—because of the huge potential in the growing intergenerational wealth transfer.

3. Focus big-gift fundraising on the new generation of wealthy people who increasingly wish to establish their own foundations before they die.

4. Systematically review all activities to determine whether they could be financed from new sources of funding (for example, by borrowing working capital).

5. Strengthen their financial departments with skills in understanding and using the new sources of finance.

6. Adjust the fit between sources and uses of funds in order to exploit new sources and release unrestricted funds for new ventures.

7. Conduct periodic board-level reviews of the sources of and applications for the organization's funds; determine whether different mixes would open up new opportunities.

8. Review current funding against a list of all the options for nonprofit funding to generate fresh ideas for exploiting the new sources of funds.

5

Leading with Integrity

L eadership is one of the most discussed and most documented aspects of management. The shelves of bookstores burst with titles setting out a wide range of views on the topic. There are books written by leaders based on their own experience, books promoting particular approaches to leadership, and many biographical books that feed people's curiosity about how business leaders make their organizations successful.

Leadership is viewed as immensely important in nonprofit organizations. A Brookings Institution survey of 250 researchers and providers of management assistance highlighted leadership as the single most important ingredient of effective organizations: "Leadership does appear to be the answer, but not the sparkly, charismatic leadership celebrated in glossy best-sellers. . . . Rather it is a participatory, democratic leadership that draws upon strengths inside and outside the organization" (Light, 2002, p. 69).

One of the first people to promote specific leadership strategies in the nonprofit sector was Peter F. Drucker. In "Leadership Is a Foul-Weather Job," the second section of his 1990 book, *Managing the Nonprofit Organization*, he makes these pertinent points:

- The first task of the leader is to make sure that everybody sees the mission, hears it and lives it.

- In the nonprofit agency, mediocrity in leadership shows up almost immediately.

- The new leader of a nonprofit doesn't have much time to establish himself or herself.

Throughout the 1990s, the Drucker Foundation (now renamed the Leader to Leader Institute) did much to promote understanding of leadership and to offer training and practical support to nonprofit leaders.

The late John W. Gardner, founding chair of INDEPENDENT SECTOR, also recognized the importance of leadership in nonprofits. In his book *On Leadership,* also published in 1990, he described what successful nonprofit leaders must do to instill confidence, morale, and motivation in those who look to them for the future.

More recently, Burt Nanus and Stephen Dobbs wrote *Leaders Who Make a Difference* (1999), in response to "the paucity of professional guidance available to leaders of nonprofit organizations" (p. x). They argued that leadership of nonprofits is different from leadership of business and government organizations. First, nonprofits have unpaid board members, many deliver their services through volunteers, and most staff consider their salary secondary to the "psychic income" they derive from working for a cause. "Leading these kinds of people requires much more reliance on inspiration, passion, coaxing, persuasion and peer pressure than upon authority, financial incentives or fancy job titles." Second, "success in nonprofit organizations is measured not in terms of profits and fulfillment of legislative intent, but in terms of social good. This is a more value-laden and less clearly defined criterion than . . . other organizations must meet, leaving considerable room for nonprofit leaders to exercise judgment, intuition and innovation." Finally, Nanus and Dobbs argue that "working with the board— some might say leading the board—is a much more critical part of the leader's job in nonprofits than in other types of organizations. The sheer number of people to be led is far larger in nonprofit organizations than in business or government agencies with similar-sized budgets" (p. 12).

Leadership is not just about the person at the top of the organization, though the behavior of that person clearly has a huge influence on the values and style of the organization and its management. It is about the delivery of leadership in all parts of the organization. Everyone in a position of authority has a responsibility to provide leadership for his or her area of work and to contribute to the wider leadership of his or her department or division and the organization as a whole.

This chapter demonstrates that people who succeed in leadership positions learn to

- Be a leader

- Mobilize around the mission

- Focus people on results

- Build a small, focused team

- Invest in leadership and management development

Be a Leader

The leaders and others I interviewed and the literature stress the importance of leaders' behavior. Leaders have to embody the values of the organization in what they do and how they do it. They have to be conscious of the need for complete congruence between the organization's values and their own behavior. Leaders are being watched all the time—and small differences between their deeply held values and the actions they take will be noticed. "Leaders are the embodiment of the mission and values in thinking, action and communication," according to Frances Hesselbein, chair of the Leader to Leader Institute. Hesselbein, Goldsmith, and Beckhard (1996) recommend that leaders always think about what their legacy will be. In their view, leaders need to understand "how to be." This involves leaders' "quality, character, mind-set, values, principles, and courage." Leaders who appreciate how to be "build dispersed and diverse leadership and hold forth the vision of the organization's future in compelling ways that ignite the spark needed to build the inclusive enterprise" (p. 122).

This view is echoed by Parker Palmer, author of *Let Your Life Speak* (1999). Interviewed in the journal *Leader to Leader,* he said, "The best leaders work from a place of integrity in themselves, from their hearts. If they don't they can't inspire trustful relationships. In the absence of trust, organizations fall apart. . . . It takes courage to lead from the heart because you're putting your own identity and integrity into the public arena. You're standing for things you believe in. You're professing values that are important to you—and in the public arena you will always draw slings and arrows for doing that. But you will have the best chance of creating something of true and lasting value" ("Leadership and the Inner Journey," 2001, pp. 27–28).

Leaders have to fulfill a number of roles. Nanus and Dobbs argue that leaders' attention needs to be focused in four directions:

1. *Inside the organization,* where the leader interacts with the board, staff and volunteers to inspire, encourage, enthuse, and empower them.
2. *Outside the organization,* where the leader seeks assistance or support from donors, grantmakers, potential allies, the media or other leaders in the business or public sectors.
3. *On present operations,* where the leader is concerned about the quality of services to clients and the community, and also organizational structures,

information systems and other aspects of organizational effectiveness.

4. *On future possibilities*, where the leader anticipates trends and developments that are likely to have important implications for the future direction of the organization [Nanus and Dobbs, 1999, p. 17].

Nanus and Dobbs (1999) argue that focusing attention in these four directions requires leaders of nonprofit organizations to be proficient in six essential roles:

1. *Visionary*. Leaders work with others to scan the realm of future possibilities, seeking clues to a more desirable destination. "Great leaders have great visions, and great visions, when they are widely shared, are the principal engines of organizational growth and progress" (p. 17).

2. *Strategist*. Leaders are responsible for ensuring that nonprofit organizations have strategies that position the organization to be most effective in meeting present and future challenges. Leaders ensure that their organizations adopt strategies that hold the most promise of fulfilling the vision and achieving the greatest social good.

3. *Politician*. Leaders are *super networkers* who champion the organization's cause and use their contacts to further the organization's mission.

4. *Fundraiser*. Leaders of nonprofits have an important role in raising funds from the public, foundations and corporations. Nanus and Dobbs call this role *campaigning*, reflecting the common use of the term *campaigning for funds*.

5. *Coach*. Leaders empower and inspire individuals and help them to learn, grow and realize their full potential.

Figure 5.1. The Roles of Nonprofit Leaders.

Outside the
organization

Politician   Visionary
and fundraiser   and strategist

Present   Future
operations   operations

Coach   Change
                                agent

Inside the
organization

Source: Nanus, B., and Dobbs, S. *Leaders Who Make a Difference: Essential Strategies for Meeting the Nonprofit Challenge.* San Francisco: Jossey-Bass, 1999, p. 18. Copyright © 1999 John Wiley & Sons, Inc. Reprinted with the permission of John Wiley & Sons, Inc.

6. *Change agent.* Leaders initiate change that positions the organization for the future, introducing changes externally around the clients, the services offered and the means of financing them, and internally around the organization's structures and processes.

The focus of leaders' attention and the roles they need to perform can be related as illustrated in Figure 5.1. Effective leaders recognize that they need to discharge all these roles all the time. Being brilliant at one role does not compensate for lack of skills in the others. Leaders are constantly juggling these different roles and taking actions that advance their agenda for each one.

In delivering these roles, leaders have to gain the trust and respect of the people who are being led. A series of seminal studies asked managers from all sectors what values they looked for and admired in their superiors. The results consistently showed the same characteristics (Kouzes and Posner, 1987, p. 17):

Characteristic	% of Managers Selecting This Characteristic
Honest	83
Competent	67
Forward-looking	62
Inspiring	58
Intelligent	43

The lowest-rated characteristics were ambitious, determined, self-controlled, loyal, and independent.

Chief executives whom I interviewed stressed the importance of openness and honesty. "It is important to be up front with people," according to Michael Flood, executive director of the Los Angeles Regional Foodbank. "I strive to be both honest and ethical in all that I do." Buck Parker of Earthjustice, a $23 million national organization that uses the legal system to protect the environment, concurred: "You need to get to know people and build trust. I always try to be seen to be fair and to talk the truth." (Also see Exhibit 5.1.)

Being honest is not always as easy as it sounds. Leaders have information that they may not be able to share with everyone at the same time: for example, plans for restructuring staff, discussions about a potential contract, or disciplinary matters. Leaders sometimes have preliminary thoughts that they wish to test on close colleagues without communicating them more widely. So, even though leaders should strive to be as open as possible and people increasingly expect greater openness, in practice there are boundaries that need to be respected. However, hiding behind such rationales rather than being open during difficult decisions or conversations will damage the trust and respect that people have in their leaders. Michael Flood stressed to me that "you can't be a leader if you dislike conflict. People respect you if you have honest conversations,

Exhibit 5.1. Raising and Resolving Conflict: The LightHouse.

Anita Aaron is the executive director of the LightHouse, the leading provider of services for visually impaired people in San Francisco. She believes that a key part of the executive director's role is to spot areas of conflict, bring them to the surface, and ensure that they are resolved.

"People used to bring problems and differences of opinion to me and expect me to make judgments and take decisions," she said. "They also wanted closed-door discussions about issues and other people. To begin with I acquiesced, but I soon came to realize that my judgments were not always the best and that people were being encouraged to dump their problems on me.

"I now see my job as bringing these issues out into the open. Sometimes I get the relevant parties around the table and make them talk about the issue in front of each other. In other circumstances I send individuals or groups of people away to discuss the issue and come back to me with their preferred solution.

"I have taken this a step further and see my job as identifying potential areas of conflict and raising it with the relevant people. I had to learn how to have open and honest conversations with people who report to me. I may be less popular, but I believe that I am more respected.

"An important element of my job is conflict resolution, and the [conflict resolution] training I attended gave me the confidence to manage difficult conversations in a constructive way."

Source: Interview with Anita Aaron, LightHouse executive director.

and if their work is not good enough, it is important to say so." He also emphasized the need to admit one's own mistakes and encourage others to admit theirs. (Also see Exhibit 5.2.)

Mobilize Around the Mission

Great leaders have a clear vision for the future of their organization and a clear understanding of the organization's mission. The terms *vision* and *mission* have been defined in a number of ways. A succinct

Exhibit 5.2. Being a Leader in a Crisis: Elderhostel.

In 1979, James Moses took on a short-term job with Elderhostel. At the time, the organization had six employees. Today it provides extraordinary learning adventures for nearly 250,000 people aged fifty-five and over in over 100 countries every year. Having worked for Elderhostel in many different positions for twenty-three years, Moses was given the challenge of a lifetime. The organization had recently parted with its previous chief executive. The 2001 recession had led to a significant drop in bookings, and the organization faced a cash crisis. Staff had to be laid off, and offices had to be closed. Staff morale was at an all-time low. To cap all this, the tragedy of September 11, 2001, led to a further reduction in bookings as people stopped traveling.

Moses is a thoughtful man. He is not a management guru and admits to not being well versed in management literature. He works from his instinct, and this is what he did when the organization faced its crisis:

- He was encouraged by staff to apply for the chief executive post, and when he was appointed, he kept his previous senior vice president salary, despite pressure to take the chief executive salary.

- He brought the staff together for a meeting to identify a few simple priorities to guide the organization through the crisis (such as building lists of potential participants and being fiscally conservative).

- He bought everyone coffee and doughnuts from his own funds.

- He expressed his passion for the cause.

- He initiated a fortnightly newsletter to staff, which focused on business performance and included messages from clients for whom the organization had made a big difference.

As a result of his actions, his senior staff decided not to take their annual raises. The atmosphere this created enabled him to make further budget cuts, but this time without layoffs. Taken together these actions were immensely important to staff.

Exhibit 5.2. Being a Leader in a Crisis: Elderhostel, Cont'd.

Six months later the finances started to turn around. Moses consulted with each of his senior staff individually on what to do about salaries. He took a salary halfway between his VP salary and the CEO's salary, and his senior staff took their raises.

He saw one of his roles as working to develop other people's skills. He talked to people a lot and made sure they were clear about what he wanted them to do. He used his ability to have difficult conversations. He took a questioning approach and believed people were honest when he was open.

Source: Interview with James Moses, Elderhostel chief executive.

definition comes from Nanus and Dobbs (1999), who describe *vision* as "a realistic, credible, attractive and inspiring future for the organization. . . . A vision does not show you how to get somewhere, but it does present a clear and exciting image of what the world might be like when you arrive" (p. 78). The mission is "a brief delineation of the organization's reason for being" (p. 82).

One of the more notable aspects of leading-edge nonprofits is that their missions are pervasive. They are framed in the office entrance hall; they are on business cards, on the organization's Web site, on screen savers, and on directions for visitors; they are highlighted in all strategy and planning reports; and they appear on documents the organization publishes. Leaders ensure that they are omnipresent. In these organizations the mission is also referred to frequently in conversation. It is alive, well understood, and trips off people's tongues. According to John Bryson (1995), author of a best-selling book on strategic planning for public and nonprofit organizations, a clear and living mission creates "a habit of focusing discussion on what is truly important." Thomas Holland (2002) noted in his research into board behavior that in "the middle of intense discussions on some complex issue before the group, it was not unusual for someone to remind the others of how their mission, core values and ethical responsibilities were key guideposts in these deliberations. In a variety of ways, members of these boards recognized that their board's actions were the embodiments of those values and their meetings the place where they could translate the mission and values into responsible decisions" (p. 415).

Leaders use missions to motivate people throughout the organization. Missions are used, along with strategies and plans, to keep managers focused on the organization's primary objectives. Missions are also actively used in decision making. Leaders encourage managers and board members to use the mission statement to inform strategic decisions. If there are major questions about strategic direction or about corporate priorities, the mission statement is the touchstone to which people refer. The first question Raymond Considine, president of the Boston-based Medical Foundation, always asks when considering a new initiative or a new contract bid is, "How well does it fit with our mission?"

It is widely accepted that missions are more important in the nonprofit sector than in the for-profit sector. Mission is a management idea that has much greater salience in the nonprofit world than in the business world. Mission is the raison d'être for the non-profit organization. From a managerial perspective the mission has three main purposes:

1. It sets the boundaries on the organization's work—the mission should answer the question, What is provided, and for whom?

2. It motivates staff and donors—the mission should be formulated to "carry the ideology of the organization, to serve as a flag around which the organization can rally" (Oster, 1995, p. 23).

3. It assists assessors to evaluate the impact of the organization—the mission should be the starting point for measuring performance.

Organizations at the leading edge review their missions regularly to confirm that they are up-to-date, relevant, and continue to encapsulate the organization's purpose. This usually happens at the annual board strategic planning retreat. If the mission is clear, relevant, and appropriate for current circumstances, it will be confirmed. If not, it will be adjusted. Leaders who champion the mission will then seek more and more ways to promote it—on invoices, on contract documents, on e-mail signatures, in staff manuals, and so on. It will remain central to the daily lives of everyone involved in the organization. (Exhibit 5.3 presents examples of mission statements.)

Focus People on Results

Leaders have to manage strategy and its implementation. This is the management competency that is critical to high performance. Clarifying the mission, establishing top-quality strategic and operational plans, creating teams to deliver the plans, and establishing systems of accountability are widely seen as the indispensable elements of strong leadership. What these elements all boil down to is ensuring that everyone at every level of the organization understands his or her roles and priorities and is held accountable for his or her contribution to the achievement of the mission. These are the management arrangements that are absolutely essential to effective nonprofit organizations. They have to be implemented to the highest standard to build the backbone onto which other managerial actions can be added.

Use Planning as a Focusing Tool

When asked how they focus their nonprofit organizations on achieving the mission, chief executives invariably say that the annual cycle of planning, budget setting, and performance reviews is their most powerful management process. "Strategic planning is the strongest lever I have on the organization. It helps to clarify the vision and the goals. It enables us to focus on the things we can control," said

Exhibit 5.3. Examples of Nonprofit Mission Statements.

Mission statements are short, precise, and most critically, a central part of organization life. They are real, used, and regularly reviewed.

American Diabetes Association
"To prevent and cure diabetes and to improve the lives of all people affected by diabetes."

The Nature Conservancy
"To preserve the plants, animals and natural communities that represent the diversity of life on Earth by protecting the lands and waters they need to survive."

March of Dimes
"To improve the health of babies by preventing birth defects and infant mortality."

Goodwill Industries of Southern California
"To enhance the quality of the lives of people who have disabilities and other vocational disadvantages by assisting them to become productive and self-sufficient through education, training and job opportunities."

America's Second Harvest
"To feed hungry people by soliciting and distributing food and grocery products through a nationwide network of certified affiliate food banks and food-rescue programs and to educate the public about the nature of and solutions to the problem of hunger in America."

Jewish Vocational Service
"To link employers and individuals together to achieve their employment goals by providing the skills necessary for success in today's workplace."

INDEPENDENT SECTOR
"To promote, strengthen and advance the nonprofit and philanthropic community to foster private initiative for the public good."

The Alliance for Nonprofit Management
"To increase the effectiveness of individuals and organizations that help nonprofits build their power and impact."

Donna Feingold, executive director of Toolworks, the San Francisco-based organization that provides training and job opportunities for disabled people. Paul Jansen, a director at McKinsey & Company, agreed: "The most powerful lever for management is getting the performance cycle going—setting goals, evaluating people against goals, linking this to compensation and next year's goals."

Clarifying objectives and holding people accountable for results does not mean putting people in a straitjacket. Circumstances do change, experience brings understanding of what works and what does not, and plans have to be modified. The characteristic of well-led organizations is that such changes are explicit and clearly relate to agreed strategies and goals.

Strong leaders ensure that strategies are well integrated with implementable operational plans. "Tight linkage between the strategic plan and implementation is the key handle the CEO has for managing performance," according to Doug Barr, chief executive of Goodwill Industries of Southern California. "I ensure that people make their strategic plan commitments measurable and know that they will be held to account for their delivery." This view was echoed by other observers, who also believe that more progress needs to be made in tightening up the links between a realistic mission, robust strategies, and clear action plans. In their view there is still too much sloppy thinking about making these elements of management work as a unit.

Strategic and operational plans in leading-edge organizations also demonstrate how the organization capacity needed to support implementation will be built. "Strategizing and good planning lead to increased focus, but organizations tend to move straight from goals to programs," according to Christine Letts, associate director of the Hauser Center for Nonprofit Organizations at Harvard University. She told me, "The 'business planning' stage is left out, and business planning is about developing organization capacity to deliver the mission."

It is easy to create well-intentioned objectives. The critical leadership activity is to require managers to map out the essential steps for achieving them—identifying the actions required and the obstacles to be overcome. This should be done rigorously, and "each departmental manager must know exactly what his or her department is trying to achieve," according to Los Angeles Regional Foodbank executive director Michael Flood. Furthermore, "the process must allow identification of areas where departments impact on each other for plans to be really robust."

Effective leaders ensure that plans are thoroughly scrutinized before being approved. In some organizations, board subcommittees, such as the planning and performance review committee, will be involved in reviewing plans before they are submitted to the main board. In others the examination will happen at the annual board planning retreat, and in yet others it will be undertaken by both a subcommittee and the board as a whole.

Well-managed organizations do not set their plans in stone. "Strategic plans are needed to provide a clear structure, but the environment is increasingly volatile," said Mary Emmons, president and CEO of the Los Angeles–based Children's Institute International, "so we also need capacity to be responsive to new opportunities as well." The Los Angeles Regional Foodbank works on a similar premise and expects managers to leave 15 percent of their time unallocated to activities and therefore available for unanticipated activity.

Link Plans to Performance Reviews

Once robust plans are in place effective leaders ensure managers are held to account through a performance review process that connects plans with individual and corporate performance. Many organizations have a quarterly performance review cycle. Doug Barr of Goodwill Industries said to me, "I hold my staff clearly accountable for achieving plan targets, and I expect them to hold their staff accountable, thus creating a clear hierarchy of accountability through the organization." When individuals are held tightly to account for performance against plans, the organization as a whole can be held to account, initially by the chief executive and subsequently by the board.

Boards play an important role in establishing high expectations for the planning and performance cycle. Evidence for the increasing importance attached to evaluation comes from the number of boards that have established committees for planning and performance review. These boards expect their planning and performance committees to oversee the planning process and continuously improve reporting mechanisms so the full board has top-quality reports on the overall performance of the organization. In some cases the performance evaluation of the CEO is based on strategic plan achievements as reported to the board. Doug Barr's evaluation, for example, "is based on the Strategic Plan Monitoring Committee report."

Manage Costs Tightly

Managing for social results does not absolve leaders and managers from being held accountable for financial results as well. One of the characteristics of the nonprofit world noticed by managers in the for-profit sector is that costs are not managed nearly as tightly as they are in the business world. "Private sector organizations in the same fields as nonprofits have a much better understanding of costs and whether expenditure is delivering value for money," I was told by Jeff Bradach, cofounder and managing partner of the Bridgespan Group, a nonprofit consulting firm linked to the global, for-profit consultants Bain and Company. "Understanding nonprofits' cost structure is increasingly important. In my view many nonprofits are managing with false books of account."

Leaders of some nonprofit organizations have begun to treat departments as *profit centers* and to hold managers accountable for the bottom line that shows how the department performed, taking into account both income and expenditure. These leaders ensure that managers are provided with financial reports that set out the income and expenditure streams associated with their departments. They expect managers to control both income and expenditure even if a significant proportion of income comes from "corporate" funds, those held by the center of the organization. According to John Graham, CEO of the American Diabetes Association, "this concentrates people's minds on all the possible income-raising opportunities they should be exploiting."

Leaders in these organizations also seek productivity improvements every year. The American Diabetes Association, for example, expects budget holders to find efficiency savings every year. "Even if a department is experiencing double-digit growth," Graham said to me, "we will expect infrastructure costs to rise by less than 3 to 4 percent." This approach led the organization to merge all phone and IT lines, saving a substantial sum every day. (Also see Exhibit 5.4.)

Build a Small, Focused Team

Leaders cannot deliver social results on their own. To fulfill their many roles they need a team, and the shape and composition of that team and its ability to perform at the highest level are critical to success.

Composition of the Top Team

Having a group of people who share the same mission, work together well, focus on corporate results, and provide effective leadership is a major determinant of organizational effectiveness. A key decision for chief executives, therefore, is to determine the number of people who sit on this top team and which roles should be represented. If the team has too few people, there may not be sufficient diversity of thought. If it has too many, it runs the risk of giving insufficient attention to external matters.

Exhibit 5.4. Using the Budget as a Leadership Tool.

The Wildlife Conservation Society saves wildlife and wildlands through careful science, international conservation, education, and the management of the world's largest system of urban wildlife parks, led by the flagship Bronx Zoo. With an annual income of $125 million and assets of over $500 million, managing costs can make a significant difference to the Wildlife Conservation Society's performance.

President and CEO Steve Sanderson argues that the budget can be used as a key lever for change. He recommends six actions, which must be managed flexibly and collegially:

1. Link the budget explicitly to the mission by funding activities that contribute most to achieving the mission. Use unrestricted funds strategically.

2. Require each part of the organization to manage the net of its income and expenditure (that is, its bottom line), even when it receives funding from the center.

3. Expect managers to find cost savings each year, even when total income and expenditure are growing.

4. Give incentives to departments that exceed their budget targets by allowing them to keep part of any "surplus" that the department makes.

5. Penalize departments that do not meet budget targets by rolling losses over into the following year and expecting those departments to recover them.

6. Recognize that the enterprise should absorb any large changes in income and expenditure outside its control, but treat these circumstances as exceptional and be transparent about making such changes.

Source: Interview with Wildlife Conservation Society president and CEO Steve Sanderson.

The chief executives I interviewed state that somewhere between three and five direct reports is the ideal number in most circumstances. Having more than five can lead chief executives to become too internally focused. The LightHouse's Anita Aaron, for example, established a team of eight people but quickly realized that was a mistake. "I became a supervisor and could not provide the organization with effective leadership. The structure drove me to be internally oriented. Even though I neglected external relationships, I was still not able to provide all the managers with sufficient support." She quickly reverted to a structure with four direct reports, representing

- Programs

- Development (fundraising)

- Finance

- Administration

A chief executive can hold only a few people tightly to account. The smaller the group, the easier it is for the chief executive to have clear expectations and to be adequately supportive. John Graham, CEO of the American Diabetes Association, has three direct reports:

- Chief scientific and medical officer

- Chief of field operations

- Chief operating officer

All three attend and participate as equals in board meetings, creating a model that emulates the joint executive and nonexecutive board that is more common in the corporate sector.

The US Fund for UNICEF has an even smaller team of two, who report to organization president Charles Lyons:

- Vice president marketing

- Chief operating officer

This group is supplemented by a wider operations committee that meets every one or two weeks and does not include the chief executive. "People like the arrangement because it gets faster decisions," according to Lyons.

A small team at the top usually requires the appointment of a chief operating officer (COO) to take command of a range of functions. The position of COO is increasingly widespread. There are three models for organization structures incorporating a COO. The most common one incorporates all back-office functions of finance, human relations, IT, and facilities under one senior post. A variation on this model excludes finance but puts all other back-office functions under one person. A third and less common alternative puts all service delivery functions under one person. The California-based Trust for Public Land has adopted this model, with a team consisting of the

- Chief operating officer

- Chief finance officer

- Development director

- Marketing director

The organization's seven regional directors all report to the COO.

The position of COO is not an easy post to fill, particularly when it is first created. Some of the chief executives interviewed reported difficulties finding suitable candidates and people with whom they could work effectively. A number recommended taking this critical step only when there is an internal candidate ideally suited for promotion to the position.

Skills to Look For

Chief executives stress that members of the top team must have strong management skills. Functional expertise is not sufficient at this level. "We look for people who have effective supervision skills, can work collaboratively, are good at holding people to account, and who can establish realistic and measurable goals," Amnesty International USA's senior deputy executive director, Curt Goering, told me. "We do not appoint campaigners as managers unless they demonstrate clearly that they have management skills."

Good communication is of key importance, so regular meetings of this top group are seen to be critical to success. Most top teams meet weekly, supplemented by regular retreats away from the office to address big issues. "Mutual respect and good communications are critical," according to Michael Flood. This is echoed by other chief executives who also stress the importance of excellent relationships between members. "We encourage candid speaking and have regular dinners together," said Curt Goering, who also takes the responsibility for running all senior team meetings. Mary Emmons, CEO of Children's Institute International, expressed this view even more strongly: "The key is to have a senior team with an agency-wide perspective. To achieve that there has to be a high level of trust between members; [they have] to have great confidence in each other, an ability to share problems and to maintain strict confidentiality when required by the team."

Interviewees frequently spoke about leaders' skills in getting high performance from their teams. Doug Barr stressed the importance of "ensuring that people feel challenged and that their successes are acknowledged." Roni Posner, executive director of the Alliance for Nonprofit Management, saw her role as "being the greatest cheerleader for every member of staff. I expect people to excel and I work with them to help them excel. My job is to provide staff with resources and to make people feel they are special."

Leaders stress the need to see people's strengths but also to recognize that sometimes it is necessary to move them to jobs that better fit their skills and interests. "It is important to let people know if they are underperforming," according to Roni Posner. Doug Barr agreed, "If someone is struggling, the first step is to get them support, for example from a national body or from consultants. I give people a number of chances but I also recognize the need to be decisive when the time comes to let someone go."

Rewarding Performance

Leaders need to recognize and reward excellent performance by members of their teams. The most important reward for nonprofit managers is knowing that their organization is achieving its mission and that they are able to make a significant contribution. Job satisfaction is usually much more significant than money. Nevertheless, some nonprofits are devising systems to reward senior managers for effective performance. Performance-related pay is a tricky issue for nonprofits. There is public sensitivity over the idea of bonus payments, particularly if rewards persist when performance falters, and some organizations say they will never countenance the idea of performance pay.

The interviewees identified two essential prerequisites of a successful performance-related pay system. First, staff objectives must be clear and measurable so that the system is fair and transparent. Second, everyone must have a high level of trust in the performance evaluation system and its results. Performance-related pay can work well only in organizations where it fits the culture and where other management processes are secure and well respected. With these prerequisites in place, a number of organizations are introducing performance-related pay. The United Way of Greater Los Angeles allows bonus payments for all top managers. These managers are evaluated on standard corporate criteria in addition to individual functional criteria. The evaluations are carried out by the board's personnel committee, and payments do not exceed 10 percent of salary. President Joseph Haggerty said that this approach "keeps the senior team focused on the agreed corporate objectives." Goodwill Industries of Southern California has performance-related pay for its top 150 managers. The chief executive's performance pay is linked directly to the achievement of agreed corporate strategic objectives. Performance pay for other managers has an element related to functional performance. According to Paul Jansen of

McKinsey, "It is not necessarily about the money, but the payment is the clearest communication a manager can give about a subordinate's performance." (See also Exhibit 5.5.)

However, as mentioned earlier, although some nonprofits are now using financial incentives, others would never consider such a move. James Moses, chief executive of Elderhostel, is firmly against it: "Nonprofits have to challenge self-interest. We have to express different underlying values from business and government, and one way to do this is to make working for nonprofits distinctively different." Buck Parker agreed: "[Earthjustice] will never have bonus payments. It would conflict [with] our ethos and would be a headache to implement."

Invest in Leadership and Management Development

Leading nonprofit organizations invest in leadership and management development. They are taking many different approaches to support people's growth, however, and this reflects the fact that there is little evidence demonstrating which approaches are most effective.

A common starting point is a *360-degree review,* which helps people with leadership responsibilities to identify their development needs through feedback from many people that they deal with. Earthjustice, an organization providing lawyers to fight key environmental campaigns, is one nonprofit that uses 360-degree reviews. "It was the best investment we ever made," Executive Director Buck Parker told me, "and we use it as the basis for promotion decisions."

Role-specific training is used by Children's Institute International (CII), which has identified three very different roles that its key service delivery managers play:

- Maintaining professional relationships with clients

- Maintaining managerial relationships with staff

- Effectively handling administrative issues, contracts, and budgets

**Exhibit 5.5. Increasing Productivity
at Children's Institute International.**

Children's Institute International (CII) is committed to the prevention,
identification, and treatment of all forms of child abuse and neglect.
Based in Los Angeles and with a $21 million annual budget, CII
employs teachers and social workers to provide training and therapy.

When managed care packages were extended to individuals supported by human service providers, CII's grant funding was replaced by
fee-for-service payments. CII therefore had to start recording how its
professionals used their time. Management calculated that for CII to
remain viable, service delivery staff would have to charge for more than
two-thirds of their time. A time-recording system was introduced, and
although the change caused considerable anxiety at the outset, it has
now become an accepted way of working. The bigger challenge was
to ensure that everyone was achieving or exceeding his or her targets.
Management introduced an incentive payment system (known as
CASH), which made payments of $40 per hour for every chargeable
hour that each member of staff delivered above his or her target of
68.5 percent of total time.

The approach did not sit comfortably with the culture of a nonprofit dedicated to meeting the needs of poor families. Much time was
therefore invested in communicating with staff and listening to their
concerns before the new arrangements were introduced.

This discussion about the need for change and how it would affect
staff was time well invested, and the system has proved to be remarkably
successful.

- The organization has benefited financially because it charges
  its funders (mainly the county and the state) $120 for every
  extra hour delivered.

- Management now has much greater flexibility in delivering
  services. Instead of working second jobs elsewhere, staff now
  work overtime with CII to fill gaps in capacity caused by sickness, maternity leave, and promotions.

**Exhibit 5.5. Increasing Productivity
at Children's Institute International, Cont'd.**

- Because good supervision is essential to ensure that quality is maintained, supervisors, who also deliver services, have lower targets. The strong culture of delivering the highest-quality services and effective management by supervisors ensures that quality is maintained.

- The top management challenge has changed. Rather than trying to persuade people to deliver chargeable hours for the agency, managers now work to remove any obstacles that made it difficult for staff to achieve and exceed their targets.

- People who deliver the highest-quality work have the highest rates of extra chargeable time and the lowest no-show rates among their clients.

The next step for CII is to introduce a system of incentives for directors, because the staff incentive system now discourages people from seeking promotion.

Source: Interview with Mary Emmons, president and CEO of Children's Institute International.

CII provides managers with training on the distinction between client relationships and staff relationships to help them perform their different roles with different mind-sets. It has also hired a consultant to help individual managers improve their communication skills and in particular to learn how to give difficult messages to staff.

Many nonprofit managers select learning programs from the wide range of open and tailored *management training courses* on offer. Over ninety universities and colleges now provide courses in non-profit management. "They are creating people who are skilled in the technical elements of managing nonprofits, such as fundraising, financial management, and governance, though many are not creating people with vision who understand public policy and can provide organizations with leadership," Pablo Eisenberg of Georgetown University told me.

Some organizations rely on *coaching*. For example, Amnesty International USA gets experienced managers to coach the less experienced. It has an employee professional development program that relies on staff identifying their needs. It also gives individuals sabbaticals to overcome the problem of burnout, offering them five months off after five years' service, provided they commit to returning for two years.

Most organizations have *training budgets* that managers can apply to for development funding. Some go one step further and give individuals personal financial allocations. Toolworks gives managers personal training budgets to attend accredited training courses. The budget grows from $300 per year after two years' service to $1,000 per year after ten years' service. These training and development measures may be supported by *regular meetings of all middle managers*. Many organizations have quarterly meetings of middle managers; others arrange half-yearly or yearly meetings. When these meetings are carefully planned and well structured, they encourage communication across functions, keep the managers focused on corporate aims, and provide further opportunities for supporting these middle managers.

Chief executives' development was reported as taking a variety of forms. Some chief executives attend leadership courses, at institutions such as Harvard and the Center for Creative Leadership, that are specifically for nonprofit leaders. Others attend business and public sector leadership development courses. "Some training is good," according to Audrey Alvarado, executive director of the National Council of Nonprofit Associations. "The challenge is the application of the learning when you return to the office."

Some chief executives read extensively about leadership. "I read about the theory of leadership and study examples of excellent leadership and strive to apply the lessons in my work," said Linda Whitlock, president and CEO of Boys & Girls Clubs of Boston. "I also reflect a lot on my actions." Peter Shiras of INDEPENDENT SECTOR stressed that "leaders need time to reflect, and it is not easy to create that time in the maelstrom of daily activity." Some use one or more coaches to support their reflecting, help them learn, and develop their leadership skills. Linda Whitlock has a *Jedi council*, five to seven people whom she uses as a sounding board and consults on difficult issues. Some leaders network with other leaders at meetings sponsored by state, regional, and national intermediary bodies. They share their issues and learn from each other.

Together these actions support leadership and management development throughout organizations. They strengthen management capacity, and they reflect that individuals now expect continuous personal development. Strong leaders recognize that their organization benefits from carefully chosen investments in the development of themselves and their staff.

Summary

Be a Leader

- Leaders embody the values of the organization in what they do and how they do it.

- Leaders need to focus their attention inside and outside the organization and on present operations and future possibilities.

- Leaders fulfill six roles: visionary, strategist, politician, fundraiser, coach, and change agent.

- Leaders have to gain the trust and respect of the people they lead.

- Leaders have to be open, and they have to have honest conversations.

Mobilize Around the Mission

- Great leaders have a clear vision for the future of the organization.

- Leaders use missions to motivate people.

- Mission statements are short, precise, and distinctive.

- Leaders ensure that missions are omnipresent, used, and reviewed.

Focus People on Results

- Planning and performance review are the most powerful levers leaders have to drive performance.

- Leaders ensure that strategies, operational plans, and individual work plans are tightly integrated.

- Leaders ensure that plans are closely scrutinized before being approved.

- Leaders use regular performance reviews to hold managers to account.

- Boards enhance the quality of planning and performance review.

- Leaders also hold managers accountable for costs and expect departments to be managed on bottom-line performance.

Build a Small, Focused Team

- Leaders create line-reporting arrangements that enable them to lead.

- The top team tends to have between three and five members.

- Chief operating officer posts are increasingly prevalent.

- Top teams meet regularly and hold regular retreats.

- Trust, confidence, and excellent communication are the hallmarks of an effective top team.

- Some nonprofits use performance-related pay; others reject the idea.

Invest in Leadership and Management Development

- Leading organizations are taking many different approaches to leadership and management development.

- Leading organizations get all their managers together regularly.

- Leaders invest in their own development by attending courses, reading extensively, using coaches, and networking with other leaders.

Action Checklist

Strong yet subtle leadership is essential to the long-term success of every nonprofit organization. Leaders who want to strengthen their abilities should

1. Create space to reflect extensively on their own actions and behaviors, and take time to learn from their experiences.

2. Strive to ensure that their values are entirely congruent with those of the organization.

3. Promote the mission more often than may seem necessary, because it can get lost in the maelstrom of organization activity.

4. Create a small team of senior managers, each of whom focuses sharply on clear and achievable objectives.

5. Ensure that the organization invests in the development of the leadership skills of the leader, the senior management team, and the board.

The board chair should support chief executives and help them to deliver effective leadership. The board should

1. Develop an open and trusting relationship with the chief executive.
2. Encourage conversations about leadership styles.
3. Seek and provide clear feedback on the leader's performance.
4. Ensure that board members take actions to strengthen and not undermine the leader's role.
5. Conduct a 360-degree appraisal of the chief executive once a year.

6

Strengthening Governance

Demands on the boards of nonprofits have grown dramatically over recent years, and there is every expectation that the challenges will continue to increase in the future. Donors and the wider public expect boards to hold organizations to account for the quality and effectiveness of their work and the probity of the organization. The high profile that the press now gives to the small number of scandals in the nonprofit sector means that people's expectations are rising further. Spectacular failures in the corporate sector have added to pressure for high performance. The downfall of Enron, WorldCom, and Arthur Andersen has signaled to everyone that effective governance is important, and these messages are trickling down to the nonprofit sector. They are reminders that the boards of nonprofit organizations are expected to provide the public with trust and confidence and to maintain organizations' reputations. Trust, confidence, and reputation are hard-won features, secured primarily through effective governance.

The quality of nonprofit governance in the United States has improved significantly over the last fifteen years. Definitions of governance have been clarified, requirements of board members have been defined, induction for new members has been introduced, and the need to manage the performance of the board itself has been established. Much of the momentum for these improvements originated from the establishment of BoardSource (founded, as the

National Center for Nonprofit Boards, in 1988), an organization that has set standards for nonprofit governance and whose work has attracted worldwide interest. A huge body of research and writing on nonprofit governance has been developed during this time. A recent review of governance research cited over 120 works reporting research on nonprofit governance (Ostrower and Stone, 2001), and more books exist on how to govern nonprofits than on the core task of managing them. Yet in a recent survey of nonprofit chief executives, only 37 percent rated their boards as highly effective (National Center for Nonprofit Boards, 2000). There is a widespread view that much work has to be done to further improve the governance arrangements of nonprofit organizations. "All the evidence suggests that the interest in boards will continue to grow" (Ostrower and Stone, 2001, p. 2).

In a seminal 1996 article, "The New Work of the Nonprofit Board," Barbara Taylor, Richard Chait, and Thomas Holland argued that nonprofit "boards are often little more than a collection of high-powered people engaged in low level activities." They suggested that individual "board members may not bring themselves fully to the task of governance, because board membership generally carries little personal accountability. And often the powerful individuals who make up the board are unpracticed in working as members of a team." The new work of boards, they proposed, "concerns itself with crucial, do-or-die issues central to the institution's success . . . is driven by results that are linked to defined timetables . . . and has clear measures of success" (p. 4).

Nonprofit boards in the United States have a number of distinctive features. First, members are expected to make financial contributions to the organization. BoardSource research shows that almost half of board members have to pay for the privilege of joining, and more than half have to fundraise as well. As Harvard Business School senior associate dean John Quelch told me, "Board members are left in no doubt about the amount they are personally expected to donate, and the most prestigious boards have the highest tariff." Second, joining a board is an essential element of career development for many people working in any of the three sectors. Individuals set goals for the types of boards they wish to join. Organization and agency recruiters expect to see membership on boards of increasing prestige on individuals' résumés as their careers progress. When people have had insufficient nonprofit experience, they may be advised to seek board positions to expand their horizons and develop new skills. Third, people seeking positions on more influential boards are expected to have experience from membership on lesser boards or to have contributed as nonboard members of a board committee. One chief executive of a comparatively small organization said to me, bluntly, "We want people with experience of governance, so we don't accept first-time board members."

This chapter demonstrates that leading-edge organizations

- Ensure that board roles are crystal clear

- Structure the board around governance tasks

- Take actions to enhance board performance

- Deepen the board chair–chief executive relationship

- Continuously review board performance.

Ensure That Board Roles Are Crystal Clear

One of the enduring characteristics of nonprofit boards is that they are all different and there are no one-size-fits-all solutions to improving board performance (see, for example, Exhibit 6.1). According to Ostrower and Stone (2001), "Boards are complex entities that defy sweeping generalizations. They are heterogeneous, subject to internal shifts and respond to multiple—and sometimes conflicting—influences" (p. 2). BoardSource director of consulting and training for Europe and Asia, Marilyn Wyatt, told me, "There is no one model and flexibility is the key. Boards need to go through

Exhibit 6.1. Governance of Amnesty International USA.

Amnesty International is a membership organization. It has a board of eighteen people, each of whom can have a maximum of two three-year terms. All board members have job descriptions, and are expected to have "no unexcused absence" from board meetings.

The board has a nominating committee that interviews people interested in standing for election. Some people decide not to stand once they understand the requirements Amnesty is seeking and the commitment required. Alternatively, any member who is unsuccessful at the interview stage but still wishes to stand can do so by petitioning 100 members to support his or her candidacy.

Board performance is reviewed regularly. After every meeting members complete a questionnaire that includes an opportunity to comment on board and member performance. The chair compiles these comments and feeds back the results as one way of encouraging open discussion about performance. Board members also participate in an annual retreat with senior management and an external consultant to review performance.

Source: Interview with Curt Goering, Amnesty International Senior Deputy Executive Director.

a process of discovery to find out what works best at their particular stage of development." Board development is therefore a never-ending process of discovery, because governance arrangements appropriate for one stage of an organization's development will need to evolve to accommodate its next phase. Ideally, governance arrangements should anticipate organizations' future requirements.

The starting point for board development is the clarification of roles. Boards have many roles, and the trend is undoubtedly toward boards that focus sharply on their unique roles and discipline themselves to stick tightly to them. The roles of the board are best conceived in terms of board accountability to different stakeholder groups. Leading boards recognize that funders, consumers, staff, and the public all have legitimate interests in the organization, that the board has to understand their views and consider them explicitly in its deliberations. Although boards may be called on to offer judgment and wisdom on many matters, it is widely accepted that at the heart of good governance is high-standard delivery of these four essential functions:

1. Determining the organization's mission, strategy, and policies

2. Appointing and overseeing the chief executive

3. Monitoring organization performance

4. Managing governance processes

Although these roles overlap with management roles, they are also distinct from management roles. Some leading thinkers on governance believe there should be a very strict division between the roles of governance and of management. John Carver (1997) argues that the secret of new governance lies in policymaking and that "policy clarification is the central feature of board leadership" (p. 22). Carver has developed the *policy governance* model, which proposes that boards should limit their work to the establishment of policies about

- Ends to be achieved

- Means to achieve those ends

- The board-staff relationship

- The process of governance itself

In Carver's view, once the board has established policies in these areas, it should be strict in empowering management to deliver the implementation roles. Carver's books are widely read, and he has caused many boards to clarify the purpose and functions of governance. However, other leading thinkers see dangers in taking this distinction too far. William Ryan, a Research Fellow at Harvard's Hauser Center for Nonprofit Organizations, argued in an interview that "boards can become 'sealed off' if policy governance is applied too rigidly. The management-governance boundary needs to be clear, but there needs to be a degree of fluidity. Boards can become remote if they only consider strategic issues and feel they can't raise detail." Richard Chait, a leading governance expert at the Harvard School of Education, agreed: "There is evidence that ruthless separation of *means* and *ends* is not helpful."

There is nevertheless widespread agreement that effective boards strive to maintain clarity about their roles and continuously monitor their own performance to ensure that they are not inadvertently slipping into management roles. An analysis of interviews, consultations, and meeting observations involving 169 board members identified practices that enhance board performance, the first of which was clear expectations. "Some boards had developed explicit statements of expectations and responsibilities of the board as a whole as well as of its individual members. . . . Nominating Committee members engaging in discussions with potential candidates said they drew upon these documents to explain what the board expected of its members and what context of mission, values and obligations underlay its work" (Holland, 2002, pp. 414–415).

When the unique roles of the board have been defined, the board chair has the critically important responsibility of ensuring that the board sticks to its roles and of calling members to account when they transgress the boundary. "The Chair needs to have the courage to correct, admonish and corral" (Robinson, 2001, p. 102). Carver (1997) agrees: "the chairperson bears a peculiar responsibility with respect to board process. . . . However, the entire board cannot avoid its share of responsibility. The existence of a chairperson does not relieve other board members from contributing to the integrity of the process" (pp. 129–130). Chairs need to be continuously alert and to remind members promptly of the board's role when necessary. Chief executives also play a crucial role in keeping boards focused on governance. When chief executives ask boards to advise on management issues or when they provide information on management issues, the board inevitably slips into managerial tasks. When they focus their boards on governance issues, board members are much more likely to stick to their defined roles.

Although leading boards maintain crystal clarity over their roles, this is not the norm in much of the sector. "Complacency about the board itself appears to be the norm and action the exception," reports Holland (2002, p. 422) in light of his extensive studies. William Ryan agreed, "There is in many cases an accountability vacuum. Some boards exhibit dysfunctional politeness, when what they really need is to be equipped to challenge increasingly competent management. They should be asking the scary questions about performance and avoid being too courteous." Pablo Eisenberg, a distinguished nonprofit sector commentator and Senior Fellow at the Center for the Study of Voluntary Organizations and Service at Georgetown University, also concurred: "We need feisty boards, not rubber stamps."

Structure the Board Around Governance Tasks

Traditionally, boards have structured their committees to mirror the organization's functions, such as services, finance, personnel, and fundraising. However, this encourages boards to do management tasks, so leading organizations are now structuring their board committees around the key functions of governance and around the organization's strategic priorities. They are delegating aspects of governance work to subgroups that undertake particular responsibilities on behalf of the board. They keep committee structures lean by establishing a limited number of permanent committees and delegating all other governance work to task groups that disband when the job is done.

So committees in leading organizations have functions very different from those found in traditional governance structures. These new governance committees might include the

- *Audit committee*, which provides specialist recommendations to the board on financial controls.

- *Nominating committee*, which takes responsibility for managing the board's skill and experience matrix and identifying talented and experienced people to stand for election to the board.

- *Governance committee*, which takes responsibility for monitoring and enhancing the performance of the board and its committees. It oversees the performance review process and, when necessary, recommends changes to governance structures and processes. This committee also takes responsibility for electoral and nominating processes.

- *Strategic planning and performance committee*, which takes responsibility for managing the board's input into strategic planning. Some organizations link this function with oversight of the organization's performance management systems.

- *Compensation committee*, which takes responsibility for benchmarking and setting senior salaries.

Some boards have committees structured to reflect the organization's strategic priorities. These are likely to be time limited and to focus on the achievement of one of the organizational goals. They disband when the objective has been achieved. Given the special role board members of U.S. nonprofits play in fundraising, most organizations will also have a permanent fundraising committee.

A significant challenge for many boards is balancing their decision-making role with their representation role. Carrying out both roles increases the size of the board and inevitably changes its function. Boards have to consider whether particular stakeholders, such as people representing regions of the country, organization branches or chapters, specific professions, or gender and ethnic groups need to be included. This is a significant issue in membership organizations, and it can lead to demands for a large and potentially unwieldy board. A number of leading organizations are therefore separating the functions of governance and representation to resolve the problem of having a board small enough to provide effective governance and yet large enough to represent a wide range of views. "Representation is a big issue because of the escalation of identity politics," according to Harvard's Richard Chait. "There is a growing demand for mechanisms that allow representatives to make an input to the board without being members of the board." Consequently, some boards have established one or more groups of representatives who advise the board. This enables key stakeholder groups to make their views known in a structured way so the board can take them into account in decision making. It also provides a channel through which the board can communicate its views back to those stakeholder groups.

Larger boards are better suited to a broad policy-setting role and tend to debate the policy issues. Although some traditional nonprofits have large boards of forty to sixty or even more members, some leading commentators argue that smaller boards provide more rigorous accountability. Some organizations with large boards vest considerable responsibility for governance in a small executive committee, which is accountable to the larger board.

Board size is also influenced by the mix of skills and expertise that the organization believes it needs on its governing body. Boards of leading organizations define the skills and experience needed, sometimes producing a *skill matrix*. This exercise sets criteria to use when seeking new members. In addition to people with financial and legal skills, boards also require people with a high level of professional expertise in the organization's field of work. Many boards also look for members who are executives of other nonprofits and who bring their experience from similar organizations. The *Nonprofit Governance Index* finds that although a majority of nonprofit board members are employed in the private sector, almost a fifth are employed in the nonprofit sector, as shown in the following list (National Center for Nonprofit Boards, 2000).

Employers	% of Board Members
For-profit organizations	43
Nonprofit organizations	19
Self-employed	14
Retired	12
Government organizations	9
Other	4
Total	100

The expectation that board members will make significant donations themselves and raise funds from others adds to the pressure to maintain a large board. Some organizations overcome this problem by establishing a separate board with responsibility for fundraising and giving it some power to influence the ways the funds it raises are spent.

Diversity is a significant aspect of board structure and particularly of board composition, and it is widely held that a more diverse board is more likely to deliver effective governance than is one that does not reflect the diversity of the communities in which the organization works. Despite best intentions, diversity is still not being achieved in practice. Women are more likely to serve on the boards of smaller and less prestigious organizations and less likely to be found on the boards of hospitals, colleges and universities, and policy-related organizations. They are more likely to serve on human service and cultural boards (Ostrower and Stone, 2001). *The Nonprofit Governance Index* states that although their numbers are growing, minorities constitute only 15 percent of board members and that most within this 15 percent are African Americans (National

Center for Nonprofit Boards, 2000). Foundation boards are even less racially diverse—90 percent of their members are white, according to research by the Council on Foundations (2002). However, there is some evidence that minorities are better represented in the less formal community organizations that are not captured in this research. (Exhibit 6.2 summarizes some additional board facts.)

Take Actions to Enhance Board Performance

Boards of leading organizations are striving to enhance their performance, and they are adopting a wide range of measures to increase their effectiveness. Evidence that an effective board contributes to a strong organization is also growing. However, measuring board effectiveness is fraught with difficulties. It is possible to ask board members and staff to rate effectiveness against agreed criteria for board performance. It is harder to demonstrate a specific connection between board effectiveness and organizational effectiveness because that effectiveness is dependent on many factors. Consequently, some are asking whether strong boards create strong organizations or whether it is just that strong organizations tend to have strong boards.

Holland and Jackson (1998) asked boards to assess their own performance before and after board development initiatives and compared these assessments with assessments from boards that did not make such developmental investments. These researchers demonstrated that over a three-year period, the experimental group showed significant improvements in performance that were not evident in the comparison group. They concluded that

> focused and sustained efforts to improve board perfor-
> mance can realize measurable gains. Such efforts take
> long-term work by a board, they involve moving mem-
> bers out of familiar territories and comfortable habits and
> supporting their experimentation with new ways of

Exhibit 6.2. More Data on Board Composition and Functioning.

BoardSource carries out regular surveys on the composition, structure, roles, and practicalities of boards. The most recent survey gathered data from over 1,300 chief executives and 200 board members and included 89 interviews. Although this is not a weighted national sample, the findings give interesting insights into boards in the United States.

In the 2000 survey the median size of boards was seventeen people. Board members were predominantly male (57 percent) and aged between forty and fifty-nine (64 percent). A majority of boards were self-perpetuating (66 percent), and most members served three-year terms (68 percent).

Almost half of the boards required members to make personal financial contributions (48 percent), and over one-third of respondents said that their entire board contributed annually. Half required board members to identify donors or solicit funds (52 percent) and to attend fundraising events (49 percent).

Boards spent most of their time on major policy questions (33 percent) and planning for the future (32 percent). Chief executives were most satisfied with board members' understanding of the organization's mission and least satisfied with board members' understanding of the board's role and responsibilities.

Among the board members surveyed:

- 69 percent identified policymaking as the primary role of the board.
- 44 percent said the board is an oversight body ensuring accountability.
- 42 percent felt their boards were effective.

Factors cited as contributing to board effectiveness included strong relationships with the chief executive, highly active and committed board members, and strong board member participation.

Source: Reprinted with permission from the *Nonprofit Governance Index* written by BoardSource and Stanford University, a publication of BoardSource, formerly the National Center for Nonprofit Boards. For more information about BoardSource, call 800-883-6262 or visit www.boardsource.org. BoardSource © 2000. Text may not be reproduced without written permission from BoardSource.

doing business. Ongoing attention by a board to its performance leads to a culture of active responsibility for continuous improvement in the quality of its work and greater satisfaction among members. It enables the board to improve its leadership of the organization and demonstrates to others inside and outside how the board expects value to be added to the organization [p. 133].

Enhance Induction

BoardSource found that only 40 percent of new members receive formal orientation when joining a board (National Center for Nonprofit Boards, 2000). However, top-quality induction for new members is recognized as a starting point for enhancing board performance. Some board members may require orientation on board roles and functions, and some may need support in developing their governance skills. Others may have governance skills but require an introduction to the organization's field of work and the services it offers. Organizations that do provide orientation are adopting a wide range of delivery methods, including

- A skills audit to determine the skills each new member may need to develop

- Premeetings to brief new members before board meetings

- Appointing a mentor to guide new members during their first year

- A board orientation workshop, when a number of new members join at the same time

- A board handbook containing all relevant background papers

- Visits to see the organization's work on the ground

- A review after six months to check how new members are feeling about their role and about the way the board works

- A briefing on the board performance assessment process

Keep the Board Focused on Priorities

Board members' time is precious. A board meeting quarterly for one day puts in 1,200 to 1,440 minutes of meeting time per year. Twelve to fourteen minutes lost because someone raised a point of detail means 1 percent of the board's annual meeting time has been spent inappropriately.

Leading boards work hard to ensure that their time and energy are focused on the organization's priorities. This work starts with gaining a thorough understanding of the organization's strategic plans and appreciating how these plans affect the board's work. Holland's research (2002) found that on some boards, members "were more active participants in identifying the most important issues facing the organization and setting priorities among them for the board's attention. These boards were careful to put in place procedures that would help them keep their time and attention focused on their own goals and deal with attempts to divert energy onto other issues" (p. 416). He cites one board that put its goals on a large poster that hung in the board meeting room, so all eyes would be on the priorities at every meeting.

Richard Chait told me that he gets boards to ask themselves, "What are the three most important questions this board needs to address over the next twelve months?" Getting members to agree on the key questions starts to shape the high-level board agenda for the year. Having a discussion about the questions is a necessary prerequisite if board members are to engage with the issues they raise. Another way Chait gets boards to think about board performance is to ask, "What would be the gravest consequences of this board not operating for the next three years?" This question focuses people's minds on the nontransferable functions that the board should carry out to the highest standards. With a clear view of the essential functions of the board, members can discuss how the board's work should be organized to perform these tasks.

Encourage Members to Work as a Team

Board teamwork is seen as critical for effective governance, and teamwork skills require continuous development. Board members need to work as a group, listening closely to each other, using each other's strengths, and striving to find agreement. Chait, Holland, and Taylor (1996) have noted that "the stronger the board members, the harder it is just to get them to meld into the group (p. 5)." So board members have to work to create a culture that is respectful and supportive while also ensuring that the group delivers high-quality governance.

Use Many Approaches to Enhance Performance

Interviewees described a wide range of approaches that enhance board performance:

- Organizing an education hour before each meeting

- Holding a *fireside chat* with the chief executive (this is particularly valuable for preliminary rumination about an issue)

- Encouraging members to attend industry conferences

- Auditing member skills, and then offering training or coaching in areas where members need to enhance their skills

- Arranging learning exchanges with comparable organizations to share policy discussions and to compare methods of working

- Holding an annual board and senior management retreat to review performance and to shape future strategy

- Giving members opportunities to improve their understanding of the organization (making site visits, carrying out specific tasks, observing meetings)

- Developing a *dashboard* of key indicators for improving board performance, and reporting quarterly on progress

- Asking experienced members to mentor new members

- Inviting representatives of stakeholder groups to observe the board

- Allowing stakeholder representatives to sit on selected committees

- Pairing board members with senior executives, and giving these pairs joint responsibility for representing different stakeholder views

- Offering new chairs a coach to assist them in delivering this demanding role

Ensure Thorough Preparation for Board Meetings

Board meetings are at the heart of good governance. The quality of the preparation by the chair and the chief executive, the thought that goes into board papers, and the development of an agenda that gets to the nub of the critical issues are all essential ingredients of effective meetings (see, for example, Exhibit 6.3). Good performance here is very dependent on the senior management team and on the person responsible for board administration. Successful meetings are much more likely when

- Staff prepare well-argued papers that are circulated in sufficient time for members to ask questions of clarification before the meeting.

Exhibit 6.3. One Meeting:
Two Styles at the American Diabetes Association.

The American Diabetes Association (ADA) has a main board of fifty-five people that meets three times per year. This board is supported by an executive committee of ten people that meets six times per year. The main board is "the conscience of the organization," according to CEO John Graham.

Meetings of the main board last for four hours. The first two hours are spent discussing one major strategic issue, for example, the association's position on stem cell research. The setting is informal, the room layout is cafeteria style (to support small-group discussion), and the aim is to discuss all aspects of the issue and to begin the process of developing a consensus. The relevant committee will take the "feel of the meeting" and draft a policy statement on the issue.

The second two hours are formal and structured. The board moves into a different room with a conference table and works through a tightly structured agenda with an agreed time allotted to each item. There are no committee reports—these are distributed beforehand and are not up for discussion in the board meeting itself.

Source: Interview with John Graham, American Diabetes Association CEO.

- The agenda is carefully constructed and prioritized.

- The board chair and chief executive are clear about the outcomes they desire from each item on the meeting agenda.

Deepen the Board Chair– Chief Executive Relationship

A sound relationship between the board chair and the chief executive is a linchpin of a well-run organization. The importance of managing this relationship was stressed by a number of interviewees, though, surprisingly, it is not an issue explored in the literature. When this relationship starts to break down, many aspects of good governance and management become increasingly difficult as conversations become more closed and positions more entrenched. It is not easy for these two people to establish a solid working relationship, because they frequently do not select each other. They are chosen by different people and at different times. Chairs have to build a relationship with an incumbent chief executive when they are appointed and may later have to form a relationship with a new chief executive. Frequently, chief executives need to work with a number of different chairs during their term of office.

Chairs and chief executives of leading organizations invest time and effort in managing and strengthening their relationship. First, they have an explicit discussion of each person's expectations of the other—covering both what they want and what they would find unacceptable. These expectations may even be written down for future reference and can provide the basis for an annual review of the relationship. By setting clear expectations, both parties ensure that there will be plenty of honest, fast, and accurate communication, and minimize the opportunities for misunderstandings. Mary Pearl, executive director of the Wildlife Trust, reported, "I talk to my [board] chair every Monday, almost without fail." Roni Posner, executive director of the Alliance for Nonprofit Management, said she takes a similar approach: "I have a weekly phone call, I e-mail the board chair regularly, I seek her guidance, and I give her credit when it is due."

Extensive and open communication sets a foundation for developing a deeper and more trusting relationship. Both parties will increasingly find that they can confide more private thoughts to each other. Unformed ideas around possible future directions for the organization, reflections on the performance of board members and senior managers, visions of possible future management and committee structures, and even plans for their individual personal futures become topics that can be discussed in confidence.

Creating this depth in the relationship ensures that neither party surprises the other or that if one does so inadvertently there is sufficient trust and confidence to ensure that mistakes do not become big issues. It also enables each individual to convey respect for the other's roles to the board and to senior management.

Of course chairs and chief executives do change, and when this happens the relationship building has to start all over again. And as no two relationships are the same, the existing partner has to adjust his or her approach and style to suit the new chair or chief executive.

Continuously Review Board Performance

Leading boards in the United States are overcoming their traditional reticence about discussing their own performance and are finding that they can improve performance by putting it at the heart of their agenda.

Boards are typically making assessments of three elements of performance:

1. Meeting performance
2. Performance of the board as a group
3. Individual performance

Assess Meeting Performance

Leading boards review their meeting performance, either orally or with anonymous written comments. A wide range of the issues that make for high-value meetings may be addressed, including

- The quality of the information provided to the board

- The relevance of agenda items

- The clarity of the issues raised

- The balance between presentation time and discussion time

- The overall allocation of time to different issues

- The opportunities for everyone to participate

- The clarity of the decisions made

- The follow-through on previous decisions

- The role of the chair

In some cases written comments are analyzed and reported back to the next meeting along with proposed actions to address the problems raised. In this way performance review is established as a regular activity that is integrated with other board work and is not seen as a separate and one-off activity.

Assess Board Performance

Boards are increasingly establishing annual objectives for their own performance and reviewing their achievements against those goals. Self-assessment of board performance, often by a questionnaire, is common. Holland's research on a large number of boards and board members led him to suggest that boards should consider the following questions to enhance their performance:

- How is this group adding value to the organization, beyond the contributions of staff and administration?

- Have we identified the most important issues facing this organization?

- Are we spending time and energy on those key issues?

- Have we set clear priorities and then stuck with them in our meetings?

- What specific expectations do we have for ourselves individually as members of this board and of the group as a whole?

- Are the issues and questions coming before us clear, and do we have the right information for working on them?

- Have we listened to the concerns of those affected by our decisions and understood the impact of our work on them?

- What specific steps should we take to improve the performance of this board and increase the value we add to this organization?

- What criteria or indicators would be appropriate for monitoring and demonstrating the improvements in our group's performance?

- How will we obtain and use such information to make further improvements in our work? [Holland, 2002, p. 423]

Although off-the-shelf self-assessment packages are available (from BoardSource, for example), experience suggests that each assessment needs to be tailored to suit each board's circumstances at that particular moment in time. The core assessment issues will be the same, but each organization has unique circumstances and idiosyncrasies that need to be incorporated into performance reviews.

There is also growing evidence that boards tend to be less critical in self-assessments than they are in external assessments. "In a survey of 280 boards that did self-evaluation, the overwhelming majority reported similar performance on all variables except relationships with the CEO. This suggests that there is a 'socially acceptable' performance level," Richard Chait told me. Most boards would not accept self-evaluation as the only form of staff performance review, so to be consistent they should not accept it of themselves.

Chait suggested that "a self-review may be a good starting point, but an external input allows boards to be more honest about performance." External reviewers can also return after an agreed period and ask board members to report, openly, on progress. This gives the board improvement program life and vitality, preventing it from becoming a bureaucratic process.

Assess Individual Performance

There is a growing trend for boards to review not only the performance of the board as a whole but also the performance of individual members. A prerequisite for such reviews is that individuals have been clearly informed about what is expected of them and have been given a description of their role—sometimes cast in the form of a board member's job description. The task of reviewing individuals' performance is often delegated to the nominating or governance committee. Rather than being an annual event, these reviews are most commonly held when someone's term of office is up for renewal. At this point the nominating committee reviews the individual's performance on the board, attendance record, and overall contribution. The chair of the nominating committee may ask the individual for his or her reactions to the experience of being a board member, whether he or she has any concerns, and whether he or she is seeking promotion to a leadership position. This helps to build an open discussion about the future.

For example, the nominating committee of the US Fund for UNICEF board has established a set of performance criteria for board members. It evaluates each person's performance against these criteria at the end of his or her first term of office. If any member is deemed not to have made sufficient impact, the committee chair has a discussion with that person about the board's expectations and his or her future involvement. At this point the person often agrees to stand down. The person is generously thanked for his or her efforts and allowed to move on with dignity. Another board asked its nominating committee to develop the leadership skills of all members after they came onto the board. The committee was responsible for collecting individual assessments and discussing each member's self-assessment and plans for the coming year in light of the needs of the full board. The committee met with each member to offer suggestions about improving the quality of his or her contributions and developing greater leadership skills. Developmental actions included "rotating committee assignments, serving as an understudy in another board role, attending a conference on a specific issue, and talking with members of other boards to identify alternative approaches to a complex issue" (Holland, 2002, p. 420).

Develop Performance Review in Stages

Board members often find it difficult to enter discussions about their own performance. They may be skeptical about the value of these assessments, they may feel the board has more important priorities to address, or they may feel threatened or insecure.

Reviewing meeting behavior is the easiest starting place. With the findings from that review, the board can establish objectives for its own performance over the coming year. These objectives then become the basis for an annual review of the performance of the board as a whole. When members are comfortable with that, and when there are strong and trustworthy relationships between members (in particular between members and the chair), individual performance review can be considered. Research suggests that when people do start working on board performance, they are more comfortable talking about the board's roles and responsibilities and its contribution to organization strategy than they are talking about teamwork and interpersonal relationships. For example, Holland and Jackson (1998) found that only "as they began to experience more focused, productive and satisfying meetings were some participants ready to revisit . . . the interpersonal dimension" (p. 133).

As to what is next in governance, Richard Chait sees a need for boards to move beyond their traditional controlling role. "They need to move beyond oversight to have a duty to provide the curiosity and creativity that can make a significant difference to organization impact."

In the long term the most critical tasks in enhancing the quality of governance are to

- Institutionalize the key processes for finding high-caliber members

- Provide training and development opportunities

- Monitor board performance

When these activities are an integral part of the way the board works, the conditions are right for top-quality governance.

Summary

Ensure That Board Roles Are Crystal Clear

- Although the quality of governance has advanced significantly over the last fifteen years, there are growing calls for further improvements.

- There are no one-size-fits-all solutions to enhancing board performance.

- The key roles of the board are to

    Determine the organization's mission, strategy, and policies

    Appoint and oversee the chief executive

    Monitor the organization's performance

    Manage the governance process

- Boards of leading organizations explicitly define their unique governance role and monitor their performance to ensure that they remain focused on this role.

Structure the Board Around Governance Tasks

- Traditionally, board structures mirrored staff structures. Leading boards are structuring committees according to governance tasks and according to the organization's strategic priorities.

- Governance committees take responsibility for the audit, nominations, governance processes, strategic planning and performance review, and compensation.

- A number of different approaches are used to balance decision-making functions with representation.

Take Actions to Enhance Board Performance

- Studies have shown that investment in board development leads to better board performance.

- Actions boards are taking to improve their performance include

  Enhancing induction

  Focusing board time sharply on the organization's priorities

  Explicitly agreeing on key governance questions for the year ahead

  Adopting a range of measures to encourage board members to engage in continuous development of their knowledge and skills

Deepen the Board Chair–Chief Executive Relationship

- A sound relationship between the chair and chief executive is a linchpin of an effective nonprofit organization. In leading organizations these two people invest time and effort in clarifying expectations of each other and communicating honestly, openly, and quickly.

- Extra effort is required when the incumbent in either position changes.

Continuously Review Board Performance

- Leading-edge boards review meeting performance, the overall performance of the board, and individual performance.

- Establishing a performance review regime tends to start with a meeting performance review. This develops into board performance reviews, and finally the board engages with individual performance issues.

Action Checklist

Efforts to enhance the quality of governance will grow over the coming years as the expectations of nonprofit organization stakeholders increase. Board members who want to strengthen their organization's governance should

1. Set objectives for the performance of the board itself.
2. Establish an annual program, to ensure that the board works on different topics at different times of the year.
3. Annually review the performance of the board against the agreed objectives.
4. Ensure that all members are totally clear about the role of the board.

Individual board members who want to enhance their own governance skills should

1. Insist on an induction when joining the board, and ask for a "buddy" with whom they can discuss matters between meetings.

2. Ask the organization to offer a skills self-assessment so that board members and the organization together can identify skill areas requiring attention.

3. Ask for training to strengthen their skills in selected areas.

4. Offer to shadow an experienced board member in another organization.

5. Ask for informal feedback from other board members.

6. Encourage the board to establish a system for giving and receiving individual performance feedback once a year or every two years.

Senior managers who want to strengthen their organization's governance should

1. Ensure that the board is given top-quality support (including clear informational materials and concise reports of performance against objectives, all circulated well in advance of meetings).

2. Ensure that the chair is fully briefed before meetings and kept in close touch with the organization's progress.

3. Ensure that board members are given many opportunities to see the organization's work on the ground.

7

Reflections of an Outsider

This book has set out approaches that leading-edge organizations are taking to enhance their management and governance. It has attempted to draw together the strands of current thinking and make an assessment of the state of the art.

This final chapter offers some reflections on the development of these cutting-edge practices and comments on their potential contribution to the future management and governance of nonprofit organizations in the United States and more widely.

Perspectives on the Role of Nonprofit Organizations

There is a vibrant debate across the United States about the roles that different kinds of nonprofit organizations should play in civil society. From my research it became clear that there were two very different perspectives on the roles of nonprofit organizations and therefore on approaches to their development.

One view, which I call the *citizen action* perspective, is that the primary role of the nonprofit sector should be as a bulwark against the power of the state and inappropriate actions by private companies. Advocacy, activism, and empowering people are all critical in this view. People who take this view believe that social justice is best advanced by grassroots organizations that enable individuals to campaign for the causes that matter to them, and that provide services that fit with the culture, religion, and circumstances of the local community. These people argue that the development of nonprofit organizations should occur from the bottom up and be driven by a desire to empower and strengthen marginalized groups. They stress the importance of the representational functions of nonprofits and value consultation and consensus-style decision making. They believe that diversity is a great strength of the sector and that nonprofits should network with each other, share good practices, and come together as movements rather than in mergers. They argue that many major social changes, such as the end of slavery, women's emancipation, and environmental protection, resulted from campaigns by a large number of smaller organizations that networked together to achieve social justice. People holding this view suggest that the seeds of the next social changes are growing in grassroots organizations across the country rather than in the organizations sitting at the top of the nonprofit league tables.

The other view, which I call the *managerial* perspective, is that the primary role of the nonprofit sector should be to provide a wide range of essential services, often delivered on behalf of the government, for disadvantaged people. Efficiency, quality, and effectiveness are all critical in this view. People who take this view believe that the sector needs fewer and stronger organizations, ones that can command the resources required to have a significant impact on the great social issues that the nation faces. They see considerable wastage of resources in duplicating governance and central management infrastructures across a large number of small organizations. They believe that small organizations cause stress and early burnout among managers and staff who find themselves trying to fill needs that far exceed the scale of the resources at the organization's disposal. They argue that effectiveness would be increased if there were fewer and larger organizations that provided staff with appropriate training and support and held them to account for their performance in more effective ways.

This debate spills over into arguments about different approaches to governance and management. Proponents of the citizen action viewpoint believe that investment should focus on identifying social entrepreneurs and community leaders and supporting their efforts to mobilize groups and individuals. They believe that people with the potential to create significant change are the most critical resource and that these individuals should be nurtured and supported. They place a priority on investment in developing individuals' skills and in building the capacity of small and medium-sized organizations. They argue for more unrestricted funding to empower organizations to do what each one believes is best in its local circumstances.

People who take the managerial perspective believe that the key to having maximum effect is to build stronger organizations that can mobilize more resources and create the structures, systems, and organization capacity needed to deliver substantial social impact. They argue that the benefits of scale are significant. They talk about finding ways to *scale up* ideas that have proven effective. They believe many organizations could achieve more by integrating back-office functions or merging with similar bodies. They are interested in targeted investment, performance indicators, and funding linked to outcomes.

These two perspectives lie behind many of the different views about the best ways of increasing the impact of the nonprofit sector. Yet, clearly, they are not mutually exclusive. Although some people tend to support one end of the spectrum or the other, in practice many organizations combine elements of both perspectives. For example, local chapters may be more concerned with citizen action, and national offices may take a more managerial perspective.

These different perspectives set the context for the concluding comments in this chapter and demonstrate that different approaches to enhancing nonprofit performance will be required in different circumstances. There is no magic elixir, and no single paradigm applies across this diverse sector. There are, nevertheless, some important trends that emerge from my research.

In this final chapter I suggest that

- Capacity building will become more contingent on circumstances

- Performance management should focus on tailor-made balanced scorecards

- Managing strategic alliances will become a vital skill

- Patterns of funding will continue to change

- Leaders will need to invest more in skill development

- Governance will become more demanding

Capacity Building Will Become More Contingent on Circumstances

Some components of organization capacity are required for all high-functioning organizations, whether their developmental aspirations derive from the citizen action or the managerial perspective. All organizations benefit to some extent from having plans for the future, from ensuring the quality of their activities, from having effective internal communication systems, and from clarifying team and individual responsibilities and accountability. However, my research confirmed what I suspect many know from experience: the value of the various elements of organization capacity varies according to an organization's circumstances. Different types of capacity are required for organizations

- In different subsectors of the nonprofit sector (for example, human services, religion, or the arts)

- With different purposes

- At different stages of evolution

- With different geographic reach

The critical challenge in capacity building is therefore to determine which component of capacity will bring the greatest improvement in organizational effectiveness. Making this determination requires the ability to accurately assess existing capacity. This is a major responsibility of the board and of senior management, because such investments consume significant management time and organization resources and can be critical to long-term success.

Coming to this judgment is not straightforward. Boards bring together a range of people from different walks of life, with varying degrees of understanding of organization capacity. Board members may not comprehend the inner workings of the organization well enough to make the best decision. Senior managers will know much more about the organization, but they face the danger of being too close to it to take a broad perspective. Both face the problem that management practices can seldom be proven to work, so it is hard to distinguish between the latest management fad and techniques that produce tangible benefits.

The starting point for making a diagnosis is to review the quality of the organization's current capacity. Organizations usually have most of the components of capacity in place, to a greater or lesser extent. The critical issue is whether each element of capacity is thought to be making a significant contribution to the organization's success or to be just part of routine administrative activity. Table 7.1 sets out the two ends of this quality spectrum and provides the basis for a preliminary assessment of capacity. A more sophisticated diagnostic tool is the Capacity Assessment Grid developed by McKinsey & Company (2001) (as discussed in Chapter One). It provides a rigorous approach for assessing organization capacity, but it is still a generalist tool and does not distinguish between the different elements of capacity needed by different organizations in different circumstances.

The second step is to determine which elements of capacity the organization most needs in order to achieve its mission. As described earlier, these elements will vary according to the organization's

Table 7.1. High-Level Capacity Assessment.

Essential Capacity	Useless Bureaucracy
A **mission** that is sharp, realistic, and widely used	Much debated missions that are not sufficiently specific, are over-ambitious, and are seldom used
Boards and committees that add high value at every meeting	Boards that consume time and effort and cost more than they contribute
Strategic plans that are precise, prioritized, and tightly linked to operational plans	Strategic plans that are too long, not well prioritized, and unrealistically ambitious
Managers and staff with a limited number of objectives organized into an integrated hierarchy from the organization's goals to individuals' objectives	Managers and staff with many objectives that are not tightly linked across the whole organization
Leaders and managers who delegate and empower staff	Leaders who slip into doing managers' jobs, and managers who slip into doing staff jobs
Leaders and managers who use supervision to hold people to account for meeting their commitments, coach their staff, and expect staff to learn from experience	Supervision that is not related to objectives and not viewed as a learning opportunity
Performance reports that lead to decisions and new priorities	Performance reports that do not result in action
Short, well-planned **meetings** that have clear objectives, have effective leadership that draws on everyone's perspectives, and deliver specified outcomes	Long, poorly planned meetings that are unfocused and skirt around the real issues because people do not speak openly

Table 7.1. High-Level Capacity Assessment, Cont'd.

Essential Capacity	Useless Bureaucracy
Training and professional development directly linked to the organization's objectives	General training linked to individuals' interests
Personal appraisals that are well prepared, give honest feedback, and lead to action	Appraisals that are polite, not supportive, and do not address poor performance
Timely **financial management information** that relates directly to people's responsibilities and the resources that they control and that focuses people on the key numbers	Management accounts that are full of numbers people do not understand and that include resources they do not control
Risk assessment that is engrained in organization culture and leads to amelioration measures for all high-risk activities	Cursory risk assessments, lacking systematic analysis and not leading to actions to offset risk

subsector, purpose, stage of development, and geographic reach. For a clearer picture of the line of thinking that evolved as my research progressed, consider organizations with different *geographic reach*:

- Community-based, neighborhood, and local organizations

- Larger organizations operating at city, state, regional, or national levels

And consider organizations with different *purposes*:

- Service delivery

- Social change

Smaller *community-based organizations that deliver services*, on the one hand, need to have the capacity to deliver quality activities without reinventing them from scratch. Some are well suited to delivering prepackaged projects that build on experience acquired across the country but can also be tailored to suit local circumstances. Examples are drug treatment programs and youth activities. This capacity could be called *franchisee* capacity (using the term *franchisee* in a general rather than narrow legal sense). It is the capacity to plug into expertise while maintaining local independence.

Smaller *community-based organizations that promote social change*, on the other hand, need the capacity to network with other organizations championing similar causes. They should be able to link together to establish new movements that create public awareness and change public policy. They need to coordinate action but do not require the types of systems and processes used by service delivery organizations.

In contrast, *larger organizations that deliver services* across a city, a state, a region, or the nation as a whole require robust and sustainable delivery capacity. They need marketing, quality management, and performance-reporting systems that enable the systematic application of tried and tested approaches. They need a deep understanding of *what works*, how to deliver services economically, and how to have significant impact. Dividing complex activities into manageable tasks and giving people challenging yet realistic jobs are the critical aspects of their long-term success.

Finally, *larger organizations that deliver ongoing campaigns* on matters of national concern such as civil liberties, human rights, and environmental protection need the capacity to mount and sustain campaigns over extended periods. Their output is ideas, so they need to capture people's imagination and change views and behaviors. They depend on creativity and publicity.

The critical capacities in each of these circumstances differ significantly and can be summarized as illustrated in Table 7.2. In practice, of course, many organizations both deliver services and

Table 7.2. Predominant Capacity Requirements.

	Service Missions	Social Change Missions
Community-based organizations	Franchisee skills	Networking skills
Larger organizations	Delivery skills	Campaigning skills

promote social change. However, most tend to work predominantly in one or the other field, so their capacity investment should be focused on their primary purpose.

This is just one set of examples, and many other combinations of organization settings could be considered. It leads me to conclude that the next stage in developing the theory of capacity building is to get a much deeper understanding of the fit between organizations' circumstances and the types of capacity building that will bring them the greatest benefits.

Nevertheless this contingent approach to determining capacity building priorities should lead to efforts that are chosen because they will significantly boost achievement of the organization's mission. In the past, decisions about which elements of capacity to build were based on the direct experiences of the organization's leadership and a great deal of "gut feel." A more rigorous approach to linking capacity requirements with the organization's mission will emerge from the current efforts to develop the theory and practice of capacity building.

Performance Management Systems Should Focus on Tailor-Made Balanced Scorecards

Performance management is an element of capacity that is crucial for some types of organizations. Since the mid-1990s there have been growing demands for greater accountability among nonprofit organizations after a series of scandals rocked public confidence. In

1995, William Aramony, president of United Way of America, was convicted of defrauding the organization of $1 million. In the same year the Foundation for New Era Philanthropy, which had attracted investments of over $41 million, was discovered to be an elaborate ruse and collapsed into bankruptcy. In 2002, Oral Suer, leader of United Way of the National Capital Area, pleaded guilty to stealing $500,000 from the organization during his twenty-seven years with it. In addition, the destruction of the World Trade Center in 2001 was followed by heated debate about the use of funds raised by the American Red Cross to aid the affected individuals and families. This too fueled the growing debate about donors' rights and their need for information to hold organizations to account.

This debate is now moving on from concerns about reporting on expenditures to demands for greater accountability for outcomes. There are increasingly strong calls for organizations to report on what they have achieved, particularly service delivery organizations that work to the managerial perspective described earlier. Most observers believe that these demands will rise.

More fundamentally, there are signs of an important cultural shift, from the assumption that activities undertaken by nonprofit organizations are inherently good to the assumption that what matters is outcomes, whether they are achieved by nonprofit, private, or public organizations. Private sector encroachment into areas of human service delivery that used to be exclusively the domain of nonprofit organizations is taking away the psychological safety net that used to support the sector. It is challenging the sector to demonstrate that it can achieve the impacts that its donors and contractors require.

However, although there is growing demand for accountability, measuring and monitoring the performance of nonprofit organizations is at an early stage of development. The champions of performance management believe that having some measures to monitor performance is better than basing judgments on feel and opinion. They argue that most outcomes can be defined numerically and that boards and management should hold people accountable for achieving the desired results. They see performance management as essential to the public accountability of nonprofits, and they argue that future resources should be allocated on the basis of past achievements.

The critics of performance management argue that measures or metrics will never describe nonprofit activities precisely and that searching for such metrics will not yield managerially valuable information. They point out that measurement can be expensive, particularly when new data are required. Obtaining measures such as social return on investment requires significant investment, and some argue that this is not a good use of resources. They also point out that organizations that deliver a range of services face particular difficulties, as the measures used for different services can not usually be added together, making it difficult to obtain an overall picture of an organization's performance. They also point out that lobbying successes can seldom be ascribed to the work of one organization.

It is nevertheless clear that the demands for greater accountability and therefore for better measures of performance will grow. Performance measures may not be as good a proxy for performance as managers might like, but the art is at an early stage of development, and if nonprofit sector people contribute to the development of these measures, they will undoubtedly become more closely aligned with performance.

From my research I have concluded that the balanced scorecard with various metrics is the most pertinent and powerful tool for tracking nonprofit performance that has been developed to date. However, the balanced scorecard was originally developed for the corporate sector (Kaplan and Norton, 1996), and the four key dimensions of performance it examined were financial, internal business processes, learning and growth, and customers. These are insightful parameters for businesses, moving attention away from the traditional focus on historical financial reports and toward the drivers of future performance. These dimensions of performance do have resonance in the nonprofit world (and some nonprofit organizations have tried to squeeze accounts of their performance into these categories), but for many nonprofits they do not relate closely enough to the organization's particular circumstances.

The balanced scorecard may therefore need to be more closely tailored to the needs of different types of nonprofit organizations. Managers will need to select both the dimensions of performance and the individual performance metrics within each dimension that best describe their achievements and the health of their organizations. In my experience the critical performance metrics for nonprofits are

- Social outcomes

- People

- Fundraising

- Finance

Social outcome metrics define what the organization has achieved, and although they are often difficult to pin down to a few performance measures, they are critical to describing what an organization has achieved in service delivery and in its wider social mission.

People metrics define the performance and opinions of the organization's staff, board, and chapters. They might measure staff turnover, staff satisfaction, sickness levels, and board, staff, and chapter performance. They describe the human aspects of the organization's health.

Fundraising metrics describe income raised and the returns on fundraising investments. They are perhaps the simplest to prepare, as they are inherently amenable to quantification. In addition to measures recording the achievement of fundraising targets, organizations may include metrics that are future oriented, such as measures of brand recognition and donor satisfaction.

Financial metrics define economic performance and the financial strength of the organization. Examples include income, expenditure, activity analysis, unit costs, financial reserves, and cash flow.

I believe that nonprofit managers and board members will get better value from a balanced scorecard that uses dimensions of performance that fit their organization's particular circumstances than they will from one adopted, albeit sometimes modified, from business. Having defined the appropriate dimensions, managers and board members then need to determine what the key performance metrics can be and fit them into the agreed categories.

Getting the performance dimensions and metrics right is only the first step. The key to performance management is acting on the results. The essential notion of specifying what the organization wants to achieve and then managing against those objectives sounds simple, but that is deceptive. It is a challenge to put this idea into operation. Creating simple systems to track performance, report on it, and take action based on outcomes has proven to be extraordinarily difficult, and according to my research there are still remarkably few examples of well-developed systems that are deeply embedded in their organizations and used to report on performance to external stakeholders.

The single most important element leading to success is the establishment of an organization performance culture in which board members, managers, and staff are tightly focused on linking all activities to evidence about the achievement of the mission and on identifying potential actions to increase mission impact.

Many organizations are already striving to find ways of boiling down reports on their overall achievements to a meaningful and manageable set of data. They are also attempting to find ways to report on their health as well as their financial performance. The clamor for greater accountability and growing public expectations for performance information means that organizations that make progress now will have significant fundraising and public relations advantages over those that wait until they are required by external forces to improve their performance monitoring and reporting.

Managing Strategic Alliances Will Become a Vital Skill

Strategic alliances are important both to organizations with the citizen action perspective and to those with the managerial perspective. However, the types of relationships they pursue are likely to be very different.

Making the Alliance Decision

It is natural that people managing and governing a nonprofit organization focus most of their thinking around that organization and its mission. However, it is all too easy to become habituated to thinking within the organization's own context and to miss the opportunities for making step changes that come from taking a wider perspective. It is clear that there are many instances when the mission can be achieved more effectively or more efficiently by organizations working together. This applies to organizations right across the nonprofit sector.

Managers and board members therefore need to step back periodically from the day-to-day priorities of the organization and review whether the current configuration of organizations in a particular field is the best way to achieve the mission. Might one organization be better able to develop services originally established by another? Could back-office services be delivered more efficiently in collaboration with other organizations? Would an alliance bring together the amounts and types of resources needed to have greater impact? Should a merger with another organization be considered? A growing body of evidence demonstrates that organizations can achieve their missions more effectively when they form a range of strategic alliances, undertaking different types to suit different circumstances. These alliances may be with other nonprofits, businesses, professional groups, or public sector agencies. We are living in an age when organizational boundaries are becoming fuzzy and fluid. When organizations are young, their founders clearly need to focus on creating the fundamental elements of management and governance. However, once the essential elements have been created, collaboration with other organizations may be the most effective way of advancing the mission. The range of alliances that many organizations have now is larger than is commonly recognized. Evidence from my research suggests that both the numbers and the types of relationships are growing exponentially.

Strategic alliances are most effective when they are put together by organizations that are secure managerially and financially and have built substantial capacity of their own. Effective alliances are properly resourced and professionally managed. Two weak organizations do not make a strong one. Alliances are demanding, and organizations contemplating one need to have "spare" capacity if they are to be able to invest time and money in managing and governing the alliance and ensuring that it is effective.

The form of a strategic alliance will depend on whether the organizations' primary purpose is service delivery or social change. Among service delivery organizations operating from a primarily managerial perspective, alliances are likely to be formal and long term. Among social change organizations they are likely to be concerned with the establishment of networks, sharing expertise, and working together to achieve particular political objectives. *Strength in numbers* and *breadth of interest* are both particularly important when campaigning for change.

The evidence from my research is that the theory around making strategic alliances effective is not well developed. It is clear that the governance and management skills required to make alliances a success are somewhat different from traditional management skills, but as yet these new skills are not well documented. The challenge for the sector over the next few years will therefore be to develop a robust analysis of the different types of alliances and the best ways to make them effective. Only then will it be possible to spread the necessary knowledge widely across the sector. Eventually, the management and governance of alliances should be as well understood as the management and governance of single organizations is today.

The Special Case of Mergers

Sometimes the logical conclusion to a strategic alliance is a merger. Mergers arouse strongly opposing views in the nonprofit sector that deserve special note.

Proponents of mergers argue that there are far too many nonprofit organizations chasing the same funds and delivering similar services. They see the sector as fragmented and inefficient and believe that mergers should be as common as they are in the corporate sector.

People who are more skeptical about nonprofit mergers point out that organizations often have very different value bases and provide different services to different user groups, so the real opportunities for mergers are fewer than might at first sight appear to be the case. These critics are also likely to highlight the value of diversity and plurality in a sector that depends for its lifeblood on its ability to motivate individuals. They also argue that independence is a much cherished attribute for the people working and giving their time as board members and that this can be a powerful deterrent to mergers. Managers, staff, and board members may view a potential merger as a threat to their autonomy and freedom to act. Skeptics see mergers as a time-consuming and costly business as well. A merger may distract both organizations from their core businesses for a significant amount of time. There are often difficult issues to resolve, such as which organization will supply the board chair, chief executive, and senior managers.

So mergers are comparatively rare in the nonprofit sector. Frequently, the word *merger* is a euphemism for the *takeover* or absorption of a smaller, ailing organization by a larger, more successful one. However, a dispassionate assessment must conclude that fears of loss of autonomy should not prevent mergers and takeovers. Ultimately, organizations' missions are more important than their independence. The key question in each case must be whether or not the merger will increase the probability of achieving the mission.

My outsider's view is that the objective of achieving critical mass, the value of having a strong brand, and the pressing need to achieve and report significant impact will combine to drive more nonprofit organizations to consider mergers. In time the knowledge and experience of making a success of a nonprofit merger will grow, and the loss of independence may not be as significant as feared. Merging does not always mean total absorption into another organization. Organizations can become part of a federation that works under one name and develops one brand but allows individual units the freedom to manage their own affairs. Similarly, organizations might become part of a group structure that provides greater financial security and spreads risk across a number of organizations while still allowing subsidiaries considerable latitude in managing their services or campaigns. I conclude that there will be many more mergers among nonprofit organizations over the coming years.

Patterns of Funding Will Continue to Change

Sources of finance for nonprofit organizations have changed dramatically in recent years, and this is likely to continue. The landscape of nonprofit finance will also look very different in ten years' time.

Commercialization

Over the last twenty years, nonprofit organizations have earned a growing proportion of their income from fees paid directly by users or indirectly by government (Table 7.3). This trend has been driven partly by changes in government policies that have reduced payments to providers for delivering services and replaced them with vouchers for users to purchase services. In addition nonprofits have found a variety of ways to sell their services directly to customers. Consequently, fee income has grown faster than all other sources of income. There is no evidence that this trend is slowing, so I conclude that nonprofits are likely to become more commercialized over the coming years.

Table 7.3. Changing Structure of Nonprofit Revenue, 1977–1997.

Revenue Source	% Change 1977–1997	% Share of Total Revenue 1977	% Share of Total Revenue 1997	% Share of Revenue Growth 1977–1997
Fees and charges	145	46	47	47
Government	195	27	33	37
Philanthropy	90	27	20	16
TOTAL	144	100	100	100

Source: Salamon, 2002, p. 31. Reprinted with permission.

Competition

Competition from for-profits will also affect nonprofit income streams. The creation of markets for the provision of social services has attracted for-profit organizations to fields traditionally dominated by nonprofits. Many for-profits have grown successful because of their ability to raise capital, their management and marketing skills, and their willingness to invest in technology. For example, "Between 1977 and 1992 for-profit firms captured 80 percent of the growth in day care centers, and in home health and clinic care for-profit firms captured close to 90 percent of the growth of facilities" (Salamon, 1999, p. 71).

Increased competition is anticipated in future as businesses recognize the commercial opportunities in areas that used to be considered open only to nonprofit organizations. Salamon (2002) suggests that nonprofits "can hold their own only where they have well established institutions, where they can secure capital, where they manage to identify a meaningful market niche and a distinctive product, and where individual consumers or those paying on their behalf value the special qualities that nonprofits bring to the field" (p. 43). Interestingly, nonprofits may have a greater capacity than for-profit organizations to survive the ups and downs of markets that are driven primarily by government decisions on fee reimbursement levels. They tend to have lower borrowing and have the cushion of donor income to subsidize the provision of services where costs exceed contract payments. Nevertheless, the winds of competition are likely to blow even harder on nonprofit organizations as the delivery of services within a business model becomes increasingly common.

New Types of Funding

Further changes in the financing of nonprofit activities have been driven by new types of funding. Venture philanthropy and high-engagement funding have both had an impact on grantmaking (an impact out of all proportion to the value of their funding), and these types of funding have influenced debates about the relationship between funders and funded organizations. The jury may still be out on whether strong support combined with tough accountability is a formula for long-term success, but there is no doubt about the impact of venture philanthropy on the way people think about this crucial relationship.

New Approaches by Foundations

Another change is being driven by the new approaches to funding taken by foundations. The calls for foundations to increase their payout rates are growing, particularly at present when income from government and business is no longer growing at previous rates and in some cases is falling. The 5 percent of their capital that foundations are required to pay out each year is often treated as a maximum as well as a minimum. A change in this practice or a legal requirement to pay out a greater percentage would release significant new money for nonprofits.

In addition, as foundations now have $1 trillion in invested assets, there are also growing calls for more of these funds to be used to address today's pressing social problems rather than invested so they can be spent on future problems (Jansen and Katz, 2002).

Finally, concern that foundations invest their funds in financial markets at a time when some nonprofits are taking loans at commercial rates has led some foundations to make small but significant capital investments directly into nonprofit organizations.

The Nonprofit Capital Market

Together, all these changes in the types of funding and the nature of relationships have led to the beginning of a debate about the *nonprofit capital market* (described in Chapter Four). Early discussion suggests that this is an inefficient market, characterized by poor information flows about what works and what does not work. There are propositions that the sector as a whole could have greater impact if this market could be made more effective.

In addition, increasing thought is being given to the capital structure of nonprofit organizations. Although not a new subject, it is now being more widely discussed (Miller, 2003). Most nonprofit organizations have few borrowings compared to their assets (they are not *highly geared* in the technical jargon), and many use donors' funds for capital investments when borrowing might be a more appropriate form of financing.

My reflection as an outsider is that people in the nonprofit sector tend to focus most of their energy on services and campaigns and comparatively little on financial structures. The private sector puts greater effort into ensuring that different financial instruments are used for different purposes. I suggest that we are seeing the beginning of a seismic shift that will point toward

- Loans being more widely used for capital investment and for working capital

- Donor income being focused more sharply on direct benefits to users

- Financial reserves being invested in social benefit organizations rather than with banks and in the financial markets

All this will require new thinking by people in many departments of nonprofit organizations. Directors of fundraising will have to be much more imaginative in the ways they think about potential sources of funding; directors of finance will have to develop more sophisticated financial information systems to link sources and uses of funds, and boards will have to be more astute in assessing risk and finding ways of ameliorating it.

Leaders Will Need to Invest More in Skill Development

There is growing discussion about leadership, the role that it plays in creating successful nonprofit organizations, and in particular the leadership role of the chief executive. A key challenge for chief executives is managing many issues simultaneously. Chief executives talk about the challenge of

- Building and maintaining a rich network of external relationships, and keeping a close eye on changes in the external environment

- Keeping a really tight grip on every stage of the planning and performance cycle

- Keeping the quality of the board and its work at the highest level

- Raising funds, and maintaining personal relationships with key funders

- Building the senior team, investing in personal relationships, and supporting members of the team

- Demonstrating a personal commitment to all strategic alliances

- Taking actions that can catalyze change (speaking, writing, and so forth)

This is a hugely challenging job, and one that has to be done in consultation with a wide range of stakeholders, all of whom have a legitimate interest in the organization.

To give the chief executive time to deliver these roles, an increasing number of organizations are appointing a chief operating officer and switching some or all of the chief executive's direct reports to this new post. Although the COO's role may be defined in a number of ways, its primary purpose is to reduce the demands on the chief executive. Like all structural arrangements, it is critically dependent on good personal relationships and in this case on the highest levels of trust and openness between the CEO and the COO. Because of the impact on senior managers' reporting lines, and the potential for them to believe they have been demoted, this change can be difficult to introduce successfully. However, its popularity in larger organizations implies that it can often relieve the pressure on chief executives and enable them to discharge their leadership roles more effectively.

Many organizations are investing in leadership development. The size of the nonprofit sector has enabled it to develop many resources for leaders. There is a body of literature devoted specifically to the leadership of nonprofit organizations, and there are organizations devoted to nonprofit leadership, most notably the Leader to Leader Institute. Some nonprofit management education includes courses on leadership, and there is strong evidence that managers want better leadership development. In a survey of the leading public policy and administration schools, graduates reported that leadership was the second most important skill in helping them to succeed in their jobs. However, even though 76 percent rated leadership as very important, only 39 percent said that their schools had been very helpful in teaching that skill (Light, 1999).

The challenge for the sector is therefore to encourage more organizations to recognize the critical importance of top-quality leadership and to secure funds to invest in developing leadership skills. Better training and stronger support are required to attract and retain people willing to take on leadership roles and to make these jobs more doable and enjoyable. Although there is continuing debate about the extent to which leadership skills can be taught, the leaders I interviewed had all invested significant time and effort in their own development. They read voraciously, attend courses, seek feedback, use coaches and mentors, and reflect extensively on their own performance. All this suggests that they believe their skills are improved by their own development efforts and that they will be more effective leaders as a result.

Governance Will Become More Demanding

Ten years ago the United States led the world in driving the modernization of nonprofit governance. The establishment of BoardSource, with its publications on governance and its annual conference that attracts people from around the globe, created a driving force for a new agenda for governance. The propositions that BoardSource promoted are now being implemented in the United States and more widely. The area of greatest development is currently the assessment of the performance of the board as a whole and of the individuals who constitute the board. Boards recognize that because they now expect every part of the organization to evaluate its achievements, the board itself should review its own performance and identify the value that it adds to the organization. Leading-edge boards are using board self-assessment tools to review their performance. These can be obtained (sometimes via the Internet) from organizations delivering governance improvement. The emerging learning is that these self-assessments need to be tailored to individual organization circumstances if they are to provide valuable insights into board performance. Unfortunately, oganizations cannot rely on a one-size-fits-all assessment tool.

Individual feedback is a further means of enhancing board performance. It is appropriate when the board is clear about its role and when individual members are unambiguous about what is expected of them. Ideally, job descriptions for board members should be in place so there is no doubt about the requirements. In addition board members must have confidence in the chair or other person who is chosen to give the feedback. Feedback from board members to their colleagues can be sought at the same time that data are gathered on the performance of the board as a whole. It can be collated by the person giving the feedback or an external adviser. It can include feedback both from fellow board members and from members of the senior management team.

A further development is for boards to talk about their performance review process. An open discussion can identify the strengths and weaknesses of the review process and can pinpoint improvements to be made for future years.

My overall impression is that over recent years board effectiveness has increased significantly. However, the journey from governance that was comparatively amateurish to skilled governance that reflects the needs of organizations and the wider demands of the community will take time. There is a long way to go before a majority of boards and board members deliver governance at the highest standard and add maximum value to their organizations.

Focus on the New Agenda

Powerful forces are shaping the context in which the nonprofit sector operates:

- The public sector is withdrawing from providing services and is instead focusing on funding and regulating those services.

- Profit-seeking firms are being attracted to providing services that were previously the preserve of the public and nonprofit sectors.

- Social enterprise is emerging as a new way of tackling social problems, and it straddles the traditional boundaries between the private and nonprofit sectors.

- New forms of funding and financial instruments are emerging and opening opportunities for organizations to structure their finances in different ways.

These and other changes point to the challenges managers and board members will face over coming years. In summary, when I stand back from the work I have undertaken over the last two years, I conclude that managers and board members will need to focus on the following tasks:

Invest in building strong organizations that have the skills, experience, and capacity to have a significant impact on the social issues they exist to address. Managers and board members need to recognize the potential for step changes in organization performance and not assume that the status quo is sufficient.

Know what organizations are achieving, so they can learn much more from experience and orient every aspect of management to what works and to delivering results. Managers and board members need to understand the key drivers of performance and ensure that everyone in and around the organization is focused on successful outcomes. They also need to provide greater accountability to funders, other stakeholders, and the wider public.

Work strategically with other organizations to maximize the potential to be unleashed by combining the resources of two or more organizations. Managers and board members need to seek out alliances and put their organization's mission ahead of its autonomy and independence.

Diversify funding to exploit a range of new sources of finance and therefore obtain greater leverage from existing funding. Managers and board members need to create a much better fit between activities and investments on the one hand and the sources of funding used to pay for them on the other.

Provide leadership at every level to get the best from the organization's people. Managers and board members need to recognize that most staff feel they are not well managed, that the key components of top-quality management are well known, and that people will increasingly expect these components to be applied.

Enhance the quality of governance through a sharper understanding of the unique roles of the board and through higher standards for board members in delivering those roles effectively. Managers and board members need to use every tool available to improve their own performance.

Resource A

A Brief History of the Nonprofit Sector

The current issues in the management and governance of U.S. nonprofit organizations emerge from a historical context, which is briefly summarized here.

The Roots

As the first American states were once British colonies, the roots of nonprofit organizations in the United States can be traced back to England's Statute of Charitable Uses of 1601. Up to the time of the War of Independence (1775 to 1783), colonial legislatures did not have the power to create corporations. The immense difficulty of creating formal organizations meant that charitable activity was carried out primarily in the sphere of personal action rather than through organizations.

After the war, private corporations were formed to serve public purposes such as the construction of bridges, turnpikes, and canals. These corporations were delegated powers by the state, but their existence was time limited and they were viewed more as stewards of public funds than as organizations created to make profits. States' policies toward corporations differed, ranging from encouragement

Natalia Leshchenko, a doctoral student at London School of Economics, did the research that led to this summary, which draws on the work of Peter Hall and others who have written about the history of the sector.

in New England to hostility in the South. There was much tension between the role of private corporations and that of the state.

In the early years of the nineteenth century, views on the need for nonprofit corporations were divided. The Federalists believed in strong government and argued for the delegation of state power to groups of respectable individuals. The dissenters remained stead-fastly hostile to private nonprofit corporations (Hall, 1987).

The Federalist view began to prevail as churches, Bible societies, lyceums, and teachers' institutes all began to reach out for public support and a culture of organization began to take hold. Develop-ment was strongly influenced by those who favored the nonprofit role. "Wherever an orphanage, a library, a college, a hospital, an academy or a professional society originated, it was almost invari-ably the work of a migrant New Englander with evangelical con-nections" (Hall, 1982, p. 7). However, it was not until 1844 that the U.S. Supreme Court placed private nonprofit corporations under federal law, a decision that began the process of creating a uniform set of regulations around nonprofit activity.

The growth of private businesses that wanted to operate on a national scale led to demands for a more educated workforce, which in turn led businesses to fund nonprofit organizations, in particular institutions of higher education. Universities and colleges were funded by businesses, and academic research centers gathered and interpreted social information needed by for-profit companies. Gifts and bequests to Harvard University reached almost $6 million in the five years preceding 1890. Other fields also benefited, as busi-nesses and individuals financed the growth of libraries, hospitals, and professional organizations. The middle and lower classes also contributed to the burgeoning nonprofit sector through the estab-lishment of labor unions, mutual benefit societies, volunteer fire companies, building and loan associations, and even cooperatively owned nonprofit businesses (Hall, 1987).

The processes of industrialization and urbanization and the eco-nomic liberalism of the nineteenth century facilitated and encouraged the growth of philanthropic activity. Although this growth led to further debate about the relationship between the nonprofit sector and the state, nonprofit activity was unequivocally seen as an alternative to welfare support provided by the government. "Private non-profit corporations became the main form of social palliative, dislodging the competing idea that it should fall into the sphere of governmental competence" (Hall, 1987).

The nineteenth century has been referred to as the "golden age of philanthropy," reflecting the social, cultural, and economic conditions of that period. However, the concept of a distinct and separate nonprofit sector emerged only toward the end of the century (Salamon and Anheier, 1997). Reformers started to rationalize organizations by creating *united charities*, which combined the resources of small organizations and state organizations known as *charity commissions*. This began a period of professionalization and management improvement that led to the creation of today's nationwide organizations such as the Red Cross and the United Way.

Key Modern Developments

At the opening of the twentieth century Americans remained averse to government solutions to social and economic problems. Private solutions were voluntary, and their survival and success depended on how efficiently organizations were run, not on government legislation. These views were strengthened by the many disreputable and uncontrollable aspects of U.S. politics, which discouraged people from giving greater powers to government (Hall, 1987).

Also around the turn of the century, wealthy Americans began creating a new type of philanthropic institution, the charitable foundation (Hall, 1987). In 1889, steel industry tycoon and generous philanthropist Andrew Carnegie wrote an influential essay entitled "The Gospel of Wealth," which argued that philanthropy should orient itself not to the cure but to the prevention of social problems. This led to the establishment of a new type of organization, known as an *open-ended* foundation. The contributors provided money to a panel of experts who chose the projects to support. The first open-ended foundation in the United States was the Sage Foundation (1907), and it was followed by the Rockefeller Foundation (1917).

The establishment of these foundations was controversial. There were fears that they might have undue influence on public policy, and this made them very cautious in their funding decisions. It was left to a few, such as the Brookings Institution (1916) and the Twentieth Century Fund (1919), to address public policy issues directly.

The dominant model of social welfare during the first quarter of the twentieth century was known as *welfare capitalism*. Starting in the 1880s, welfare capitalism aimed to encourage firms to work more efficiently and more equitably. It involved both the construction of company towns and investments in people to make them more productive and enable them to identify more closely with their employers. As a result the role of the nonprofit sector in social welfare provision was considerable and often greater than that of the government.

Until 1930, private sector welfare provision was also seen as the main means of thwarting socialism. The dominant paradigm was known as the *associative state*, developed under the influence of Herbert Hoover's 1922 book, *American Individualism*. This model encouraged reliance on cooperative institutions (Hall, 1987). An important feature of the model was the National Recovery Administration, an agency that produced a system of agreements through which the government guaranteed stability to for-profit and non-profit corporations in return for their work in generating employment and delivering social services.

The "private" alternative did not withstand the economic depression of 1929 to 1933. As businesses became less able to provide social services, the government stepped in. The foundations of the social welfare system were established in Franklin D. Roosevelt's New Deal program. The main services included the provision of old-age pensions, unemployment insurance, and needs-tested cash assistance for elderly and disabled people and families with dependent children.

These welfare policies, with increased taxation of the rich on the one hand and encouragement of charitable donations on the other, spawned a rapid increase in the number of foundations, from 239 in 1930 to 535 in 1939 (Foundation Center, 1970). Private nonprofit organizations continued to perform a significant role due to the patchy nature of public provision, but in the general atmosphere of insecurity, nonprofits were not seen to be particularly innovative during this period.

The Second World War led to greater government involvement in the provision of social services. Before the war, the nonprofit and for-profit sectors provided basic social, cultural, and welfare services with encouragement from government. After the war, the government assumed greater responsibility for the provision of social services, and it employed the nonprofit sector to deliver them.

The 1960s were a period of significant expansion of federal programs, including Medicare, the federal health insurance program for the elderly, and Medicaid, the program to finance health care for poor people. Support for research at universities and new social service and community development programs also grew rapidly. However, because of ingrained hostility to centralized government, new services were delivered by a mixture of state and city governments and most notably by nonprofit organizations, reflecting the long-standing interrelationships between government and nonprofit organizations stretching back to colonial times (Nielson, 1979). Moreover, even when states and cities received funding, they often subcontracted delivery to the nonprofit sector.

In the 1970s, the relationship between government and private philanthropy, including nonprofits, was scrutinized in a number of governmental and private reports, including the 1973 Filer Commission report. They arrived at similar conclusions about the necessity of continued government support for the sector and the expediency of tax incentives to encourage charitable giving (Salamon, 1990).

By the late 1970s, nonprofit organizations were delivering a larger share of government-financed human services than all levels of government combined, and income from government support grew to almost twice the income from private charitable donations. It seemed that a consensus was emerging on the value of government-nonprofit partnerships.

This understanding was changed during the 1980s and early 1990s when the traditional conservative commitment to limiting the role of the state and minimizing social spending had a huge impact on the nonprofit sector. The government's withdrawal from social service provision was presented during the Reagan years as "freeing the field," or creating opportunities for nonprofits. Further tax incentives for charitable giving were introduced.

As government spending on social service provision fell, so did nonprofits' income. It is estimated that the nonprofit sector (outside the health field) lost $17 billion in government support between 1982 and 1985, with a reduction of up to 36 percent in federal support for social service organizations (Salamon, 1990).

In 1992, Bill Clinton was elected to the presidency and growth in some programs resumed, particularly support for children and families and programs to encourage low-income people to become more self-sufficient. From 1989 to 1994, the expansion of eligibility for Medicaid and the widening of Medicare payments to include home health care contributed to a real increase of 39 percent in health spending. Income assistance spending increased, and social service spending grew by 19 percent during this five-year period (Salamon, 1999).

Overall income to the independent sector grew by 17 percent in real terms from 1992 to 1998 (the most recent year for total income figures) (INDEPENDENT SECTOR and Urban Institute, 2002), driven mainly by increased fee income for nursing home care and children's day care. Income from donations, for which more recent data are available, also showed an acceleration toward the end of the decade and registered a small decline in real terms in 2001 (AAFRC Trust for Philanthropy, 2002). Following the bursting of the stock market bubble and the slowdown in the U.S. economy, it became clear that the boom years of the 1990s had come to an end and that the nonprofit sector was again facing a tougher period.

# Resource B

People Interviewed for This Book

A total of sixty-five individuals in the United States participated in structured, face-to-face interviews for the research reported in this book. The organizations with which they are affiliated include twenty-three nonprofit organizations, ten intermediary bodies, nine university departments, and four consulting firms.

Organization	City	Name	Job Title
Nonprofit organizations			
American Diabetes Association	Washington, D.C.	John Graham	CEO
Amnesty International USA	New York	Curt Goering	Senior Deputy Executive Director
Big Brothers Big Sisters	Long Island	Bill Tyman	Executive Director
Boys & Girls Club of Boston	Boston	Linda Whitlock	President & CEO
Children's Institute International	Los Angeles	Mary Emmons	President & CEO
Earthjustice	San Francisco	Buck Parker	Executive Director
Elderhostel	Boston	James Moses	Chief Executive
Goodwill Industries of Southern California	Los Angeles	Doug Barr	President & CEO
Jewish Vocational Service	San Francisco	Abby Snay	Executive Director
KIPP Schools	San Francisco	Mike Feinberg	Cofounder & CEO
LightHouse for the Blind and Visually Impaired	San Francisco	Anita Aaron	Executive Director
Los Angeles Regional Foodbank	Los Angeles	Michael Flood	Executive Director
The Medical Foundation	Boston	Raymond Considine	President
National Urban League	New York	Hugh Price	President
Origin	New York	Jeffrey Jablow	President & CEO
Toolworks	San Francisco	Donna Feingold	Executive Director
Trust for Public Land	San Francisco	Ralph Benson	Senior Vice President
US Fund for UNICEF	New York	Charles Lyons	President

Organization	Location	Name	Title
Volunteers of America	Washington, D.C.	Charles Gould	National President
Wildlife Conservation Society	New York	Steven Sanderson	President & CEO
Wildlife Trust	New York	Mary Pearl	Executive Director
YWCA	New York	Margaret Tyndall	CEO

Intermediary organizations

Organization	Location	Name	Title
Alliance for Nonprofit Management	Washington, D.C.	Roni Posner	Executive Director
Aspen Institute	Washington, D.C.	Alan Abramson	Director, Nonprofit Sector and Philanthropy
BoardSource	Washington, D.C.	Marilyn Wyatt	Director of Consulting and Training for Europe and Asia
BoardSource	Washington, D.C.	Outi Flynn	Consultant
Center for Nonprofit Management	Los Angeles	Peter Manzo	Executive Director, General Counsel
CompassPoint	San Francisco	Jan Masaoka	Executive Director
Council on Foundations	Washington, D.C.	Char Mollison	Vice President, Constituency Services
Council on Foundations	Washington, D.C.	Dorothy Ridings	President
Council on Foundations	Washington, D.C.	Joanne Scanlon	Senior Vice President, Professional Development
Foundation Center	New York	Loren Renz	Vice President for Research
Foundation Center	New York	Sarah Engelhardt	President
INDEPENDENT SECTOR	Washington, D.C.	Peter Shiras	Senior Vice President
Leader to Leader Institute	New York	Frances Hesselbein	Chairman of the Board

Organization	City	Name	Job Title
National Council of Nonprofit Associations	Washington, D.C.	Audrey Alvarado	Executive Director
National Council of Nonprofit Associations	Washington, D.C.	Lora Pollari-Welbes	Director of Member Relations and Services
Urban Institute, Center on Nonprofits and Philanthropy	Washington, D.C.	Elizabeth Boris	Director
Urban Institute, Center on Nonprofits and Philanthropy	Washington, D.C.	Francie Ostrower	Senior Research Associate
Funders			
Ford Foundation	New York	Michael Edwards	Director, Governance and Civil Society
Meyer Foundation	Washington, D.C.	Mary Ann Holohean	Director, Nonprofit Sector Advancement Fund
New Profit Inc.	Boston	Kelly Fitzsimmons	Managing Partner & Cofounder
New Schools Venture Fund	San Francisco	Kim Smith	Cofounder & CEO
REDF	San Francisco	Melinda Tuan	Managing Director
United Way of Greater Los Angeles	Los Angeles	Joseph Haggerty	President
Universities			
The Center for Social Innovation, Stanford Business School	San Francisco	Jed Emerson	Lecturer

Affiliation	Name	Title	Location
Center for the Study of Voluntary Organizations and Service, Georgetown University	Pablo S. Eisenberg	Senior Fellow	Washington, D.C.
Center for the Study of Voluntary Organizations and Service, Georgetown University	Virginia Hodgkinson	Professor	Washington, D.C.
Harvard Business School	Allen Grossman	Professor of Management Practice	Boston
Harvard Business School	James Austin	Chair, Social Enterprise Initiative	Boston
Harvard Business School	Jane Wei-Skillern	Visiting Assistant Professor, Social Enterprise Group	Boston
Harvard Business School	John Quelch	Senior Associate Dean	Boston
Harvard Graduate School of Education	Richard Chait	Professor of Higher Education	Cambridge
Hauser Center for Nonprofit Organizations, Harvard University	Christine Letts	Associate Director	Cambridge
Hauser Center for Nonprofit Organizations, Harvard University	William Ryan	Research Fellow	Cambridge
Institute for Nonprofit Organization Management, University of San Francisco	Michael Cortes	Director	San Francisco
Johns Hopkins University	Stefan Toepler	Associate Research Scientist	Baltimore
New School University	Dennis Derryck	Professor of Professional Practice	New York
New School University	Rikki Abzug	Assistant Professor of Nonprofit Management	New York

Organization	City	Name	Job Title
Consulting firms			
Bridgespan Group	Boston	Jeff Bradach	Cofounder & Managing Partner
Human Interaction Research Institute	Los Angeles	Thomas Backer	President
La Piana Associates	San Francisco	David La Piana	Principal
McKinsey & Company	Washington, D.C.	Les Silverman	Director
McKinsey & Company	San Francisco	Paul Jansen	Director
McKinsey & Company	Boston	Stephanie Lowell	Manager of Nonprofit Practice

Resource C

Some Comparisons with the U.K.

The aim of my journey to the United States was to get an overview of the nonprofit sector. I came with over twenty years' experience of the sector in the United Kingdom, so my perspective was inevitably influenced by that knowledge and understanding. This resource takes my experience from both countries and makes some comparisons between the nonprofit sectors.

A Brief Historical Comparison

Charitable activity in the U.K. can be traced back to medieval times and earlier. However, the formal definition of charity is generally traced to the 1601 Statute of Charitable Uses. This law also applied in Britain's American colonies, so in both countries the early definition of charity had the same roots.

From that point the development of nonprofit activity followed two different paths. In Britain charitable activity grew and diversified away from religious causes into education, child welfare, and moral discipline. It was mostly associated with the urban middle classes and was sustained by civic pride and civic rivalry (Smith, 1995). The notion of charity in Britain is based on a deeply held assumption that people with resources should assist those with less. Today British people give proportionately more than Americans to international causes, use the word *charity* to describe giving, and talk about the *voluntary sector*.

In the United States a distinct nonprofit sector emerged only in the late nineteenth century, and it was rooted in a tradition of cooperation and a mistrust of central authority (Salamon and Anheier, 1997). Nonprofit organizations were created to solve community problems, including infrastructure building and providing essential medical, educational, and financial services. Americans give proportionately more than British people to local causes, they use the word *philanthropy* to describe their giving, and they talk about the *nonprofit sector*.

For nearly four hundred years each country has adopted policies from the other. Until the twentieth century much of the learning that crossed the Atlantic was from the U.K. to the United States (Block, 2001). The English 1601 Statute of Charitable Uses provided an early definition of philanthropic activity. The idea of foundations that use an independent group of people to oversee the distribution of funds and the notion of granting tax relief to individuals and companies that donate money also originated in the U.K.

In the twentieth century the U.K. attempted to import ideas that originated in the United States, including community foundations, payroll giving, contracting for the provision of public services, and more recently, program-related investment and venture philanthropy. However, it is fair to say that none of these ideas have transferred easily into the U.K. culture or have been as successful there as they are in the United States.

The transfer of management and governance ideas from the United States to the U.K. has been more significant and more successful than the adoption of U.S. approaches to policy. Many of the great general management thinkers whose work determined how people today conceive of management were American. Consider, for example, the work by Frederick Taylor on *scientific management*, Abraham Maslow on the *hierarchy of needs*, Frederick Hertzberg on *motivators* and *hygiene* factors, Douglas MacGregor on *Theory X* and

Theory Y, Peter Drucker on *management by objectives*, and Warren Bennis on *leadership*.

It is not, however, a one-way street, and there is much that the United States could still learn from U.K. experience in the non-profit field. The U.K. has a long history of government working in partnership with voluntary organizations, and recently, clear principles were established for the ways voluntary organizations and government should work together. The agreement containing these principles is known as the Compact. A monitoring program is in place to determine the extent to which the principles are being applied in practice. The U.K. has also pioneered the involvement of users in many aspects of voluntary activity. Organizations "for" disadvantaged people are increasingly frowned upon and organizations "of" the same people are in the ascendancy. (Figure C.1 summarizes some key events in this history.)

Similarities and Differences

Today the U.K. and the United States have much in common. We share the same primary language, though the use of Spanish in the United States and of a variety of minority languages in the U.K. is growing. We have a common and deeply held commitment to the principles of democracy, freedom, and liberalism, and to capitalism within regulated boundaries. We share the "special relationship" that speaks to the many bonds between the two countries. We divide our economies into the three broadly similar categories of the business, government, and nonprofit sectors. We share a largely similar understanding of charity and philanthropy, and we have established similar taxation arrangements to encourage people and companies to make donations.

However, there are significant differences in the role of the state in the two countries, and these have in part defined the different roles of the U.K. and U.S. nonprofit sectors. In the U.K. the government has taken on much wider roles in health, education, housing, and social welfare, particularly since the Second World War.

Figure C.1. Major Events in the History of the U.S. Nonprofit Sector and U.K. Voluntary Sector.

U.S.	U.K.
	1793 Rose's Act encouraged formation of mutual aid societies
1844 Private nonprofit corporations placed under federal law	
	1853 Charity Commission established to supervise charitable trusts exempt from income tax
	1869 Charity Organization Society created to improve effectiveness of charities with scientific approach
1894 Congress-supported tax exemptions for charitable, educational, and religious organizations	
1900 First community foundation set up in Cleveland	**End of the nineteenth-century** Income tax privileges extended to all charities
1907 The first open-ended foundation (the Sage Foundation) established	**1905–1909** The Royal Commission on the Poor Laws proposed larger governmental involvement
1917 Charitable tax deductions for individuals	
1936 Charitable tax deductions permitted for corporations	**1919** National Council for Social Service, umbrella organization for charities, created (later called NCVO)
1948 National Security Council and the Council of Economic Advisors–first governmental bodies with a planning function	**1948** Beveridge report *Voluntary Action*; major social services provided by statute; National Health Service took over charitable hospitals
1954 Establishment of Section 501 of the Internal Revenue Code recognizing tax-exempt organizations	**1960** Charities Act enhanced powers of Charity Commission
1965 Establishment of Medicare and Medicaid	
1969 Tax Reform Act placed foundations under federal oversight	
1973–1977 Filer Commission highlighted lack of knowledge about the sector	**1978** Wolfenden Committee report emphasized necessity of voluntary-government partnership
1980 INDEPENDENT SECTOR, umbrella body for the sector, founded	**1992** Charities Act gave greater powers to Charity Commission, introduced a new accounting regime
1982 Verity Task Force founded to stimulate higher levels of giving and voluntary effort	**1994** Gift Aid, individual charitable tax deduction for up to £250, introduced
	1996 Deakin commission proposed concordat between state and voluntary sector
	1998 Compact signed between government and voluntary sector
	2000 Limits on tax deductions for individual donations abolished
2001 CARE proposed an Act supporting faith-based organizations and a charitable deduction for nonitemizers	**2002** Cabinet Office review of charity law and regulation, *Private Action, Public Benefit*

Indeed for part of that time the role of the U.K. voluntary sector was seen as an *adjunct* to state provision of services. That is now changing as the government is viewed in many areas as a funder and regulator of services that may be provided by either the public, private, or nonprofit sectors. Consequently, there has been huge growth in the provision of housing by the nonprofit sector as housing stock has been transferred to housing associations. A similar trend is taking place in social services and is just beginning in Britain's much-cherished health service. As the state withdraws from service provision, opportunities for voluntary organizations are growing, and the sector is developing characteristics that are increasingly similar to those found in the U.S. nonprofit sector.

Turning to the nonprofit organizations themselves, in both countries they (Hudson, 2002):

- Exist primarily for a social purpose rather than for profit making

- Are independent of government, because they are governed by an independent group of people

- Reinvest all their financial surpluses in the services they offer and the organization itself

The nonprofit sectors in both countries responded in similar ways to moves by government to fund and regulate more of the public services and to provide fewer services themselves. Here the United States has a great deal more experience than the U.K., resulting from a long tradition of the government contracting with nonprofit organizations (Gutch, 1992). This trend has been given further impetus by the recent *reinventing government* initiative.

Both countries have created task forces to carry out periodic reviews of their nonprofit sectors. The United States had the Filer Commission and the Verity Task Force, and the U.K. had the Wolfenden Committee and the Deakin Commission. The U.K.

government recently published *Private Action, Public Benefit* (The Strategy Unit, 2002), a fundamental review of the legal and regulatory framework for charities and the broader nonprofit sector that proposed wide-ranging change, including updating and expanding the list of charitable purposes, increasing the range of organizational forms legally available to charities and social enterprises, developing greater accountability and transparency, and ensuring independent, open, and proportionate regulation.

There are also many similarities in the ways nonprofits organize and manage themselves. Both countries have a rich infrastructure of national, regional, and local organizations that make similar distinctions between management and governance, have boards that govern in somewhat similar ways, struggle with the issues around encouraging effective representation and providing good governance, face tensions between consultation and decision making, and are populated by people who have broadly similar values. The debate about *core costs* in the U.K. is mirrored by a similar debate in the United States about *capitalization* and *capacity building*. (Exhibit C.1 presents some variations in terminology.)

Different Sizes

There are also many differences, the single biggest being size. The United States has 5 times as many people, 6.7 times as much economic activity, 1.4 times as much income per head, and 1.6 times as much personal disposable income as the U.K. (see Table C.1).

Comparing the absolute size of the nonprofit sectors is difficult because each country has its own definition of almost every dimension of size. Furthermore the data for the United States are considerably less up-to-date than those for the U.K. The figures set out in Table C.2 should therefore be treated as indicative. They suggest that the sector in the United States is somewhere between ten and twenty times the size of the sector in the U.K. Greater size allows the U.S. sector to support a much larger academic community and provides more funds for research on the issues and practices of governing and managing nonprofits.

Exhibit C.1   Terminology Differences.

Although the U.K. and the United States have many similar concepts about nonprofit organizations, the terms used in each country are often different. The following are the most commonly used terms. Note, however, that although the concepts behind the terms in each pair are similar, they are not necessarily identical.

U.S.	U.K.
Nonprofit sector	Voluntary sector
For-profit or private sector	Private sector
Corporation	Company
Philanthropy	Charity
Foundation	Trust
Bequest	Legacy
Program	Service or activity
Constituent engagement	User involvement
Parent corporation	Group structure
Executive director	Chief executive
Thrift store	Charity shop
Human services	Social services
Citizen participation	Voluntary work
Dues	Membership fees
Compensation	Remuneration

Table C.1. Key Statistical Comparisons, 2001.

	U.S.	U.K.
Population	285 million	60 million
Gross domestic product (GDP) at current purchasing power parity (PPP)	$9,809 bn	$1,461 bn
Per capita GDP at current PPP	$35,600	$24,480
Disposable income per capita	$24,600	$16,000

Note: This information represents the most recent data available at the time research for this book was undertaken. Figures in pounds converted to dollars at £1 = $1.60.

Source: Organization for Economic Cooperation and Development, 2003. OECD copyright 2003. Used with permission.

Table C.2. Comparisons of Absolute Sector Sizes.

U.S.	U.K.	Ratio
1,600,000 formally	140,000 general charities	11
constituted organizations	188,000 registered charities	8.5
$486 bn revenues (1998)	$25.6 bn gross income	19
10.9 million paid employees	563,000 paid employees	19
$226 bn volunteer time	$24 bn volunteer time	9

Note: Figures in pounds converted to dollars at £1 = $1.60.

Sources: U.S. data: INDEPENDENT SECTOR and Urban Institute, 2002; U.K. data: The Strategy Unit, 2002; Jas and others, 2002.

The nonprofit sector in the United States is not only larger in absolute terms, it also accounts for a greater percentage of economic activity (Table C.3).

Different Composition

In both countries the nonprofit sector consists of an extraordinary array of organizations that exist to help people, to entertain them, and to protect the environment. Variety is an enduring character-istic of the sector, so it is not surprising that the mix of activities in each country is very different. In the United States the sector is dominated by health services, and the next largest recipient of income is education and research. Religion is central to life in the United States, and this is reflected in religious organizations' accounting for 12 percent of the sector's income. In the U.K., in comparison, education receives a tiny 1 percent of the income of the top 500 charities because further education is provided almost exclusively by the state. In the U.K., social services accounts for the largest proportion of nonprofits' income, followed by medical and health causes, many of which are concerned with medical research. International causes are, in comparison much more significant in the U.K. than the U.S. (Table C.4).

Table C.3. Comparisons of Relative Sector Sizes.

U.S.	U.K.	Ratio
6.9% of GDP[a]	2.2% of GDP	3.1
7.8% of workforce[b]	2.2% of paid employment	3.5

[a]This figure from the Comparative Nonprofit Sector project is used to obtain a consistent comparison with the U.K.

[b]This is the nonagricultural workforce.

Sources: U.S. data: Sokolowski, 1999; U.K. data: Kendal and Almond, 1999.

Table C.4. Comparisons of Distribution of Income by Subsector.

U.S.	%	U.K.	%
Health services	49	Social services	25
Education and research	18	Medical and health	21
Religious organizations	12	International	14
Social and legal services	12	Children and youth	10
Civic, social, and fraternal	3	Religious organizations	9
Arts and culture	2	Heritage and environment	7
Foundations	5	Animals	5
		Benevolent funds	4
		Culture	3
		Education	1

Sources: U.S. data: INDEPENDENT SECTOR and Urban Institute, 2002; U.K. data: Pharoah, 2003, and private correspondence with the author (the best available data at the time of writing).

Different Relationships with Government

In the United States, citizens have a right to form a nonprofit organization. The major benefit of registering such organizations is that a qualifying organization is exempt from paying corporation taxes and can receive tax-exempt private and corporate donations. The primary federal regulatory body is therefore the Internal Revenue Service, which grants this exemption and in return requires an annual submission of financial data (IRS Form 990).

In England and Wales, charities have to demonstrate to the Charity Commission, a body that is semi-independent from government, that they have charitable objects, and they also have to receive approval from the Inland Revenue. The commission is the regulator of nonprofit organizations with charitable status, and it can initiate inquiries into organizations' affairs. (The arrangements are different in Scotland.) Proposals have recently been made to redefine the fundamental definition of *charity* and to sharpen and enhance the role of the commission. If approved, the definition will build on the four "heads of charity" (the relief of poverty, the advancement of education, the advancement of religion, and other purposes beneficial to the community) and require demonstration of the delivery of "public benefit."

In the past, organizations in both countries have faced similar issues around the relationship between government and the nonprofit sector, including potential constraints on organizational campaigning for policy and legislative change at the same time as the organization is receiving funds from government.

There is concern among many nonprofits in the United States about engaging in advocacy when government is often on the receiving end of such campaigns. In 1995, U.S. Congressman Ernest Istook proposed legislation that would bar organizations that receive government funding from engaging in advocacy. Although it has been defeated five times, this proposal has caused great concern about federal limits on advocacy. However, recent research on advocacy in human service organizations concluded that the extent of advocacy is largely a function of an organization's inclination, the commitment of its leaders, and its capacity to conduct research. This research concluded that the threat of biting the hand that feeds the sector is more perceived than real (Ryan, forthcoming).

Relationships between the government and the voluntary sector have been the subject of much work in the U.K. following publication of the Deakin Commission report in 1996 highlighting the problems (Deakin, 1996). Since then, as mentioned earlier, the voluntary sector and the government have signed the Compact, a written understanding creating a framework for their relationship. The Compact sets out undertakings by both government and the voluntary sector. The government undertook to

- Recognize the independence of the voluntary sector.
- Pay attention to the need for strategic funding, and develop a code of good practice for government funding of the voluntary sector.
- Take account of effects of new policies on the voluntary sector; consult the sector on issues likely to affect it; take account of those parts of the sector that represent women, minority groups, and socially excluded people; and develop a code of good practice for consultation.
- Promote effective working relationships between government and the sector; review the operation of the Compact and promote the adoption of the Compact by other public bodies [National Council for Voluntary Organisations, 2003].

The voluntary sector undertook to

- Maintain high standards in funding and accountability, respect and be accountable to the law, and develop quality standards.
- Ensure that service users, volunteers, members, and supporters are informed and consulted about activities and policy positions.
- Promote effective working relationships with government; involve users in activities and services; and promote best practice and equality of opportunity [National Council for Voluntary Organisations, 2003].

Codes of practice to support implementation of the Compact have been jointly developed to address government funding, consultation and policy appraisal, black and minority ethnic groups, and volunteering and community organizations. Local compacts mirror the national Compact, and are being drawn up in consultations between local voluntary sector organizations and local councils and other public bodies. An annual meeting between government ministers and voluntary sector leaders reviews the operation of the Compact. These arrangements are now being further strengthened following publication of the Treasury department's *Cross Cutting Review on the Role of the Voluntary and Community Sector in Service Delivery*. Although implementation is currently patchy, there is no doubt that this initiative has established a secure basis for the future relationship between government and the voluntary sector. This is one of the significant areas where the United States could learn from U.K. experience.

One result of this partnership approach in the U.K. is that many of the recent programs to address social issues have been developed and delivered jointly by government and the voluntary sector. Examples include the Sure Start program for early education, the Neighbourhood Renewal Strategy, some of the programs financed by the New Opportunities Fund, and FutureBuilders, the £125 million (US$200 million) government fund for strengthening the voluntary sector. Inevitably, there have been some tensions but there have also been genuine attempts to involve the voluntary sector in policy formulation and service delivery.

Different Tax Regimes

Although donations to nonprofits and charities are tax deductible in both countries, the way they operate is fundamentally different. In the U.K. the majority of the benefit of tax deductions is given to the charity, whereas in the United States the benefit goes to the individual making the donation. This echoes the different contexts in the two countries. In the United States a much higher percentage of people file tax returns. For these people a charitable donation produces an immediate reduction in their tax payment. It also reflects a close link in the United States between supporting community development and the promotion of self-interest.

In the U.K., tax deduction for charitable donations was until recently restricted to individuals making four-year commitments to donate and signing a witnessed covenant to keep that commitment. This restriction has now been removed, but the majority of the tax paid on donations is reclaimed by the charity from the Inland Revenue. The benefit is therefore seen to go to the charity, reflecting the more altruistic tradition of giving in the U.K.

The value of tax exemptions in the United States has been estimated to be over $17 billion. This compares with the value of tax relief on giving in the U.K., which is estimated to be worth £1.2 billion (US$1.9 billion) (Jas and others, 2002). So U.S. tax exemptions are worth nine times the value of U.K. tax relief. As a result, per capita tax exemptions in the United States are worth twice as much as the tax relief in the U.K.

Similar Patterns of Volunteering

The overall patterns of volunteering in the United States and the U.K. are similar, although there are some small but significant differences. More Americans volunteer, but as individuals they give slightly less time than British volunteers. Americans give the most time to volunteer activities in religious contexts, whereas Britons give the most time in sports contexts. A higher percentage of women volunteer in the United States, whereas a similar percentage of men and women volunteer in the U.K. (Table C.5).

Similar Development of Social Enterprises

In both countries new types of organizations are emerging that sit on the boundary between the nonprofit and for-profit sectors. These organizations have a social purpose, such as employing the disadvantaged, but earn income from their activities and operate as

Table C.5. Comparisons of Volunteering.

Category	U.S.	U.K.
No. of volunteers	110 million	22 million
% of population volunteering	55%	48%
Average time given by volunteers	3.5 hours/week	4 hours/week
% of women volunteering	61%	48%
% of men volunteering	49%	48%
Main activities	Religion	Sports
	Education	Education
	Youth development	Social welfare

Source: U.S. data: INDEPENDENT SECTOR and Urban Institute, 2002; U.K. data: Smith, 1998.

businesses rather than charities. Examples of the activities they engage in are furniture or bicycle repair and janitorial or landscaping services. In the U.K. the government has moved swiftly to propose the creation of a new legal form, the *community interest company* (CIC). The assets of CICs must be used for public benefit. CICs will not have access to the tax relief available to charities.

Summary

In summary, although nonprofits in the two countries exist for similar reasons and have similar arrangements for their management and governance, there are great differences in their size, composition, relationships with government, and tax regimes.

My overriding experience in carrying out the research for this book is that the similarities between our nonprofit sectors are far greater than the differences. Our two countries have a common language and a commitment to democracy, liberalism, and capitalism. We have nonprofit organizations with broadly similar goals, and they are governed and managed in much the same ways. It would therefore be surprising if there were not a great deal we could learn from each other.

However, even though our nonprofit sectors are based on similar values, there are distinct differences of ethos. In the U.K. there is greater emphasis on voluntarism, or "meeting the needs of strangers," as one report characterized the U.K. voluntary sector (Young, 1991). There is greater emphasis on involving users in every aspect of non-profit activity, including representation to government, service delivery, and campaigning and also in the organizations' staffing and governance.

In the United States there is greater emphasis on efficiency and effectiveness. Americans have a much stronger culture of commitment to management. Management training is much more wide-spread and the language of management pervades the way people think and speak. Management is more often derided in the U.K. and more widely accepted in the United States.

However, the forces that shape the context in which the non-profit sector operates are driving the two sectors to become increasingly similar. In both countries:

- The public sector is withdrawing from providing services and focusing on funding and regulating them.

- Profit-seeking firms are finding a market in providing services that were previously the preserve of the public and nonprofit sectors.

- Social enterprise is emerging as a new way of tackling social problems, and it straddles the traditional boundaries between the private and nonprofit sectors.

- New forms of funding and financial instruments are emerging and opening opportunities for organizations to structure their finances in different ways.

Resource D

The Best Reading

This resource picks out some of the best books and reports on the nonprofit sector and the management and governance of nonprofit organizations in the United States. I chose them because I found them interesting and authoritative—they offer information that I believe will stand the test of time and be relevant for many years to come.

The Nonprofit Sector

INDEPENDENT SECTOR and Urban Institute. *The New Nonprofit Almanac and Desk Reference: The Essential Facts and Figures for Managers, Researchers, and Volunteers.* San Francisco: Jossey-Bass, 2002. [www.independentsector.org]

This is the reference book for statistics on the sector, packed with figures, charts, and a clear commentary. It covers the place of the nonprofit sector in the national economy and employment trends, private giving trends, and financial trends in each of the main parts of the sector. It also takes a detailed look at reporting public charities.

O'Neill, Michael. *Nonprofit Nation: A New Look at the Third America.* (2nd ed.) San Francisco: Jossey-Bass, 2002. [www.josseybass.com]

If you want a thorough understanding of the nonprofit sector and each of its subsectors, this great book describes sector development and current issues in great detail. Written by a professor who has tracked the sector for many years and really understands what the relevant figures mean, especially in terms of the critical issues facing the sector, it is packed with quantitative analysis and is also a great read.

Ott, J. S. (ed.). *The Nature of the Nonprofit Sector*. Boulder, Colo.: Westview Press, 2001. [www.westviewpress.com]

This fascinating collection of the best writing about the sector starts with Andrew Carnegie's 1889 essay, "The Gospel of Wealth," and then offers thirty-five more chapters on the history and sociology of the nonprofit sector; its distinctive contribution to society; economic, organizational, and political theories of the sector; and in conclusion, the challenges facing the sector.

Salamon, L. *America's Nonprofit Sector: A Primer*. New York: Foundation Center, 1999. [www.fdncenter.org]

This is a wide-ranging guide to the sector, giving an overview of why it exists, discussing its scope and structure, describing its context in relation to business and government, and analyzing recent trends. It also offers a detailed analysis of each of the main subsectors (health; education; social services; arts, culture, and recreation; advocacy; legal services and international aid; and religion). It ends with an interesting glimpse into the future.

Salamon, L. (ed.). *The State of Nonprofit America*. Washington, D.C.: Brookings Institution, 2002. [www.brookings.edu]

This authoritative and comprehensive assessment of the sector by leading authors reports on each part of the nonprofit sector and the five major challenges facing the sector. It includes an excellent introductory overview by Lester Salamon.

Capacity Building

Letts, C., Ryan, W., and Grossman, A. *High Performance Non-profit Organizations*. New York: Wiley, 1999. [www.wiley.com]

This groundbreaking book makes a powerful case for capacity building and through comparisons with private sector organizations sets out areas where nonprofits could make the greatest improvements to their performance: quality processes, product development, benchmarking, and human resources. Written by three leading thinkers at Harvard University, it is an inspirational read.

Light, P. *Making Nonprofits Work: A Report on the Tides of Nonprofit Management Reform*. Washington, D.C.: Brookings Institution, 2000. [www.brookings.edu]

Drawing on confidential interviews with leaders of nonprofit management reform and other sources, Light examines four popular philosophies of nonprofit management reform. He cautions leaders to recognize the limits of the reform models and to concentrate an organization's reform energy on a handful of priorities.

Light, P. *Pathways to Nonprofit Excellence*. Washington, D.C.: Brookings Institution, 2002. [www.brookings.edu]

This book reports on a pioneering project to seek the views of 250 leading thinkers and 250 executive directors of leading nonprofits on the characteristics of effective organizations. Paul Light heads the Brookings Institution's Pathways to Nonprofit Effectiveness project and is driving new thinking in this field. The book includes the full answers to the original questionnaires and Light's lively commentary on the results.

McKinsey & Company. *Effective Capacity Building in Nonprofit Organizations*. Washington, D.C.: Venture Philanthropy Partners, 2001. [www.vppartners.org]

This first-rate report (downloadable from the Venture Philanthropy Partners Web site) sets out the seven elements of nonprofit capacity, findings based on thirteen case studies. It discusses why capacity building is important and why nonprofit organizations tend to ignore it. The authors develop the Capacity Framework and include a self-assessment tool that organizations can use to rate their own capacity.

Performance Management

Morley, E., Vinson, E., and Harty, H. "Outcome Measurement in Nonprofit Organizations." Washington, D.C.: INDEPENDENT SECTOR, 2001. [www.independentsector.org]

In the absence of a good book-length study of nonprofit performance management, readers may turn to this report, a succinct and valuable summary of the state of the art. Harry Harty is a known guru in this area, having previously worked on the United Way measures project. This report looks at current practices in the types of information collected, data collection procedures, the analysis of outcome information, and the reporting and use of that information. It also offers recommendations for the future development of outcome measurement.

Plantz, M. C., Greenway, M. T., and Hendricks, M. "Outcome Measurement: Showing Results in the Nonprofit Sector." [www. unitedway.org]. 1999. (Originally published in *Using Performance Measurement to Improve Public and Nonprofit Programs*. New Directions for Evaluation, no 75. San Francisco: Jossey-Bass, 1997.)

This report summarizes the history of performance measurement in the nonprofit health and human services sectors and defines key concepts. It also describes lessons learned about the value of outcome measurement, effective implementation, the role of funders, and using outcome measures in resource allocation decisions. Finally, it sets out the challenges for the future.

REDF. [www.redf.org]

A wide range of material on social return on investment (SROI) is available from REDF's Web site, including (1) *Analyzing the Value of Social Purpose Enterprise Within a Social Return on Investment Framework*, which describes the underlying methodology for SROI and is available in a series of PDFs; (2) an information OASIS, which describes how to implement a customized measurement system, using some of the principles and lessons from REDF's work with SROI; and (3) sample social return on investment reports.

United Way of America. Outcome Measurement Resource Network. [www.unitedway.org]

The United Way's Outcome Measurement Resource Network offers a wealth of reports and material on measuring outcomes.

Strategic Alliances

Arsenault, J. *Forging Nonprofit Alliances: A Comprehensive Guide to Enhancing Your Mission Through Joint Ventures and Partnerships, Management Service Organizations, Parent Corporations, and Mergers*. San Francisco: Jossey-Bass, 1998. [www. josseybass.com]

Jane Arsenault is an experienced consultant who has been involved in a wide range of nonprofit strategic alliances and mergers, and this comprehensive guide reflects that practical experience. She describes the many options for strategic alliances; when they are best used; the authority and control relationships; the integration of mission, values, and culture; the risks; and the management issues.

Austin, J. *The Collaboration Challenge: How Nonprofits and Businesses Succeed Through Strategic Alliances*. San Francisco: Jossey-Bass, 2000. [www.josseybass.com]

James Austin is chairman of the Social Enterprise Initiative at the Harvard Business School. This excellent book demonstrates how nonprofits and businesses establish strategic alliances that benefit both organizations. Packed with case studies, it sets out how to identify opportunities, ensure strategic fit, generate value for both parties, and manage the relationship. It also presents guidelines for collaborating successfully.

Business for Social Responsibility. [www.bsr.org]

The Web site of Business for Social Responsibility offers information about all aspects of corporate social responsibility, including community involvement, corporate philanthropy, and corporate volunteering.

La Piana, D. *The Nonprofit Mergers Workbook: The Leaders Guide to Considering, Negotiating and Executing a Merger.* Saint Paul, Minn.: Amherst H. Wilder Foundation, 2000. [www.wilder.org]

This thoughtful and practical book covers the options for structuring a merger, prerequisites for a successful merger, assessment of potential partners, difficulties and roadblocks to be anticipated, negotiating stages and strategies, and implementation. It includes a useful section of advice for consultants facilitating mergers.

La Piana Associates, Inc. [www.lapiana.org]

This Web site offers information about the Strategic Solutions project that was dedicated to achieving a major and lasting positive impact on the nonprofit sector's perception, understanding, and use of strategic restructuring.

Nonprofit Funding

Community Wealth Ventures. *Venture Philanthropy 2002: Advancing Nonprofit Performance Through High-Engagement Grantmaking. Venture Philanthropy Partners.* [www.vppartners.org]. 2002.

This is the third annual survey of organizations involved in venture philanthropy and high-engagement grantmaking. As well as presenting a series of articles on the hot topics in the field by leader practitioners, the report sets out an overview of the field and details about most of the organizations operating this type of funding. It is a great read for anyone interested in venture philanthropy.

Ryan, W. *Nonprofit Capital: A Review of Problems and Strategies*. Rockefeller Foundation. [www.rockfound.org]. 2001.

This is the reference for anyone wanting to understand the latest thinking on financing the capital requirements of nonprofit organizations. Written by a leading researcher who really understands the sector, it defines the need for different types of nonprofit capital. It sets out a series of proposals for reforming the nonprofit capital market and describes reforms that funders and nonprofit organizations themselves could introduce. It finishes with a section on expanding access to private capital markets.

Leadership and Management

Nanus, B., and Dobbs, S. *Leaders Who Make a Difference: Essential Strategies for Meeting the Nonprofit Challenge*. San Francisco: Jossey-Bass, 1999. [www.josseybass.com]

Focused specifically on the leadership of nonprofit organizations, this book establishes the key roles leaders have to discharge as visionaries, strategists, politicians, campaigners, coaches, and change agents. Each role is illustrated with a pertinent case study, making this book essential reading for current and potential leaders.

Ott, J. S. (ed.). *Understanding Nonprofit Organizations*. Boulder, Colo.: Westview Press, 2001. [www.westviewpress.com]

This compendium of the best articles about the management of nonprofit organizations contains the thinking of many of the leading academics in the field. Written during the 1990s, these articles are most useful for understanding the history and context of nonprofit management. They cover governance, the legal framework, leadership, strategic planning, fundraising, entrepreneurship, contracts, budgets, managing volunteers, accountability, and international organizations.

Governance

Carver, J. *Boards That Make a Difference: A New Design for Leadership in Nonprofit and Public Organizations*. (2nd ed.) San Francisco: Jossey-Bass, 1997. [www.josseybass.com]

This book sets out the policy governance model of John Carver, "the world's most published and provocative authority on effective board design." It addresses board job design, board-staff relationships, the chief executive's role, and performance monitoring. Although Carver's model is seen as extreme by some, it applies rigor and makes nonprofit managers and board members think through what roles the board should deliver.

Chait, R., Holland, T. P., and Taylor, B. E. *Improving the Performance of Governing Boards*. Phoenix, Ariz.: American Council on Education and Oryx Press, 1996. [www.greenwood.com]

Richard Chait, Thomas Holland, and Barbara Taylor have among them huge experience of nonprofit boards, especially the boards of educational institutions. Their first book established the basic competencies required of boards and much more besides. This book, based on extensive research and practical experience, addresses the topics of effective trusteeship, board development, board cohesion, trustee education, and improvement of board processes. It also discusses effective ways of responding to the resistance some trustees exhibit toward board development.

Robinson, M. *Nonprofit Boards That Work: The End of One-Size-Fits-All Governance*. New York: Wiley, 2001. [www.wiley.com]

Maureen Robinson is better placed than many to write a book on governance, having been director of education at BoardSource for eight years. This book encourages boards to look at the particulars of their own organization before determining the best approach to governance. It discusses the structure and substance of board work, board culture, the executive director–board partnership, and the way individual members should discharge their roles.

Glossary

Balanced scorecard A package of measures for reporting on an organization's health and performance.

Capacity building Strengthening organizations by investing internally in their people, systems, and technology and externally in new ideas, services, and relationships.

Charitable organization; religious organization An organization that can receive tax-deductible contributions, is registered under section 501(c)(3) of the Internal Revenue Service Tax Code, and has limits on its lobbying activities.

Faith-based organization An organization that is a function of a church, congregation, or other religious entity and that provides services to people in need. Under current law, if such organizations receive government grants or contracts, they cannot use those funds to proselytize their service users, and they must follow federal antidiscrimination laws in recruiting for the organization. (Not to be confused with organizations with religious origins that provide services but do not proselytize.)

High-engagement philanthropy A funding relationship in which the funder provides a range of support to organizations and expects a high level of accountability for results.

Independent sector The nonprofit sector, comprising several categories of organizations tax-exempt under U.S. law, including charitable and religious organizations, associations, philanthropic foundations, and social welfare organizations. (Not to be confused with INDEPENDENT SECTOR, an umbrella organization that represents some nonprofit organizations.)

Management service organization An organization that provides back-office services in such areas as accounting, human resources, information technology, and facilities management for a number of nonprofit organizations.

Management support organization An organization that exists at the city, state, regional, or national level to provide management and technical support to nonprofit organizations. It may be nonprofit or for profit.

Nonprofit organization An organization that is chartered under federal law, separate from government, self-governing, voluntary, and of public benefit and that does not distribute profits.

Nonprofit sector The widest term for the sector, covering independent sector organizations, cooperatives, social and fraternal organizations, business and professional associations, labor unions, and political parties.

Outcome measurement A quantitative or qualitative measure of achievement or the process of measuring outcomes.

Performance management The process of measuring and managing an organization's achievements, learning from experience, and using that knowledge to inform strategic decisions.

Program-related investment Investment of a foundation's capital directly into nonprofit organizations and social enterprises, usually as low-cost or no-cost loans for buildings or other capital improvements and sometimes for programs.

Scale deep Achieve greater impact in the local community by reaching more of the client population and finding new ways to serve it.

Scale up Replicate successful programs to increase an organization's impact and to achieve economies of scale.

Social return on investment A financial measure of the value to society produced by an organization that helps underprivileged people. It considers the reduced use of public services and the increased payment of taxes that result from the organization's efforts (defined more fully in Chapter Two).

Social welfare organization Strictly, a nonprofit organization that cannot receive tax-deductible contributions, is registered under section 501(c)(4) of the Internal Revenue Service Tax Code, and does not have limits on its spending on lobbying activities. More loosely, a charitable organization registered under 501(c)(3) of the Tax Code that often provides social welfare services.

Strategic alliance A significant, long-term relationship between organizations that share resources to achieve their missions more effectively. The term includes joint ventures, group structures, mergers, and other relationships (as defined in Chapter Three).

Strategy map A chart setting out the key drivers required to deliver impact and their associated performance measures.

Technical assistance Management, functional, specialist, and technical support provided to nonprofit organizations to enable them to achieve their missions more effectively.

Venture philanthropy A source of substantial, long-term funding and management support that is linked tightly to ambitious performance targets and rigorous accountability to the funders (explained further in Chapter Four).

References

AAFRC Trust for Philanthropy. *Giving USA 2002*. Indianapolis, Ind.: AAFRC Trust for Philanthropy, 2002.

AAFRC Trust for Philanthropy. *Giving USA 2003*. Indianapolis, Ind.: AAFRC Trust for Philanthropy, 2003.

Alliance for Nonprofit Management. *Gold Book: Success Stories in Nonprofit Management*. Washington, D.C.: Alliance for Nonprofit Management, 2000.

Andreasen, A. "Profits for Nonprofits: Find a Corporate Partner." *Harvard Business Review*, Nov.–Dec. 1996, pp. 111–134.

Arsenault, J. *Forging Nonprofit Alliances: A Comprehensive Guide to Enhancing Your Mission Through Joint Ventures and Partnerships, Management Service Organizations, Parent Corporations, and Mergers*. San Francisco: Jossey-Bass, 1998.

Austin, J. E. *The Collaboration Challenge: How Nonprofits and Businesses Succeed Through Strategic Alliances*. San Francisco: Jossey-Bass, 2000.

Austin, J. E., and Harmeling, S. *Women's World Banking: Catalytic Change Through Networks*. Harvard Business School Case. Boston: Harvard Business School Press, 1999.

Backer, T., and Norman, A. "Partnerships and Community Change." *California Politics and Policy*, 2000, pp. 39–44.

Block, S. "A History of the Discipline." In J. S. Ott (ed.), *The Nature of the Nonprofit Sector*. Boulder, Colo.: Westview Press, 2001.

Bryson, J. M. *Strategic Planning for Public and Nonprofit Organizations*. San Francisco: Jossey-Bass, 1995.

Business for Social Responsibility. [www.bsr.org]. 2001–2004.

Campbell, D. "Outcomes Assessment and the Paradox of Nonprofit Accountability." *Nonprofit Management and Leadership*, Spring 2002, pp. 243–260.

Carver, J. *Boards That Make a Difference: A New Design for Leadership in Non-profit and Public Organizations.* (2nd ed.) San Francisco: Jossey-Bass, 1997.

Chait, R., Holland, T. P., and Taylor, B. E. *Improving the Performance of Governing Boards.* Phoenix, Ariz.: American Council on Education and Oryx Press, 1996.

Community Wealth Ventures. *Venture Philanthropy 2002: Advancing Nonprofit Performance Through High-Engagement Grantmaking.* Venture Philanthropy Partners. [www.vppartners.org/learning/reports/index.html]. 2002.

Connolly, P., and York, P. *Pulling Together: Strengthening the Nonprofit Sector Through Strategic Restructuring.* New York: Conservation Company, 2002.

Council on Foundations. *Governing Boards.* Foundation Management Series, Vol. 2. (10th ed.) Washington, D.C.: Council on Foundations, 2002.

de Vita, C., and Flemming, C. *Capacity Building in Nonprofit Organizations.* Washington, D.C.: Urban Institute, 2001.

Deakin, N. *Meeting the Challenge of Change: Voluntary Action into the 21st Century.* London: National Council for Voluntary Organisations, 1996.

Dees, J. G., Anderson, B. B., and Wei-Skillern, J. *Pathways to Social Impact: Strategies for Scaling Out Successful Social Innovations.* Durham, N.C.: Duke University, Center for the Advancement of Social Entrepreneurship, 2002.

Dees, J. G., Emerson, J., and Economy, P. *Strategic Tools for Social Entrepreneurs.* New York: Wiley, 2002.

Drucker, P. F. *Managing the Nonprofit Organization.* Boston: Butterworth-Heinemann, 1990.

Edna McConnell Clark Foundation. "The Edna McConnell Clark Foundation." [http://www.emcf.org]. 2004a.

Edna McConnell Clark Foundation. "EMCF Youth Development Fund Grantmaking/Investment Process." [http://www.emcf.org/programs/youth/ifb]. 2004b.

Emerson, J. *The US Nonprofit Capital Market in Social Purpose Enterprises and Venture Philanthropy in the New Millennium,* Vol. 2: *Investor Perspectives.* San Francisco: Roberts Foundation, 1999.

Emerson, J. "Horse Manure and Grantmaking." *Foundation News and Commentary.* [www.foundationnews.org]. May–June 2002.

Etchart, N., and Davis, L. "Prophets for Non-Profits?" *Alliance,* June 2002, pp. 21–24.

Fine, A., Kopf, N., and Thayer, C. *Echoes from the Field.* Innovation Network. [www.innonet.org]. 2002.

Foundation Center. *Foundations and the Tax Reform Act of 1969*. New York: Foundation Center, 1970.

Foundation Center. *Foundation Giving: Yearbook of Facts and Figures on Private, Corporate and Community Foundations*. New York: Foundation Center, 1996.

Foundation Center. *Foundation Giving Trends: Update on Funding Priorities*. New York: Foundation Center, 2002.

Gardner, J. *On Leadership*. Washington, D.C.: INDEPENDENT SECTOR, 1990.

Global Leaders for Tomorrow. *Philanthropy Measures Up*. Davos, Switzerland: World Economic Forum, 2003.

Green, F. "When Collaborations Go Bad." *Nonprofit Quarterly*, Fall 2001, pp. 26–28.

Gutch, R. *Contracting Lessons from the US*. London: National Council for Voluntary Organisations, 1992.

Hall, P. *The Organization of American Culture, 1700–1900*. New York: New York University Press, 1982.

Hall, P. "A Historic Overview." In W. Powell (ed.), *The Nonprofit Sector: A Research Handbook*. New Haven, Conn.: Yale University Press, 1987.

Havens, J., and Schervish, P. *Millionaires and the Millennium: New Estimates of the Forthcoming Wealth Transfer and the Prospects for a Golden Age of Philanthropy*. Boston College, Social Welfare Research Institute. [www.bc.edu/research/swri/publications]. 1999.

Havens, J., and Schervish, P. "Why the $41 Trillion Wealth Transfer Estimate Is Still Valid." Boston College, Social Welfare Research Institute. [www.bc.edu/research/swri/features/wealth]. 2003.

Hesselbein, F., Goldsmith, M., and Beckhard, R. (eds.). *The Leader of the Future: New Visions, Strategies and Practices for the Next Era*. San Francisco: Jossey-Bass, 1996.

Holland, T. "Board Accountability: Lessons from the Field." *Nonprofit Management and Leadership*, Summer 2002, pp. 409–428.

Holland, T., and Jackson, D. "Strengthening Board Performance." *Nonprofit Management and Leadership*, Winter 1998, pp. 121–134.

Hoover, H. *American Individualism*. New York: Doubleday, 1922.

Hudson, M. *Managing Without Profit*. London: Directory of Social Change, 2002.

Hunt, A. R. "Social Entrepreneurs: Compassionate and Tough Minded." *Wall Street Journal*, July 13, 2000.

INDEPENDENT SECTOR. "A Conversation with Darell Hammond, CEO & Co-Founder of KaBOOM!" [www.independentsector.org/mission_market/Hammond_Conversations.htm], n.d.

INDEPENDENT SECTOR and Urban Institute. *The New Nonprofit Almanac and Desk Reference: The Essential Facts and Figures for Managers, Researchers, and Volunteers.* San Francisco: Jossey-Bass, 2002.

Jansen, P., and Katz, D. "For Nonprofits, Time Is Money." *McKinsey Quarterly,* 2002, no. 1. [www.mckinseyquarterly.com].

Jas, P., and others. *The UK Voluntary Sector Almanac.* (4th ed.) London: National Council for Voluntary Organisations, 2002.

Kaplan, R. "Strategic Performance Measurement and Management in Nonprofit Organizations." *Nonprofit Management and Leadership,* Spring 2001, pp. 353–370.

Kaplan, R., and Norton, D. *The Balanced Scorecard.* Boston: Harvard Business School Press, 1996.

Kaplan, R., and Norton, D. *The Strategy Focused Organization.* Boston: Harvard Business School Press, 2000.

Kearns, K. *Accountability and Government in Nonprofit Organizations: A Strategic Management Approach.* San Francisco: Jossey-Bass, 1996.

Kendal, J., and Almond, S. "United Kingdom." In L. Salamon and Associates, *Global Civil Society: Dimensions of the Nonprofit Sector.* Baltimore, Md.: Johns Hopkins Center for Civil Society Studies, 1999.

Kohm, A., La Piana, D., and Gowdy, H. *Strategic Restructuring: A Study of Integrations and Alliances Among Nonprofit Social Service and Cultural Organizations in the United States.* Chicago: University of Chicago, Chapin Hall Center for Children, 2000.

Kouzes, J., and Posner, B. *The Leadership Challenge: How to Get Extraordinary Things Done in Organizations.* San Francisco: Jossey-Bass, 1987.

La Piana, D. *Beyond Collaboration: Strategic Restructuring of Nonprofit Organizations.* Washington, D.C.: BoardSource, 1998.

La Piana, D. *The Nonprofit Mergers Workbook.* Saint Paul, Minn.: Amherst H. Wilder Foundation, 2000.

La Piana, D., and Kohm, A. *In Search of Strategic Solutions.* Washington, D.C.: Grantmakers for Effective Organizations, 2003.

"Leadership and the Inner Journey: An Interview with Parker Palmer." *Leader to Leader,* Fall 2001, pp. 26–33.

Letts, C., and Ryan, W. "Filling the Performance Gap—High-Engagement Philanthropy: What Grantees Say About Power, Performance and Money." *Stanford Social Innovation Review,* Spring 2003, pp. 26–33.

Letts, C., Ryan, W., and Grossman, A. *High Performance Nonprofit Organizations.* New York: Wiley, 1999.

Light, P. *The New Public Service*. Washington, D.C.: Brookings Institution, 1999.

Light, P. *Pathways to Nonprofit Excellence*. Washington, D.C.: Brookings Institution, 2002.

Light, P., and Hubbard, E. *The Capacity Building Challenge*. Washington, D.C.: Brookings Institution, 2002.

Maryland Association of Nonprofit Organizations. "Standards for Excellence: An Ethics and Accountability Code for the Nonprofit Sector." [www.marylandnonprofits.org/html/standards/04_02.as]. 1998–2004.

Mattessich, P. W., Murray-Close, M., and Monsey, B. R. *Collaboration: What Makes It Work*. Saint Paul, Minn.: Amherst H. Wilder Foundation, 2001.

McKinsey & Company. *Effective Capacity Building in Nonprofit Organizations*. Reston, Va.: Venture Philanthropy Partners. [www.vppartners.org or www.mckinsey.com/practices/Nonprofit/ourKnowledge]. 2001.

Meehan, B., and Silverman, L. "For Charities, Performance Is the New Ethic." *Leader to Leader*, Fall 2001, pp. 13–15.

Miller, C. "Hidden in Plain Sight: Understanding Nonprofit Capital Structure." *Nonprofit Quarterly*, Spring 2003, pp. 16–22.

Minnesota Council of Nonprofits. "Principles and Practices for Nonprofit Excellence." [www.mncn.org/info_principles.htm]. 1998.

Morino, M. *Red Herring*, Jan. 29, 2002, no. 109, p. 2.

Morley, E., Vinson, E., and Harty, H. *Outcome Measurement in Nonprofit Organizations*. Washington, D.C.: INDEPENDENT SECTOR, 2001.

Nanus, B., and Dobbs, S. *Leaders Who Make a Difference: Essential Strategies for Meeting the Nonprofit Challenge*. San Francisco: Jossey-Bass, 1999.

National Center for Nonprofit Boards [now BoardSource]. *The Nonprofit Governance Index*. Washington, D.C.: BoardSource, 2000.

National Council for Voluntary Organisations. [www.ncvo-vol.org.uk]. 2003.

Newcomer, K. E. *Using Performance Measurement to Improve Public and Nonprofit Programs*. San Francisco: Jossey-Bass, 1997.

Nielson, W. *The Endangered Sector*. New York: Columbia University Press, 1979.

Organization for Economic Cooperation and Development. "Population Statistics," "Gross Domestic Product," and "Basic Structural Statistics." OECD Main Economic Indicators. [www.oecd.org]. 2003.

Oster, S. M. *Strategic Management for Nonprofit Organizations*. New York: Oxford University Press, 1995.

Ostrower, F., and Stone, M. *Governance Research: Trends, Gaps and Prospects for the Future*. Washington, D.C.: Urban Institute, 2001.

Palmer, P. *Let Your Life Speak: Listening for the Voice of Vocation*. San Francisco: Jossey-Bass, 1999.

Pharoah, C. *Charity Trends 2003*. London: Caris Data, 2003.

Plantz, M. C., Greenway, M. T., and Hendricks, M. "Outcome Measurement: Showing Results in the Nonprofit Sector." [www.unitedway.org]. 1999. (Originally published in *Using Performance Measurement to Improve Public and Nonprofit Programs*. New Directions for Evaluation, no. 75. San Francisco: Jossey-Bass, 1997.)

Prager, D. *Raising the Value of Philanthropy*. Grantmakers in Health. [www.gih.org]. 1999.

Putnam, R. *Making Democracy Work: Civic Traditions in Modern Italy*. Princeton, N.J.: Princeton University Press, 1993.

REDF (formerly Roberts Enterprise Development Fund). *SROI Reports*. [www.redf.org]. 2000.

Renz, L. "PRI Financing: Trends and Statistics, 2000–2001." Foundation Center. [www.fdncenter.org]. 2003.

Robinson, M. *Nonprofit Boards That Work: The End of One-Size-Fits-All Governance*. New York: Wiley, 2001.

Rogers, J. "The Eugene and Agnes E. Meyer Foundation." In Community Wealth Ventures, *Venture Philanthropy 2002: Advancing Nonprofit Performance Through High-Engagement Grantmaking*. Venture Philanthropy Partners. [www.vppartners.org/learning/reports/index.html]. 2002.

Ryan, W. *Nonprofit Capital: A Review of Problems and Strategies*. Rockefeller Foundation. [www.rockfound.org]. 2001.

Ryan, W. *Government Funding of Nonprofit Human Service Organizations: A Review of Challenges and Opportunities*, forthcoming.

Salamon, L. "The Nonprofit Sector and Government: The American Experience in Theory and Practice." In H. Anheier and W. Seibel (eds.), *The Third Sector: Comparative Studies of Nonprofit Organizations*. Hawthorne, N.Y.: Walter de Gruyter, 1990.

Salamon, L. *American's Nonprofit Sector: A Primer*. New York: Foundation Center, 1999.

Salamon, L. (ed.). *The State of Nonprofit America*. Washington, D.C.: Brookings Institution, 2002.

Salamon, L., and Anheier, H. K. *Defining the Nonprofit Sector: A Cross-National Analysis*. New York: Manchester University Press, 1997.

Salamon, L., and Associates. *Global Civil Society: Dimensions of the Nonprofit Sector*. Baltimore, Md.: Johns Hopkins Center for Civil Society Studies, 1999.

Sawhill, J., and Williamson, D. "Mission Impossible? Measuring Success in Non-profit Organizations." *Nonprofit Management and Leadership*, Spring 2001, pp. 371–386.

Schwartz, E. "Venture Philanthropy: A Report from the Front Lines." In Community Wealth Ventures, *Venture Philanthropy 2002: Advancing Nonprofit Performance Through High-Engagement Grantmaking*. Venture Philanthropy Partners. [www.venturephilanthropypartners.org/learning/reports/index.html]. 2002.

Sievers, B. *If Pigs Had Wings: The Appeals and Limits of Venture Philanthropy*. [http://cpnl.georgetown.edu/doc_pool/Nielsen0103Sievers.pdf]. Nov. 2001.

Smith, J. D. "The Voluntary Tradition: Philanthropy and Self Help in Britain, 1500–1945." In J. D. Smith, C. Rochester, and R. Hedley (eds.), *An Introduction to the Voluntary Sector*. London: Routledge, 1995.

Smith, J. D. *The 1997 National Survey of Volunteering*. London: National Centre for Volunteering, 1998.

Sokolowski, S. "United States." In L. Salamon and Associates, *Global Civil Society: Dimensions of the Nonprofit Sector*. Baltimore, Md.: Johns Hopkins Center for Civil Society Studies, 1999.

The Strategy Unit. *Private Action, Public Benefit*. London: Cabinet Office, 2002.

Sussman, C. "Building Adaptive Capacity." *Nonprofit Quarterly*, Winter 2003, pp. 18–24.

Taylor, B., Chait, R. P., and Holland, T. P. "The New Work of the Nonprofit Board." *Harvard Business Review*, Sept.–Oct. 1996, pp. 36–46.

Tuan, M. "REDF: The Evolution of a Venture Philanthropy Fund." *Alliance*, June 2002a, pp. 28–29.

Tuan, M. *Reflections on Five Years of Venture Philanthropy Implementation. Alliance*, June 2002b.

United Way of America. *Program Outcome Measurement*. [www.unitedway.org]. 2003.

Vnenchak, M., and Weiss, S. "Parent/Subsidiary Case Study: PHMC and The Bridge." La Piana Associates, Strategic Solutions. [www.lapiana.org/project/index.html], n.d.

Whelan, D. "Rethinking Nonprofit Partnerships." *Chronicle of Philanthropy*. [http://philanthropy.com/premium/articles/v14/i18/18003601.html]. June 27, 2002.

Wiener, S., Kirsch, A. D., and McCormack, M. T. *Balancing the Scales: Measuring the Contributions of Nonprofit Organizations and Religious Congregations*. Washington, D.C.: INDEPENDENT SECTOR, 2001.

Williams, H., and Webb, A. *Outcome Funding: A New Approach to Public Sector Grantmaking*. New York: Rensselaerville Institute, 1992.

Yankey, J., McClellan, A., and Jacobus, B. W. *Nonprofit Strategic Alliances Case Studies: Lessons from the Trenches*. Cleveland: Mandel Center for Nonprofit Organizations, 2001.

Young, K. *Meeting the Needs of Strangers*. London: Gresham College, 1991.

Index